Christianity

a follower's guide

Pete Briscoe, *general editor*

Christianity

a follower's guide

With Contributions from
Calvin Miller, Charles R. Swindoll, D. Stuart Briscoe,
Max Lucado, Walter C. Kaiser Jr., Ramesh Richard,
Major W. Ian Thomas, Jill Briscoe, George O. McCalep Jr.,
Joni Eareckson Tada with Steven Estes, Dave Hall,
Kay Arthur, Brian Kluth, Henry T. Blackaby,
Captain John Cheydleur, Randy D. Raysbrook,
and John Eldredge with Brent Curtis

Pete Briscoe, *general editor*

BROADMAN
&HOLMAN
PUBLISHERS

Nashville, Tennessee

0-8054-2442-3

Published by Broadman & Holman Publishers,
Nashville, Tennessee

Dewey Decimal Classification: 230
Subject Heading: CHRISTIANITY
Library of Congress Card Catalog Number: 2001025360

Unless otherwise stated all Scripture citation is from the Holy Bible, New International Version, © 1973, 1978, 1984 by International Bible Society. Other versions cited are HCSB, Holman Christian Standard Bible, © 2000 by Holman Bible Publishers, used by permission; NASB, the New American Standard Bible, © the Lockman Foundation, 1960, 1962, 1963, 1968, 1971, 1972, 1973, 1975, 1977, used by permission; NKJV, New King James Version, © 1979, 1980, 1982, Thomas Nelson, Inc., Publishers; NLT, the Holy Bible, New Living Translation, © 1996, used by permission of Tyndale House Publishers, Inc., Wheaton, Ill., 60189, all rights reserved; TLB, The Living Bible, © Tyndale House Publishers, Wheaton, Ill., 1971, used by permission; *The Message*, the New Testament in Contemporary English, © 1993 by Eugene H. Peterson, published by NavPress, Colorado Springs, Colo.

Library of Congress Cataloging-in-Publication Data
Christianity : a follower's guide / Pete Briscoe, general editor.
    p. cm.
  Includes bibliographical references.
  ISBN 0-8054-2442-3 (pb.)
  1. Theology, Doctrinal—Popular works. I. Briscoe, Pete, 1963–
BT77 .C48   2001
230—dc21

2001025360

1 2 3 4 5 6 7 8 9 10 05 04 03 02 01

To Libby
The day we married I dreamed of
dedicating a book to you.
Fulfillment is sweet!

To my love,
with all of mine.

Contents

Part 3: Vibrant Christian Living

Acknowledgments

*T*o Gary Terashita, my partner from the beginning, tireless in his work and limitless in his patience; and Lisa Parnell and Kim Overcash, behind-the-scenes work, which few people ever see, that provides the stage for impact and growth: Thank you for making this book a reality!

Dr. Calvin Miller, you make words sing! Dr. Chuck Swindoll, after I've read your writing, theology makes sense. Thanks! Stuart and Jill Briscoe, thanks for saying yes, for getting your chapters in before anyone else, and for being more excited about this than I was! I love you. Max Lucado, no one communicates Jesus like you! Dr. Kaiser, I still remember with fondness hours of heartfelt discussion during my seminary years! To Dr. Ramesh Richard, my friend, coworker, and teacher; Major W. Ian Thomas, the greatest champion of the indwelling Christ; George McCalep Jr., willing to jump in at the eleventh hour; and Joni Eareckson Tada and Steve Estes, I'll never look at suffering the same way again.

To Dave Hall, my sweet brother, taking worship to the nations; Kay Arthur, taking Scripture to the masses; Captain John Cheydleur, taking Christ's love to the hurting; Randy Raysbrook, taking Christ to the lost; Brian Kluth, taking stewardship to the church—thank you for taking us along. Henry Blackaby, you helped me figure out where God was working, and this book is a partial result of that realization. My gratitude to John Eldredge and Brent Curtis for explaining a mystery, and clarifying the unknowable. Thanks for contributing to me!

To Becky Blanchard, your servant heart and administrative skill enable me. Thanks!

To all of you, I can honestly say this book would be nothing without you (well, not exactly "nothing," but who wants to read a book comprised of three introductory passages, an editor's note, and an afterword?).

Finally, to my first Essentials class, those wonderful new believers who taught me to love people with mounds of questions. To Wes Blackwood, my partner in teaching that class, who is my consistent reminder of the redemptive power of God's grace! And to the elders and people of Bent Tree Bible Fellowship, thanks for the freedom to spread my wings.

To God be the glory!

Pete Briscoe

Introduction

out of the starting blocks

BY PETE BRISCOE

My first day on the job as a lot boy at Foster Pontiac should have been my last. My first assignment was to drive a recently purchased Trans Am to the front of the store for the eager new owner. Taking a corner too sharply, I hit another car and ripped the driver's side door off this poor woman's new treasure. After a heart-felt apology to Mr. Foster, I was back on the asphalt, jump-starting dead batteries. Uninstructed and lacking in experience, I had sparks flying like a July Fourth fireworks display. While dodging the sparks I faintly heard the loudspeaker calling me into the office. I was inside for only five minutes, but that was long enough for someone to steal the five-hundred-dollar battery charger I had left in the parking lot.

My second apology in thirty minutes procured mercy and another assignment. Mrs. Foster had a new demo, a $16,000 black Bonneville. I was to drive it slowly to the wash bay, clean it, and deliver it to her parking space. I asked an employee for the car washing bucket, he pointed at one, and I got to work. I longed to atone for all my transgressions by scrubbing every speck of dirt from Mrs. Foster's vehicle. The suds bubbled, my mood improved, my self-esteem soared, and I was finally at peace in my new job. Then I rinsed the car, only to discover I had used the mitt, complete with steel wool, designed for cleaning wheels. I had removed all of the paint from Mrs. Foster's car! Working for two hours, I had cost the company approximately four thousand dollars!

I found out that it's easy to make mistakes when you're new, inexperienced, and lack instruction. Then if you receive poor instruction, real damage can occur. As a new believer in Christ, you have recently entered into a crucial relationship—a redemptive walk with Jesus Christ through his substitutionary atonement on your behalf. If you know what "redemptive," "walk," or "substitutionary atonement" mean in this context, you are ahead of the curve! You walk into your new church, and you may feel as out of place as I did at Foster Pontiac! The terminology confuses you, the expectations overwhelm you, the direction is sketchy, the feeling of ignorance may be embarrassing. You thought you were signing up for a relationship with Jesus, and you've been introduced to a foreign culture!

The church I serve is full of people just like you. They are available, teachable, willing, and overwhelmed. Even though you are bright, educated, an expert in your field of study or business, you may still be ignorant of the intricacies of the Christian faith. Perhaps you are heading daily into combat with relatives who don't understand your commitment to Christ and who feel hurt by what they interpret as rejection of your upbringing. Bruised and battered, you try to explain the journey you've begun, but the questions far outnumber the answers.

Our Purpose

This book is intended to acquaint you with the substance of your faith. Jesus taught that entrance into his kingdom was so simple that children were more suited for the task than adults! Anyone can admit sin, believe in Jesus, and commit to follow him. As a new believer tastes salvation, however, the appetite for closer harmony with Christ grows. We long for a deeper knowledge of our Savior, and we begin to seek answers to the legion of questions plaguing our minds. This is where it starts to get complicated.

Fifteen leaders from my church were gathered, early one Friday morning, sitting around tables in teams of five. We were doing an exercise designed to help us improve our leadership abilities. A Lego sports car was displayed for us as dozens of Lego pieces were distributed. "You have ten minutes to make this car," the facilitator said. "Go!"

We took a quick look at the model and discussed how to start the production of our duplicate. As the clock ticked, the tension rose. The other teams were struggling, too, even though we all had an exceptional model. After ten minutes had expired, all three groups shared the disastrous results: crooked chassis, incomplete structure, wobbly wheels, and decals in the wrong places. Not one of the three cars remotely resembled the prototype!

After a moment of stunned silence, the facilitator asked, "Why didn't you ask for the instructions?" We had experienced the folly of attempting to build a car using nothing but a model.

You will be tempted in your Christian walk to emulate models, people of pure Christian character with impeccable records as productive Christians. Although this may be helpful, these people are not the primary source of spiritual growth. In this book we will walk you through the essential steps necessary for "building the Christian life." Think of this book as an instruction manual, far from exhaustive, that provides an overview of the things you really need to know. Our desire is to map out the fundamentals of the faith before you get confused.

Our Presuppositions

New believers often wallow in the mire of "should know." "Should know" is that terrible feeling you get when a preacher says something that causes everyone's head to nod—except yours. You think to yourself, I should know that, but you don't. You're ashamed to ask a mature believer for fear of appearing ignorant (even though you are exactly that). "Should know" is like quicksand. As you step in, it seems safe; but the longer you stay in it, the deeper you sink. Pastors don't help much. We stand in our pulpits and extrapolate with glee, unaware that new believers are going down for the third time.

This book is for the uninformed new believer. We are assuming you don't know anything—or at least very little—about the Christian faith. Don't be offended if the book seems elementary. Getting out of the starting blocks requires careful instruction in the basics. A foundation is essential for a building, a starting gun for a race, a birth for a life, and an orientation for the new employee. Although all these activities are basic, they are also necessary for future success in the Christian life. [Note: We have provided an alphabetically arranged limited glossary in the back of this book that we hope will be of some help when you come across an unfamiliar word in the text.]

Our Plan

We had an inventor with forty-three U.S. patents to his name, a stunt man on a nationally syndicated T.V. show, a businessman with a dying marriage, and a Muslim whose first words to me were argumentative and antagonistic. All trusted Christ in the same year. These four fledgling believers from divergent backgrounds, along with sixteen other new believers, started meeting with me on Wednesday mornings to learn the essentials of the faith. This book is modeled after the format I used with this group.

In part 1 we will study Scripture, introducing you to an overview of the biblical text and helping you learn your way around this Book that is sometimes confusing to new believers.

In part 2 we will utilize the Apostles' Creed to summarize the fundamentals of Christian theology or doctrine.

In part 3 we will explain some of the elementary aspects of the Christian life that are necessary for continual growth and development.

The most useful wedding present my wife and I received was an ice pick. We use it constantly because of its versatility. It can reach things, poke things, push things, and scrape things. We hardly ever use it for ice! This book is versatile too. I've designed it to be read by an individual, but be creative as you read this book. Some ideas follow.

- Read it by yourself, looking up the Scripture passages and meditating on them.
- Ask a fellow believer to work through the book with you. One-on-one discipleship is a wonderful way to grow, ask your questions, and, many times, find answers to them.
- If you are in a small group that meets regularly, before each session read a chapter of this book and then discuss the content as a group.
- If you are in a Sunday school class at church, give the book to your teacher to see whether it would be a good curriculum for the class to share.
- If you have teenagers at home, work through the book with them. They need to know the basics of their faith so they can grasp it themselves and head off to college with a firm foundation.
- If you are a mature believer, find a new believer and use this book as a discipleship tool. Teach them and train them in the essentials of the faith. You will grow too!

Our Promise

If you diligently work through this book and continually embrace its message, you will . . .

- discover why the Bible is reliable and indispensable for the Christian;
- be able to recite a summary of Christian theology;
- be able to practice the basic elements of Bible study, prayer, worship, and service;
- understand how to live the new life to which you have been called;
- be able to distinguish true worship from flashy entertainment;
- recognize Christian terminology at church and be able to define those terms;

- be able to explain to your friends and family why you believe what you believe; and
- be able to adopt a new way of thinking about suffering.

The people who have contributed to this book may not be familiar to you, but they are highly respected in the Christian community. They are known for explaining biblical truth with simplicity and clarity. They are from different backgrounds and various denominations. Some are highly trained, while others have learned through the greatest teacher of all—experience. They share my passion—to help you burst from the starting blocks with confidence and purpose. I trust this book will help.

We begin with an overview of the most important Book ever given to man—God's Word, the Bible. Calvin Miller guides us in our exploration of our Creator's self-revelation.

PETE BRISCOE has been the senior pastor of Bent Tree Bible Fellowship in Carrollton, Texas, since 1992. He graduated from Trinity Evangelical Divinity School in Deerfield, Illinois, receiving his master's of divinity degree in 1991. Pete resides in Carrollton with his wife, Libby, and their three children: Cameron, Annika, and Liam.

part 1

God Reveals Himself

The Bible

why should I trust what this book says?

By Calvin Miller

*T*he teachings of the Hebrew and Christian faith are based on a Book so small that we can carry it to church in our pocket. The glory of this succinct Book first came to me while talking to a Hindu man who was bragging about the size of his sacred library. "From which of these books do you draw your doctrine," I asked him. "Why from all of them," he said. "We have a vast literary tradition in which all of these books are important."

"Not so with us Christians," I replied. "All of our teachings are drawn from a single Book, not much larger than some novels."

Did I feel shame that Hindus had so many sacred books and Christians so few?

Not at all.

As I walked away from him exultant, I felt good that all that Christians and Jews believe is based on so small and portable a Book. All that God intended us to know and all that we need to know to live a righteous life is contained in this one small Book. The Bible!

Yet when we first believe, even the Bible appears impossibly large and locked. It seems to be full of big words, run-on names, and

9

some very bizarre stories. In fact, when new believers first come into contact with the Bible, they often wonder how Jesus and the faith can be so incredibly simple, while the Book that leads us to Jesus is so impossibly hard to understand.

It is in the first weeks of faith that many new Christians develop a kind of *Bibliophobia*—a fear of the Word of God—that is totally unnecessary. Sometimes this fear persists throughout life. They regard the Bible as they might a stick of dynamite: It contains the power to blow away the barriers that bar their pathway to meaningful living. Still it is too thick and obtuse to be understood.

How can new Christians learn to serve God unafraid of his Word?

Here we might take a cue from children. *Bibliophobia* is much less pronounced in them. They love the Bible almost romantically. I remember as a child singing a wonderful song in Vacation Bible School.
Oh, the B-I-B-L-E,
Yes, that's the book for me,
I stand alone on the Word of God,
The B-I-B-L-E!

But when I grew older, I realized that the Bible was not nearly so romantic and easy as I thought. There were big words, difficult concepts, and long sections that defied my mind! It was then I wanted to rewrite the children's song:
Oh, the B-I-B-L-E,
Oh, goodness, my-oh-me!
Ezekiel and Leviticus,
The B-I-B-L-E!

How then shall we proceed? First we shall look at the Bible and how it came to us. Then we shall consider how this ancient Book is organized and in what way it is special. Then finally we shall discuss how we can begin to take those first steps to making the wonder of the Bible the best part of our everyday lives.

How the Bible Came to Us

All that we can know about God is what he chooses to tell us about himself. The true nature of God is completely hidden from us. We could never know him at all unless he decided to come out of his hiddenness to declare himself. This is exactly what God decided to do. The Bible is the record of God's revelation of himself to humankind.

Children play a game called hide-and-seek. When I played this game as a child, I found it exhilarating—and deceptive—to try to find a hiding place so well hidden that my playmates would never be able to find me. Finally, when they had completely given up and were in utter despair of ever locating me, I would pop out of my undiscovered hiding place and cry, "Here I am!"

God, too, would be forever hidden to us unless he decided to reveal himself by crying, "Here I am!" God is too vast for us pitiable and needy human beings ever to find him. Since we can never pull off our discovery of God, he, in his infinite mercy, decided to tell us who he is and what he is like. Part of his "Here I am" cry is found in the pages of the Bible.

The various false religions of the world are clear evidence of how poorly people fare when they try to figure out who God is on their own. Paul says that when people do try to find him on their own, their foolish hearts can sometimes become darkened, and they end up with a shoddy and shallow worship (Rom. 1:19–23). They often end up worshiping only their own bodies and base appetites.

The Greco-Roman pantheons, or systems of gods and goddesses, are evidence of how far short human beings fall when they try to discover God on their own. The Greeks and Romans first sculpted and later worshiped gods who were rather like themselves. Instead of seeing themselves to be made in the image of God (as Christians do), they created gods in their own image. They were generally more ideal than their sculptors, but rather like them. Their gods were tall and muscular. Physically, they were very beautiful in form. But what were they really like? Alas, these Roman gods were too much like their sculptors. They indulged in multiple adulteries and sexual complicities, spawning all sorts of intrigues and debaucheries.

Nonetheless, such pagans prove there is a fierce yearning in our hearts to know the living God. Augustine, a fourth-century Christian, testified that our hearts are restless until they find their rest in him. And during our furious and restless quests, we human beings are prone to manufacture only restless human gods, who have little in common with the true God of Scripture.

This God cannot be discovered. We would never know him at all except that he—like a child out of hiding—pops into our hungry spirituality crying, "Here I am!" Revelation, the final book of the Bible, is sometimes called the Apocalypse of St. John. *Apocalypse* is a word that had to do with the drawing of those drapes by which the hidden contents of the stage become at once visible for the performance which is to follow.

Think of any performance that you've ever attended. My wife and I love plays, and when we attend one, we are always in our seats well ahead of act one. As many musicals as I have seen, I have never grown weary of that magic moment of overture. The cymbals clash, the tympani rolls, the violins swell, and the musical or the opera or the play is waiting.

Then the curtain goes up.

Sometimes at this spell-binding moment, there is a visible gasp as the curtain rises and the breathtakingly beautiful stage setting is revealed. Then the actors come on, real live people, making some aspect of life real to us. We have seen what the artists and playwrights wanted us to see. We did not see this because we ran up and ripped the curtains open and peeked into the forbidden zone. No, we have seen because of the great *apokalupsis*, the revealing, the rising of the curtain that someone else performs for us to reveal the work.

So it is with God's revelation of himself.

God reveals himself in three different ways. First, he reveals himself in nature. No one can look at a brilliant sunset or a velvet, dew-laden rose and not know there is a God. It is nature that naturally proclaims him. The starry skies, said the psalmist, prove there is a God (Ps. 19:1). This testimony is so sure that only a fool, said the psalmist, would say there is no God (Ps. 14:1).

Outside of nature, the clearest way that God ever said "Here I am!" is in the person of Jesus. God became a man and revealed himself in the most direct way he could. Jesus was a very picture of God. He who has seen me has seen God (John 14:9), said Jesus. "I and the Father are one," he said (John 10:30). So anyone who has seen Jesus has seen God crying out, "Here I am!"

But now that Jesus is back at the right hand of the Father, the best way God reveals himself is in the Bible. The Bible is the most specific declaration of God that we have. As we read page after page, God pops out of his hiddenness to declare, "Here I am!"

How Did the Various Books Ever Become Included in the Bible?

The Bible itself is a condensation of the history and lives of people—first the Jews and then the Christians. This Book—and that's what the word *Bible* means—has a long and fascinating history. The story of its origin is as beautiful as it is complex. The books that comprise this small volume are but a condensation of the vast stores of literature from which it was gradually distilled across many centuries.

We know that many of the books that were written during biblical times never came to be a part of the Bible. Moses referred to "all the words of the LORD" were written in the "book of the covenant" (Exod. 24:4, 7 NASB). This book we do not have; it has been lost in time. Joshua referred to a "Book of the Law of God" (Josh. 24:26), another book we do not have. According to Paul's references, there were not just two letters written to the Corinthians but four (1 Cor. 5:9; 2 Cor. 7:8–9). It is clear from the context of these references that two of these four letters have been lost.

John the Apostle comments that while there may or may not have been other Gospels written (doubtless there were), what we know of

Jesus from the books that have been included in the Bible contain only a fraction of what might have been known about Jesus. "Jesus did many other things," wrote John, things that were not recorded. "If every one of them had been written down, I suppose that even the whole world would not have room for the books that would be written" (John 21:24).

Most Bible scholars believe there were many Gospels written, of which only the four we now have were accepted as authentic, reliable, and worthy to be placed in the Bible. In the late 1940s, the discovery of all the Nag Hammadi (Gnostic texts) was proof that the ancient world abounded with manuscripts. Many of these were false writings like those discovered in the Nile River valley. Only a few were deemed to be worthy of inclusion in the Bible.

The word that we use for those accepted books is *canon.* Early Christian councils, in trying to arrive at which books should be included and which should not, deliberated over many choices. Only those books that had clear apostolic origin (were in some way connected authentically to one of Jesus' twelve apostles) were included in what came to be the New Testament.

These books stand as those that the church throughout the ages genuinely believed should be in the Bible. They are sixty-six in number. They were written by forty or more authors over a period of between fourteen hundred and seventeen hundred years. It is easier to remember the number of books with a device my mother taught me as a child. There are thirty-nine books in the Old Testament. If you take thirty-nine and multiply the individual numbers of thirty-nine—three times nine—you get twenty-seven, which is the number of books in the New Testament.

What Does the Term Inspired *Really Mean?*

Where did Christians get the notion that the Bible was specially inspired? Why, from the Bible itself! Paul wrote to his young friend Timothy: "All scripture is God-breathed and is useful for teaching, rebuking, correcting and training in righteousness" (2 Tim. 3:16).

Peter wrote the same kind of truth in his second letter: "Above all, you must understand that no prophecy of Scripture came about by the prophet's own interpretation. For prophecy never had its origin in the will of man, but men spoke from God as they were carried along by the Holy Spirit" (2 Pet. 1:20–21).

The Holy Spirit himself is the author of the Bible.

But how?

Did he hand down the various books on plates of gold? Certainly not! All that God wrote in the Scripture was first accomplished in the lives of those who wrote the Scriptures, much as it would be accomplished in our own. The Holy Spirit spoke his word not in some outer, audible way that might have been picked up on a public address system. Nor did he say to Jeremiah, for instance, "Sit down, get serious, and take a letter!" Rather, he spoke to Jeremiah from the inside out. From the depths of Jeremiah's own love for the Lord, God spoke. Jeremiah, at the time God spoke to him, was living in a battle-scarred world, where an all-engulfing war was shortly to destroy his homeland. Jeremiah, driven by a desire to honor God with all he was—no matter the cost—listened carefully. God spoke to him in his heart of hearts, and the prophet wrote all that God said.

These whisperings of God became Jeremiah's sermons to Judah to help those to whom he preached understand that the day was serious indeed. Those sermons were preached to Israel in the sixth century B.C., and they contain the God-given truth for all of us who live in any day.

All the Scriptures are "inspired." The word *inspired* comes from two Latin words that mean "to breathe into." And just how powerful is the breath of God? It is a force beyond all imagining. Whatever God breathes into becomes alive.

In Genesis 2:7 God "breathed" into Adam, his first human being, and man the inanimate creature came alive. In fact, throughout the Old Testament the word *ruach* is the word for both "wind" and "breath." When God redeemed Israel, the Bible says that he held back the waters of the Red Sea (Exod. 14:21) with a strong east wind . . . the very breath (*ruach*) of God.

In the New Testament Scriptures, God is ever breathing, and from his breath comes life. In John 20:21–22, Jesus, back alive from the dead, comes suddenly into the midst of the frightened disciples and says, "'Peace be with you! As the Father has sent me, I am sending you.' And with that he breathed on them and said, 'Receive the Holy Spirit.'" Of course, they did. It is the breath of God that gives life.

When the Holy Spirit came on the day of Pentecost, he came as a strong wind (Acts 2:2)—the very breath of God—to infuse the church with life. When Jesus tried to describe the new birth to Nicodemus, he described the Spirit of God by which we are born again as a wind (John 3). The wind that redeems has always been Spirit wind, the breath of God. And where God breathes, there is life.

In such a way, when God breathes into ordinary pen and ink, the words come alive. That's the intent of the meaning of 2 Timothy 3:16, all Scripture is God-breathed. "The word of God is *living and active and sharper than any two-edged sword*" (Heb. 4:12 NASB, emphasis added). This word has been God-breathed. Naturally, it is a living Word. I understand exactly what the Holy Spirit does when he gives life to the words. In short, they are *inspired*.

But can't we say that when Margaret Mitchell wrote *Gone with the Wind* she was inspired? Her inspiration was good enough to result in a Pulitzer Prize. But that is an entirely different sort of inspiration than what we have in the Bible when we say that it is inspired. The Word of God is God-breathed; not so with *Gone with the Wind.* The novel may be the best of human genius, but it is not to be compared with those writings that were born over time as God's various lovers in various centuries felt his breath of inspiration. Indeed, if we were to try to read any novel as frequently as we read the Bible over a lifetime, we would quickly see that there are major differences in what the two books do. The Bible has the breath of God upon it, and it contains so much more than we could achieve in all of our lives.

God did not write the Bible merely to produce good Hebrew, Greek, or English literature. No, in the Bible, God writes to make sure that none misunderstand he is in love with his world and that he will spare no expense to make that clear. So he breathes. His believers and lovers were (and still are) enthralled at his breath. They wrote, and the world came to know that God has an agenda with humankind.

How Does God Inspire?

The question we must take up now is, How does God inspire his Book? There have been many theories proposed as to how God went about this. Some believe that God inspired it only in classic ways, such as we speak of when we call Shakespeare an inspired writer. But the Bible is even more inspired than this. There are those who hold a more specific view known as the Dynamic View. This view teaches that God inspired the writers of the Bible to write about specific things but that he did it in only general ways. This view would emphasize that while that which is written in the Bible is what God wanted said, it is inspired in only general ways that guarantee somewhat the accuracy of ideas but not the actual words of the text.

The view around which Evangelicals have traditionally gathered is the Verbal View of biblical inspiration. This was a view settled on by Evangelicals early in the twentieth century. Late in the nineteenth century (1870), the Roman Catholic Church proclaimed the infallibility of the pope. This concept of infallibility had led Protestants to be leery of calling the Bible the infallible Word for fear that they would have a "paper pope."

But early on in their history, American Evangelicals had firmly decided that the Bible was infallible. The infallible Spirit of God spoke it into being, causing it to be written in an infallible manner. From the very beginning of Evangelical history, the idea of infallibility was derived not from looking at the words of the New Testament and formulating a theory but from the belief that the Holy Spirit is

the author of the Bible and that he may not be thought of as anything less than infallible.[1]

Still the view that God inspired the Word verbally does not abro-
gate the individualism of the various writers of the Bible. The first cry
often issued by those who would castigate Evangelicals for believing
in infallibility is this: If God inspired the Bible word for word, why
do each of the forty different writers of the Bible retain a distinctive
style within their individual books? If God really inspired the whole
Bible word for word, wouldn't Matthew and Jeremiah sound just
alike?

The view that God dictated the Bible word-for-word is called the
Dictation Theory of inspiration. It is not widely accepted because it
does not allow for individual differences in genre and style.

Most scholars turn from this mechanical dictations theory, pre-
ferring to say that God inspired the Bible specifically, but he left the
matter of style to each of the particular writers. The highly differenti-
ated writing styles of the separate biblical authors remain faithful to
the individual personality of each writer, effusing the Word of God
with a rich and diverse form.

But let us make no mistake in the matter. The differences in
writing styles should never be construed as evidence that God is
not the author. God is writing what he wants said, yet he is moving through holy men of old, who "spoke from God as they were
carried along by the Holy Spirit" (2 Pet. 1:21). The Bible is not
God's Word dictated, as though God were the CEO of heaven,
ordering his human writers to lay aside their distinctive person-
hood. No, quite to the contrary, he allowed them their individualism as they were "carried along" by his Spirit.

There is something of buoyancy in this idea. After all, that's what
inspiration is—buoyancy. It is a quality of buoyancy that whisks us
along like a leaf on the surface of a river. The leaf loses none of its
integrity, but the river is what really matters. It is the river that motivates both the direction of the leaf, the speed of the leaf, and the des-
tination of the leaf.

Let us suppose that each of the writers is a different kind of leaf, for indeed they were. Jeremiah was a poetic leaf; Amos, a rustic-shepherd leaf; Mark, a journalistic-reporter leaf; Luke, a man-of-medicine leaf. Paul was a legal leaf. Each leaf differs as a maple leaf differs from a poplar leaf or a cottonwood leaf, or a palm frond. So when we read each of these biblical writers, we can tell immediately who the writer is. Their individual mannerisms of thought, their unique style, we recognize instantly. But in spite of their literary differences, we can see that each of them was moved by the same mighty river of Spirit that flows through all of the Bible.

It is the stream that is its authority. It guarantees that all the leaves have the same motivator. They all flow in the same direction. None of them may be accused of being subject to error, as though they were at liberty to move against the stream.

This view seems to be in concert with how Jesus felt about the authority of Scripture. He affirmed that "until heaven and earth disappear, not the smallest letter, not the least stroke of a pen, will by any means disappear from the Law, until everything is accomplished" (Matt. 5:18). Paul felt that Judaism in the Old Testament had been entrusted with the very words of God (Rom. 3:2). Throughout the Old Testament, each time a prophet said "Thus sayeth the Lord," he was authenticating that what he wrote had come from the very demand of God and was not subject to any human amendment or interpretation.

The Bible sees itself as the unbreakable Word of God. The apostles also claimed to have written under divine inspiration. They asserted "confidently that they spoke by the Spirit (see 1 Pet. 1:12). They ascribe both the form and the manner of their teaching to him (1 Cor. 2:13). They not only assume a divine authority (1 Thess. 4:2, 14; 2 Thess. 3:6, 12), but they make acceptance of their written commands a test of spiritual obedience (1 Cor. 14:37). They even refer to one another's writings with the same regard as for the Old Testament. Compare the identification in 1 Timothy 5:18 of a passage from Luke's Gospel (Luke 10:7), 'The laborer is worthy of his hire,' as Scripture and the juxtaposition of the Pauline epistles in 2 Peter 3:16 with the 'other Scriptures.'"[2]

Evangelicals have remained unflinching in their allegiance to the infallible truth of Scripture. The Bible is generally accorded to be "truth without any mixture of error." It is written by the Spirit and breathed over by his Spirit.

How God's Spirit Moves in Inspiration

The best part of this divine inspiration is that inspiration works on both ends of a long synapse. For instance, we know that God inspired Paul to write 1 Corinthians. The Spirit, as we have already indicated, moved in the apostle's life, breathing into him the content of this glorious, first-to-be-written book of the New Testament. And as Paul wrote line by line, Greek character by Greek character, there spilled out of his pen this wonderful letter. None in the faith can read it without understanding that it is God-breathed.

But the mere writing of it is not the end of the glory. The Spirit moved on Paul, his ancient lover, to write it; then he breathes again in our lives as we read it. Only then has inspiration done its finest work. The Spirit is moving on opposite ends of a two-thousand-year-old arc. Paul is on one end of this two-millennium arc, and we are on the other. The glory of the Holy Spirit is that he is on both ends, guaranteeing the apostle's accuracy as he writes and on our end guaranteeing our certainty as we read.

This is what I like to call the "inspiration synapse." The same Spirit who orders the writing lays heavily on the verse across the years until we, in our own needy lives and times, begin to read and grow from the God-breathed words of the Bible.

Form and Structure

Let us not, however, be sentimentalists in our view of inspiration. Paul did not speak English. He spoke in Greek. Jeremiah spoke Hebrew. Jesus spoke Aramaic. Hence, when the Holy Spirit moved in their lives, in no single case did he speak in English. The fact that we can read it in English means that some person or some group has been responsible for translating it into the language that we speak.

Further, not only did the Bible have to be translated, but it was given in a particular form that was not even the best and most classic of languages. Paul was a learned man, but he wrote in Koine Greek, the Greek used by the common people in the streets of the first-century cities.

When Jerome first put the Bible into Latin at the beginning of the fourth century, the same thing happened. Jerome (and doubtless God) decided to translate the street Greek that Paul and other biblical writers had used into street, or Vulgate, Latin. Paul had avoided the literary classical Greek of Plato or Homer. Jerome later avoided the classical Latin of Ovid or Cicero. In other words, the Bible was always passed down in the common language of common people. This all came about by divine plan. God has the awfullest urge to communicate with the common people in the street, and he waits to do it in common ways.

The Koine New Testament (in consultation with the Latin Vulgate) was at last fashioned into English by William Tyndale, an Oxford scholar. His work forged the style of the King James, which was translated by the top English scholars of the day. With his Bible, God's Word, for the first time, did come into a rather classic mode. The King James was brought into the very finest of English form, in concert with, and often compared to, the works of Shakespeare and other classic English writers. This great translation would inspire the advance of the English language throughout the enlargement of the British Empire and the global thrust of the modern missions movement. Both these movements spread the power and force of the King James Bible around the world.

In the *Story of English*, the authors confess that at the time of the publication of the King James Bible, only three million people in the world spoke English. But in the next four hundred years, the English language would become the *lingua franca* of the entire world. The authors of the *Story of English* attribute much of the widespread influence of English to the King James Bible and the plays and poems of William Shakespeare. In his play *Pygmalion*, George Bernard Shaw has Henry Higgins, the worldly-wise professor, confess on stage that English is the language of Shakespeare, Milton, and the Bible.

In recent years there have been a plethora of new translations that have moved the Bible translations back in the direction of the non-classic form in which the Bible was first translated. Newer versions of the Bible are written generally on an eighth-grade comprehension level. The King James, by contrast, is written on a twelfth-grade comprehension level.

Newer translations have been immensely more friendly to new Christians, especially in the dumbed-down culture of the West. Neil Postman constantly reminds us that since we in the West have passed from a culture of print to a video culture, our reading comprehension levels have seriously declined. While the continuing decline of reading skills in the West is lamentable, the Bible continues to be ever more accessible to the masses.

Newer translations are much more friendly to contemporary readers who often lack the reading skills of their forebears. Once more the "street language" of the Koine Bible is being achieved in less sophisticated but more readable translations.

How to Get Started Reading the Bible

How do new believers come to understand the Bible, and how can they get started reading it? The big decision every believer needs to make is this: "I will take a systematic and lifelong study of the Bible." This is the commitment of genuine discipleship. Remember the word *disciple* is from the same root as the word *discipline*. Further, the word *disciple* means "student," and a *student* by definition is "one who studies." If you are going to be a student of anything, you must certainly decide to study. This intention lies at the front of all good, lifelong Bible studies.

Once that decision is made, the next step is a gathering of tools that are to be kept in the place that you ordain as your study: good

light, pencils, pens, and a notebook in which you record and track
your invasion into God's Word. Select one single Bible translation as
the one from which you will always study. There are many good
study Bibles, and I would suggest one that answers a lot of questions
within itself. This will keep you from having to go to other books or
commentaries to get the insight that you will require from time to
time.

Take your time in looking through the many options available to
find the one that's right for you. Your local Christian bookstore can
offer valuable help in finding the right Bible for you.

A concordance is also essential. I recommend *Strong's Analytical
Concordance.* It is everywhere abundant and very cheap. Be sure also
to get a concordance that includes all the words and constructions
from the latest translations of the Bible.

There are different ways of attacking your first reading of the
Bible. What I recommend is a thirteen-week readthrough of the
entire Bible as a first read. Since the average Bible is around twelve
hundred pages, you will have to read about one hundred pages a
week to make this happen. This is somewhere over fifteen pages per
day. Be faithful in this, and do it as thoughtfully as you can.

You will sometimes find the reading tough going, as in Ezekiel or
Leviticus. Don't quit; read these passages as thoughtfully as you can.

There will be other times that the passages will fly, such as when
you are in Genesis, the Psalms, or the Gospels. But the point is that
in a determined first reading you will begin to discover that the Bible
is laid out in various kinds of books and blocks of literature. Note
this as you read.

Further, you will notice certain interesting characters appear in
your day-to-day reading. Keep track in your notebook of who these
people are and why they are given space in the Bible. Note things that
you don't understand. Try to get other Christians who have been
reading longer to help you. None of them will be offended; all good
Christians are honored when someone asks them a question, even if
they are sometimes as baffled as the asker.

Remember, the books of the Bible do not appear in the order in which they were written. Usually in your study Bible the various Bible book introductions will tell you when they were written and what was going on in the life of Israel (as in the Old Testament) or in the history of the church (as in the New Testament). Be sure to place each of the books in their category of style as you read. In the Old Testament, mark whether you are reading the Pentateuch (the first five books written by Moses), the Histories (Joshua, Judges, Ruth, the Books of Samuel, Kings, or Chronicles), the Writings (poetry such as Psalms, Proverbs, Job, etc.), or the Prophets (all of those books, short and long, that bear a personal name in the Old Testament).

In the New Testament, there are the Gospels, the Acts, the Pauline letters, and the Universal letters. The Revelation is alternately listed as prophecy and sometimes as another of the general letters to the churches. It will not be long with this kind of intention until you begin to feel the Bible is neither as long or as impossible to understand as you thought at first.

As someone has well said, learning to love the Bible goes through stages. First comes the Medicine Stage. It is in this stage that we first discover the Bible. It is hard and not as palatable to the taste as we would like, but we know it is good for us and so we choke it down.

Second comes the Mashed Potato Stage. It now tastes somewhat better, although to be honest there are other books that are more like French fries, providing more tickle for our taste buds.

Finally comes the Ice Cream Stage. Now we have developed a taste for the glory and riches of Scripture and can hardly wait until we are alone with the Book that makes all things possible and eternity real. We thrive on God's Word; it is as honey and the honeycomb. We have learned that when we are alone with this Book, our souls are renewed, our vision is repaired, our love of life is replenished with passion.

Conclusion

Still, the Bible exists at last to convince us not that we are learn-ing ever more and more about God, but as a reminder that we must still wait to know it all. Why do we never get tired of reading the Bible? It is because we know that this Book draws us toward ever greater levels of spiritual hunger, and that no matter how much we learn, we are thrown back against the knowledge that we can never know anything. The God who wrote this Book is far too vast to ever be known. The Bible never makes us feel complete in our mastery of its subject: God. Alas, we are ever thrown back against the hunger that assures us that God is more vast than his Book.

A friend of mine had his little girl ask him, "Daddy, what is God like?" My friend took his little girl in his lap and said, "Think of God this way. Suppose you took all the sand in your sandbox and scooped it into a little mountain in the yard. Then suppose you went up and down the block and got all the sand in all your little friends' sandboxes and added it to that mountain. Then suppose you went everywhere in the world and got all the sand in all the sandboxes of the world and added it to this mountain. Then, after you had gotten all the sand in all the sandboxes, let us say you went to all the beaches of the world and got all the sand from all of those beaches and continued to add it to your mountain of sand. Then, at last, sup-pose you went to all the deserts of the world and got all of that sand and added it to the mountain.

"Finally," he continued, "you would have a terribly large moun-tain. Then, let us say you licked your index finger and went up and stuck it on the side of that huge mountain. When you drew your finger back, some grains of sand would be stuck to your finger. But let us suppose that you took your other index finger and flicked away all of the grains that had stuck to your finger, except for one grain. That one grain of sand would represent what we know about God, and the mountain that was left would represent what we had yet to learn about him."

The Bible is but an introduction to our hunger to know what in some sense must always be vast and unknowable. Still, a single grain of sand is enough to tell you what the mountain is like, and God has given to our tiny finite minds a place to begin knowing him. Knowing him is all that matters. And reading his Book is how we come to know him and to trust in his wonderful Son, which is, after all, the heartbeat of his glorious Book. So let us commit ourselves to the Book! Let us read hungrily, writing and measuring our insight. We will not find this Book boring. After all, we know the author. Indeed, he is our best friend. His Book is his love letter to us. The words of that Book are ours to read until we have at last crossed the boring barrier of pointless living. And if anyone should stop and ask us how we can be so sure the mountain of sand exists, let us proudly point to the grain of sand still on our finger and say, "This is the evidence that the unseen mountain exists. We believe in the mountain, for we have the grain of sand. We believe we have a lover who awaits us; we have his letter.

Distant words from other worlds?
No!
Words born here in history,
Close enough for us to touch,
Yet hatched
In languageless infinity.
God, clothed
In papyrus and codex,
Flying over oriental fields
In whispered winds and printed spirit.

Sing! God has a stylus in his hands.
He shouts in quill and ink,
"Here I am
Within this Book
This Book of books,
This word incomparable,
This vellum currency
Surpassing excellence—
This scroll majestic.

Here is my majesty
In common nouns and verbs,
I gave to babes and warlords,
To Aramaic shepherds,
And Hittite vagabonds,
To Hebrew, Greek, and Latin monks,
To Elizabethan scholars,
And, last of all, to you.

"In this Book I come
Whispering in ink,
Breathing,
Revealing,
Disclosing.

Hold this Book to your ear
Like the conch of YHWH,
And you will hear the Red Sea roar—
The rattle of iron rims on cobblestones—
The neighing of war horses—
The soft tread of camels in the sand,
The snap of breaking loaves,
The clear, clean song of leper choirs
Singing in the streets.

Listen to the Book.
Almighty love is
Resonating through the Pentateuch,
Swelling in the histories,
Bursting symphonically
In psalms of timpani.

Our God is literate!
Our God *can* write!
He lifts his starry quill,
And ages beg for paper.
A thousand pages
Of Adam's sad biography,
And on each one
The grace-drawn portrait
Of his Son."[3]

CALVIN MILLER is professor of preaching and pastoral ministry at Samford University's Beeson Divinity School in Birmingham, Alabama. A native of Oklahoma, Miller is a graduate of Oklahoma Baptist University. He has master of divinity and doctor of ministry degrees from Midwestern Seminary in Kansas City, Missouri. He was pastor of Westside Church in Omaha, Nebraska, for twenty-five years before becoming professor of communication and ministry studies and writer in residence at Southwestern Southern Baptist Seminary in Fort Worth, Texas.

Miller is the author of numerous articles and more than forty books on religion and preaching, including Broadman & Holman Publishers' titles *The Empowered Communicator, The Empowered Leader, Until He Comes,* and *The Book of Jesus.* In addition, his devotions and notes accompany *The Christ We Knew* and *The Celebrate Jesus! Millennium Bible* (Holman Bible Publishers).

part 2

Doctrine and Theology

Introduction to Doctrine and Theology

BY PETE BRISCOE

*T*he word *doctrine* instills terror in almost all new believers. It's a word that produces images of strange-looking little men with bushy beards and Coke bottle glasses, pouring over gargantuan reference books in dimly lit, dusty rooms. Professors wax eloquently in a room full of sleeping seminary students about the dispensational view of eschatology in relation to the premillennial, pretribulational return of Christ. Wow, it makes you want to sign up, right?

Well, don't let the terminology or your imagination scare you! Doctrine isn't boring, irrelevant, or crusty! Doctrine is the intellectual foundation of our faith. To be well grounded doctrinally will allow us to be well grounded personally. The apostle Paul, when writing to his young protégé Timothy, said, "Watch your *life* and *doctrine* closely" (1 Tim. 4:16, emphasis added). The person who was helping Timothy grow in his young faith emphasized two areas of focus: his life and his doctrine. The remainder of our book will also delve into these two arenas. This next section will teach you how to watch your doctrine closely!

Doctrine can be defined as "what the whole Bible teaches about some particular subject." Why is doctrine so important?

Doctrine Teaches Us How to Live

In a passage exhorting Titus, another trainee, Paul outlined the benefits of teaching sound doctrine. (Titus 2:1, 11–13): "You must teach what is in accord with sound doctrine. . . . For the grace of God that brings salvation has appeared to all men. It teaches us to say 'No' to ungodliness and worldly passions, and to live self-controlled, upright and godly lives in this present age, while we wait for the blessed hope—the glorious appearing of our great God and Savior, Jesus Christ."

By learning biblical content concerning God, mankind, sin, grace, salvation, Christ, the Holy Spirit, redemption, the church, and the future, one can learn how to live while waiting to meet Jesus face to face.

Doctrine Teaches Us What to Believe

It is one thing to say "I am a Christian." It is a completely differ-ent thing to know what a Christian is. What does a Christian think about creation, judgment, or salvation? Perhaps your neighbor asks you, "If God is just, why would he condemn a good person to hell?" Maybe your Catholic parents want to know your thoughts on Mary's role in your newfound faith. If a professor at college challenges your position on the cross of Christ being the only source of salvation, what do you say? Doctrine gives you the ability to understand your faith, defend your faith, and enjoy your faith all at the same time.

Doctrine Protects Us against Heresy

One of the reasons creeds were formed throughout Christian his-tory was to combat heretical teaching. It is often said that there are no new heresies—just the same ones rehashed over and over. David Koresh is famous in my part of the country. His fiery demise was long a source of considerable discussion on Capitol Hill, but his legacy lives on for many grieving family members. How could a man, pas-sionately teaching exclusively from the Bible, manipulate so many people for selfish reasons? The answer is a lack of doctrine. Because his followers didn't know the true faith, they fell for a counterfeit. There is no shortage of twisted biblical teaching today. By learning the classic creed of the church, you can respond with clear biblical instruction and correction. This will keep you from being swallowed up, jerked around, or led astray.

The Creed

For centuries the church has looked to the Apostles' Creed as a summary of authentic Christian doctrine. The word *creed* is derived from the Latin *credo*, which is the first word of the Apostles' Creed. It simply means "I believe." The Apostles' Creed frames doctrine into a manageable summary.

There is biblical precedent for compressing doctrine into a memorable synopsis. "Pay attention and listen to the sayings of the wise; apply your heart to what I teach, for it is pleasing when you keep them in your heart and you have all of them ready on your lips. So that your trust may be in the LORD, I teach you today, even you. Have I not written thirty sayings for you, sayings of counsel and knowledge, teaching you true and reliable words, so that you can give sound answers to him who sent you?" (Prov. 22:17–21).

In the early church, a number of creeds arose: the Nicene, Chalcedon, Athanasian, and Apostles'. We are focusing on the Apostles' Creed not because it was written by the apostles themselves. It wasn't. It is a summary of their teaching; thus the name.

The Apostles' Creed is our choice because it is well endorsed. Saint Augustine said of this particular creed, "Say the creed daily, when you rise, when you compose yourself to sleep, repeat your creed, render it to the Lord, remind yourself of it, be not irked to say it over." Martin Luther called it "an excellent brief and accurate summary of the articles of faith." John Calvin insists it is "the summary, and as it were, the epitome of the faith."

This particular creed is also the shortest of the famous creeds. You can recite it in thirty seconds, but it summarizes the major points of Christian doctrine. Longevity is another plus. The creed as we now have it has been fixed in its present form since the sixth century.

Some people think that sincerity of belief, not the object of belief, is the most important thing. In other words, "It doesn't matter what you believe, as long as you believe it with all your heart." Nothing could be farther from the truth. You can sincerely believe the thin ice on a Minnesota lake will hold you up—and be sincerely wrong! Conversely, you can, with fearful trepidation, inch onto four-foot-thick ice that is capable of holding a large truck and find yourself safe and sound. The object of the faith is the important thing, not the degree of sincerity. We want you to know *what* to believe. We encourage you to believe it with all sincerity as we summarize it in the Apostles' Creed.

> I believe in God the Father Almighty, Maker of heaven and earth;
>
> And in Jesus Christ His only Son our Lord, who was conceived by the Holy Spirit, born of the Virgin Mary; suffered under Pontius Pilate, was crucified, dead, and buried; He descended into hell; the third day He rose again from the dead; He ascended into heaven, and sitteth on the right hand of God the Father Almighty; from thence He shall come to judge the quick and the dead.
>
> I believe in the Holy Spirit; the holy Christian church, the Communion of the saints; the forgiveness of sins; the resurrection of the body; and the life everlasting.
>
> Amen

This creed has three sections revolving around the three members of the Trinity. Our structure of this section of the book will follow this organization, beginning with Charles Swindoll discussing the

Trinity. Then D. Stuart Briscoe describes God the Father, followed by Max Lucado painting a beautiful picture of God the Son, Jesus. This section of the book concludes with Walter Kaiser explaining the Holy Spirit and his work in the lives of believers.

The Trinity

are there three Gods or one?

BY CHARLES R. SWINDOLL

There is one God, yet three distinct persons. The Godhead is coequal, coeternal, coexistent: God the Father, God the Son, God the Holy Spirit. Much of this remains a profound mystery. Don't lose sleep if you cannot unravel the truth of the Trinity. As you read and study your Bible, you will discover many things that will challenge your finite human mind. How worthy of worship would a god be if he could be fully understood?

God the Father Almighty

The revelation of an invisible, insidious disease that has infected and crippled our once-strong nation is commonly called "me-ism"— a subtle yet consuming passion to please one's self, to exalt "I, me, mine, myself." At the risk of sounding narrow and simplistic, I have a message that represents not just a different approach but an opposite one. I am more convinced than ever that life's major pursuit is not knowing self—but knowing God.

As a matter of fact, unless God is the major pursuit of our lives, all other pursuits are dead-end streets, including trying to know ourselves. They won't work. They won't satisfy. They won't result in fulfillment. They won't do for us what we think they are going to do.

You never really begin the process of coming to know yourself until you begin the process of coming to know God. The byproduct of such a process is discovering the peace you long for so desperately.

The prophet Jeremiah declared: "And they bend their tongue like their bow; lies and not truth prevail in the land" (Jer. 9:3a NASB). (In today's terms the way this would read is "because they are going from bad to worse.") Jeremiah wails, "Everywhere I turn I seek for truth and I hear lies. I look for faithfulness and I find unfaithfulness. I look for people who are gentle, kind, encouraging, and I find treachery, murder, assault, rape. I look in vain to find the things that are to characterize the people of God."

Now the disease—here's the foundational cause: "'And they do not know Me,' declares the Lord" (v. 3b).

This may seem like a very simple answer, yet it's profound. A little later the prophet continues to quote his Lord: "Let not a wise man boast of his wisdom, and let not the mighty man boast of his might, let not a rich man boast of his riches" (Jer. 9:23 NASB).

Now wait. Just pause right there.

You want to know what people pursue when their eyes are on themselves? You've got it right in that statement. They embrace a "counterfeit value system," the same dead-end pursuit—human wisdom, human might, human riches.

I ask you, Is this relevant or what? Does that description sound like today's world? Stop on most any university campus and ask, "What is your goal? What is your plan? Where are you going?" Sometimes the answers will surprise you.

I was on a university campus not long ago. I asked a student, "Where are you going?" He said, "Lunch." I was expecting some great philosophical answer. But aside from a simple answer like that, you will probably hear, "I want to be resourceful" (human wisdom). "I want to be influential" (human might). "I want to be powerful" (human riches). "I want to be successful. I want to wind up top in my company. I want to run things. I want to control people. I want to be in charge. I want to make a name for myself."

We don't read a single comment in verse 23 about the living God. But in the next statement (v. 24) the solution emerges: "But let him who boasts boast of this, that he understands and knows Me" (NASB).

Now there's the cure—plain, brief, and simple. What is it that will make an unfaithful person faithful? What is it that will make an influential person who is controlling people a servant? What is it that will cause an individual who has turned to treachery to become gentle and gracious and giving, demonstrating a heart for God? It is understanding and knowing the living God.

How about you? Do you really want to understand God's ways? I'm not referring to the kind of understanding and knowledge that is merely intellectual theology. Not that. I have in mind men and women who see life through the eyes of God, who understand life's circumstances through the lens of God's plan, who accept and believe that whatever is happening has been given by God, permitted by God, and continues under God's personal surveillance—that kind of God-understanding and God-awareness.

Now I need to confess something to you. When I sat down to write about God, I thought, *What can I say?* Returning to this theological root is an awesome journey. Much of it is beyond our comprehension.

The Importance of Knowing God
Knowing God Gives Us the Desire to Be Like Him

Interesting, isn't it, that when the Lord talks about himself, he reveals his attributes, his character traits: loving-kindness, justice, righteousness.

Knowing God Reveals the Truth about Ourselves

When we study the Lord God, we discover he's holy and we're unholy. It doesn't hurt us to know that; it helps us. We discover that he's perfect and we're imperfect; he's strong and we're weak; he's patient and we're impatient; he's impartial, yet we're prejudiced. He's in control, and our lives are often fractured by fear and worry. And something occurs in that contrast that causes his character to over-shadow our need. The result is marvelous—the knowledge of the Holy One equips us to see the truth and to change. I cannot explain how it works; I just know it does.

Do you change by spending time with people? Very little. Only a few people can impact you sufficiently to result in your changing for the good. Most people will tell you that you are so far ahead of others that you don't have anything to work on—"nothin' to worry about." Trust me, God won't leave you with that information! He'll help you see yourself—your strengths and certainly your weaknesses. And every time you turn to his Word, you'll see another flaw, another need, another weakness that needs to be addressed. God always tells the truth. And it is the truth that sets us free! When we see ourselves as we really are, we are prompted to lean on him and to trust him to make us like he is.

Knowing God Enables Us to Interpret Our World

When you get hold of the knowledge of God and begin to see that he is in charge, you won't panic every time you read the paper. You won't give up hope because there's an earthquake somewhere. You won't live in the fear of terrorism or possible diseases.

In fact, you'll sort of sing your way through the business section, the editorial page—even the sports page! Why? Because you know the God who is in control of all things.

Knowing God Makes Us Stronger and More Secure

I want to ask you a direct question. Isn't it true, more often than not, that the God you picture in your mind is old, has a long beard—

and maybe leans on a cane? Isn't that true? You picture him standing in the North with his cheeks pushing out as he blows real hard, right? Sure you do. He wears a robe, has big toes, sandals. He's not too sure about modern things like advanced nuclear physics, computers, Palm Pilots, and the NASDAQ. He's more of a kind old grandfather who is gonna be there when you need him, and you can trust him because he is wise and generous. He could handle things yesterday, and maybe he could handle most things today. But he's sort of losing touch.

If that's your God, then listen to me: *That is heresy!*

It's nothing short of *heresy* to think of God like that. He isn't old; he is eternal. He isn't intimidated: he's omnipotent. Computers don't bother him; he is omniscient! The nuclear warheads don't have him worried! He is sovereign.

So things aren't out of hand! He's in control. He can handle it. And what's more, he can handle you. Those who know their God operate in the context of confidence; they can face whatever—and "display strength and take action."

See the value of knowing God? See what it does to your perspective? See how much calmer you become? Lift your eyes. Behold his glory high and lifted up. Worthy is the Lamb that was slain to give power and authority over this place. His kingdom will not fail. That's our God.

Knowing God Introduces Us to the External Dimension of Existence

Look at John 17:3. Jesus is praying to the father as he says: "This is eternal life: that they may know You, the only true God, and the One You have sent—Jesus Christ" (HCSB).

Knowing God introduces me to the invisible world of God's kingdom. I see through eyes that aren't given to everyone. We read elsewhere: "Things which eye has not seen and ear has not heard, and which have not entered the heart of man, all that God has prepared for those who love Him" (1 Cor. 2:9 NASB).

The natural person isn't born with this insight. It's given at the new birth. That's why I often talk about coming to know Jesus Christ, believing in the Lord Jesus Christ. Because when he comes in, he introduces us to an eternal dimension for living. And that perspective lifts the mind *above* the present, irksome details of life. What we gain is an eternal dimension of life.

Loving God: Our Ultimate Response

We have spent time thinking about the importance of knowing God, which I've called life's major pursuit. Let's consider the other side of the same coin—loving God, which is clearly our ultimate response.

Tucked away in the fifth book of the Bible is a profound statement and a wonderful command. I want you to see both statement and command together in Deuteronomy 6:4–5. The command is preceded by the statement, which talks about *knowing* God, let's observe the command, which addresses the importance of *loving* God.

Deuteronomy 6:4 is one of the most familiar statements in all of Jewish liturgy: "Hear, O Israel! The LORD is our God, the LORD is one!" (NASB).

You can't see it in English, but in the Hebrew that word *one* conveys the idea of "one in multiple," one as in a "cluster" or "group." *Echad* is the Hebrew word for one, as in a cluster of grapes. "The Lord our God is one—one in Father, one in Son, one in Spirit." Moses says, "Hear, O Israel, and come to know him as your only God." That statement had to do with knowing God.

Now, the command: "Love the LORD your God with all your heart and with all your soul and with all your strength" (Deut. 6:5). How significant was this? He now explains its importance: "These commandments that I give you today are to be upon your hearts. Impress them on your children. Talk about them when you sit at home and when you walk along the road, when you lie down and when you get up. Tie them as symbols on your hands and bind them on your foreheads. Write them on the doorframes of your houses and on your gates" (Deut. 6:6–9).

God is saying, "This is something I want you to put on your heart, men and women. And then as I bring children into your family, these are the things I want you to teach them. Not simply as an intellectual exercise, but I want it to be in the warp and woof of your lives. I want it to take place when you lie down at night and when you get up. When you walk, when you play, when you work. I want these things to characterize your lifestyle. I want you to model knowing me and loving me with all your heart, with all your soul, with all your might. And I want your children to absorb the same convictions, so that they will have that impression even when you're gone."

I didn't give you six steps on how to know God. That was on purpose. Knowing God doesn't occur like that. It isn't a mechanical, step-by-step process. It's a lifetime pursuit. What it really requires is a day-by-day commitment in one's head and one's heart—a commitment that says, "Today I'm going to know God better. Today I'm going to love God more. This is going to become a regular, major pursuit of my life."

And piece by piece, little by little, day after day, it will begin to permeate your whole frame of reference. That's what Moses wanted for the Israelites, and that's what God wants for us.

God the Son: The Lord Jesus Christ

"Therefore the LORD Himself will give you a sign: Behold, a virgin will be with child and bear a son, and she will call His name Immanuel" (Isa. 7:14 NASB).

Mary was holding in her arms Immanuel—"God with us."

My friend, Jesus is God's Lamb, the Son of God. He didn't come to be packaged and offered for half price where, if you hurry, you can get him. He came as very God. And the world in its tinsel and tarnish has just about ruined the picture.

Has there been a time in your personal life when you have asked Christ Jesus to occupy your heart as he once occupied the manger? Honestly now, does he have first place? The Lord Jesus Christ is available in the same form he has been for centuries—the Son of God who died for you, who paid the price for your sin, who was raised from the dead, who is living.

When the God-Man Walked among Us

Who is Jesus Christ? You may be surprised to know that this question has continued to be asked ever since the first century when he walked on earth. His identity has never failed to create a stir. Who exactly is this Jesus? The answers have varied from demon to deity.

It is imperative that we know the right answer. Otherwise, we do not know how to interpret what he has done. And if we are unable to interpret what he has done, we will never be able to give ourselves to him as he invites us to do.

Who Is Jesus Christ?

"Now after Jesus was born in Bethlehem of Judea in the days of Herod the king, behold, magi from the east arrived in Jerusalem, saying, 'Where is He who has been born King of the Jews? For we saw His star in the east, and have come to worship Him'" (Matt. 2:1–2 NASB).

There was no question in the minds of the wise men: the birth of Jesus represented the birth of a king. The star was "his star." Clearly in their minds, he was "King of the Jews," and they had come to bow down before him in worship.

"And after being baptized, Jesus went up immediately from the water; and behold, the heavens were opened, and He saw the Spirit of God descending as a dove, and coming upon Him, and behold, a voice out of the heavens saying, 'This is My beloved Son, in whom I am well-pleased'" (Matt. 3:16–17 NASB).

There was no question in God's mind: "I have given you my beloved Son."

Later, at what we know as the transfiguration, on a mountain with some of his disciples, the same voice spoke yet again, making the same announcement: "This is My beloved Son, with whom I am well-pleased: listen to Him" (Matt. 17:5 NASB).

The wise men, along with God the Father, had no question. "He is the King of the Jews." "He is My Son."

Jesus Himself Believes

When you get to Luke 24, Jesus has gone to death and beyond. He's come out of the grave. He has victoriously risen in bodily form, and he is speaking to his disciples. I find it most intriguing that in verse 44, Jesus mentions words out of the Old Testament, words concerning himself: "Now He said to them, 'These are My words which I spoke to you while I was still with you, that all things which are written about Me in the Law of Moses and the Prophets and the Psalms must be fulfilled'" (NASB).

This is one of the few times Jesus took people through the Scriptures and explained himself to them from the law, from the Psalms, and from the prophets. "You see that? That was a reference to me. You see this? That's spoken of me. You see what the prophet said? I fulfill this."

"Then He opened their minds to understand the Scriptures, and He said to them, 'Thus it is written, that the Christ should suffer and rise again from the dead the third day; and that repentance for forgiveness of sins should be proclaimed in His name to all the nations, beginning from Jerusalem. You are witnesses of these things'" (Luke 24:45–48 NASB). Jesus was saying to his disciples: "Men, you have had a unique privilege—to have lived during transition. You've seen me carry these things out. Now I've come back from the grave. And I'm declaring to you, 'This is truth. I am who I claim to be, undiminished deity, true humanity, and in one person.'"

Or, as John writes, "The Word became flesh, and dwelt among us" (John 1:14 NASB). "The Word became flesh. God became man. And as man, he lives among us, and we give him glory. No question, he is God, he is the Son of God."

God the Holy Spirit

The Spirit Who Is Not a Ghost

Air is a force with incredible strength. It can snap a tree in two or demolish a landscape. Given enough velocity, air becomes a devastating wind. Energized by a hurricane or a tornado, it can clear out an entire mobile home park in seconds. The power in that invisible stuff! If you bottle it up in a network of hoses and valves and put it under enough pressure, it can bring a massive commercial bus or tractor-trailer rig to a screeching halt. It will even stop a locomotive pulling a hundred cars. It will break thick concrete on a driveway or a freeway if it's pushed through the right tools. It will loosen or tighten the lug nuts on your car's wheels if funneled into the right mechanism. In fact, it can lift massive amounts of weight.

How? Air. That's all, just air.

You can't feel it. You can't see it or smell it (unless you live around Los Angeles!). You can't, except in most technical ways, measure it or weigh it. But it keeps you alive every minute. If I took air away from you who are now reading this book for five minutes, you would become brain damaged. We cannot live without it. Yet when we fly, apply our brakes, or watch a mechanic work on our car, we think nothing of it. Amazing stuff, air.

Never think that because something is invisible it is therefore unimportant or weak. You may be surprised to know that the Bible talks a lot about air. As Calvin Miller pointed out, the Old Testament calls it *ruach*. The New Testament calls it *pneuma*. We get the word *pneumatic* from the New Testament Greek word. The English Bible, however, doesn't translate either one as *air*. Usually, it's *breath*. "God breathed into man the breath of life." Or it's called *wind*. "Like a mighty wind." Or it is translated *spirit*—as in the "spirit of man" or "the Holy Spirit."

A number of synonyms are used for Spirit—words like *helper*, *advocate*, *comforter*, *convicter*, *restrainer*, *exhorter*, and *reprover*. He is portrayed by symbols, too, such as a dove, fire, wind, even water. In

John 7 we read of this power being called "living water." Jesus says, "If any man is thirsty, let him come to Me and drink. He who believes in Me, as the Scripture said, 'From his innermost being shall flow rivers of living water'" (John 7:37–38 NASB).

And in case you wonder what he had reference to, the next verse explains: "But this He spoke of the Spirit" (John 7:39 NASB).

He referred to the Spirit of God, the third member of the Trinity.

Let me paraphrase verse 38: "From the believer's inner life there will be a reservoir of enormous, immeasurable power. It will gush forth. It will pour out like a torrential river that causes rapids, waterfalls, and endless movement to the ocean." That's the idea. It's not a picture of some blasé, passive force. The Spirit of God is the dynamic of life. Like air, the Spirit may be invisible—but let us never be misled by equating invisible with impotent. This Spirit is vital to life.

We are so impressed with what we can touch and weigh and see that when it comes to something invisible, we pass it off. Christians all around the world need the reminder that the most powerful force in life is something we can't even see—so powerful we are secured eternally until Christ comes, turning our destiny into reality, ushering us into eternity. And until that time, he is ready to work within us and move among us in revolutionary ways, transforming our lives.

The Spirit Is Not an "It" but a Distinct Personality

The Holy Spirit is a distinct person. He is a "him," a "he." Jesus once said: "If you ask Me anything in My name, I will do it. If you love Me, you will keep My commandments. And I will ask the Father, and He will give you another Helper, that *He* may be with you forever; that is the Spirit of truth, whom the world cannot receive, because it does not behold Him or know Him, but you know Him because He abides with you, and will be in *you*" (John 14:14–17 NASB, emphasis added).

What a helpful revelation! While Jesus was on earth, the Spirit of God was *with* the people of God. But when Jesus left the earth and sent another Helper ("another of the same kind," interestingly), like himself, the Helper came and became a part of their lives deep within. No longer near them, but *in* them. That's a mind-staggering truth. And notice he is called "he" or "him"—never "it." Nowhere in any reliable version of Scripture is the Spirit of God referred to as "it."

The Spirit Is Not Passive, but Active and Involved

"But I tell you the truth, it is to your advantage that I go away; for if I do not go away, the Helper shall not come to you; but if I go, I will send Him to you" (John 16:7 NASB).

What will he do? Lie around, take it easy, relax, casually kick back within us? No. Read very carefully what Jesus taught: "And He, when He comes, will convict the world concerning sin, and righteousness, and judgment. . . . But when He, the Spirit of truth, comes, He will guide you into all the truth; for He will not speak on His own initiative, but whatever He hears, He will speak; and He will disclose to you what is to come. He shall glorify Me; for He shall take of Mine, and shall disclose it to you" (John 16:8, 13–14 NASB).

Oftentimes we can sense that he is present. On some occasions his presence is so real, so obvious—it's almost as though we can touch him. When he moves among a body of people, he mobilizes and empowers them. They become sensitive, motivated, spiritually alive. They are cleansed. They are actively excited about the right things.

The Holy Spirit Is Not a Substitute for God, but He Is Deity

This will heighten your respect for the Holy Spirit's work, if nothing else will. Christians have been known to fight for the deity of Christ—and we certainly should. But what about the deity of the Spirit? Tucked away in the Book of Acts is a seldom-mentioned story about a couple who paid the ultimate price for their hypocrisy. Woven into their brief biography is a statement of the Spirit's deity. "But a certain man named Ananias, with his wife Sapphira, sold a piece of property, and kept back some of the price for himself, with his wife's full knowledge, and bringing a portion of it, he laid it at the apostles' feet. But Peter said, 'Ananias, why has Satan filled your heart to lie to the Holy Spirit, and to keep back some of the price of the land? While it remained unsold, did it not remain your own? And after it was sold was it not under your control? Why is it that you have conceived this deed in your heart? You have not lied to men, but to God'" (Acts 5:1–4 NASB).

Notice that when they lied *"to the Holy Spirit"* (v. 3), they *"lied . . . to God"* (v. 4, emphasis added).

Pause and ponder this, my Christian friend: The third member of the Godhead, the invisible, yet all-powerful representation of deity, is actually living inside your being. His limitless capabilities are resident within you since he indwells you.

You think you can't handle what life throws at you?

You think you can't stand firm or, when necessary, stand alone in your life?

You think you can't handle the lure of life's temptations? Well, you certainly could not if you were all alone. You—*alone*—can't do that any more than I can fly alone. But with the right kind of power put into operation—the very power and presence of God—you can handle it. You can do it. As a matter of fact, all the pressure will be shifted and the weight will be transferred from you to him. It's a radically different way to live. And because he is God, he can handle it.

I'm starting to sound a little authoritative about this awesome truth. The fact of the matter is that we know very little about how he does it—only that he is able to do it.

Don't let it trouble you if you struggle with trying to define and divide meanings of words and ideas and thoughts about the Holy Spirit. Some of these things are infinite and unfathomable.

He exists in an invisible realm. He is a power and a force you will never see, though you are convinced of the force himself. You will only see his working—the results of his enabling, his filling, his guiding. But when he, the Spirit of God, is in control, it is nothing short of awesome. When he is absent, it is dreadful. Believe me, nothing is worse than preaching a sermon without the Spirit's help. Well, maybe one thing is worse—listening to that sermon!

CHARLES R. SWINDOLL serves as president of Dallas Theological Seminary, helping to prepare a new generation of men and women for the ministry. He is also the Bible teacher on *Insight for Living,* a radio broadcast ministry that is aired daily worldwide. Swindoll's books have sold well over five and a half million copies. Some of the most important works include *Encourage Me, Come before Winter and Share My Hope, Strike the Original Match, Growing Strong in the Seasons of Life, The Bride,* and *Growing Deep in the Christian Life.*

God the Father Almighty

why does God care about me?

BY D. STUART BRISCOE

"I believe in God the Father Almighty, Maker of heaven and earth;"

*I*t is said that there are no atheists in foxholes. Atheists, you will remember, believe that there is no God. This is precisely what they choose to believe. It is a remarkable decision on their part because they have no evidence of such nonexistence on which to base it! But back to the foxhole. When people find themselves in positions of extreme danger, they tend to call out for help. Even atheists who believe that he is not there occasionally call out to God! This suggests that in times of extreme stress people have a deep need for a god of some kind. On risk's edge, feelings of competence quickly disappear, and the cry for help takes over.

A Religious Animal

But what about those whose pleasant lives have never reached the breaking point? They sense no need for a god. Occasionally when they experience the "highs" of life, such as the birth of a baby or the beauty of a sunset, they are overcome with thankfulness. But who can they thank? Certainly the joy can be shared with whoever shares the experience, but often the human heart longs to say "thanks" at a deeper level. We could call this an inbuilt impulse to worship. And worship requires a god. So whether it is prompted by agony or ecstasy, the human heart will often surprise itself in its instinctive reaching out to a god. It was the recognition of this that led Edmund Burke to say that man "by his constitution is a religious animal."

So there is an underlying sense, however vague, of an existing god in most people's lives, even though the degree of importance attached to this varies dramatically. This is understandable when we consider the widely divergent views that people hold concerning who God is, what he does, and the role he intends to play in people's lives.

I or We or Something Else?

Someone may say, "Well, as long as you believe in God, surely that is sufficient." Hardly! Ayn Rand, a Russian émigré to the West, was bitterly opposed to Soviet collectivism, and she reveled in the freedom of the individual in America. She said that she had discovered the god who grants "joy and peace and pride," and added, "This god is one word, *I!*" That's right, you read it correctly; God is I!

Shirley Maclaine, the actress and author of *Out on a Limb*, had a different opinion. She wrote, "We are god, [that] all is god," and she called those who do not agree "ignorant!" Now you can see immediately that both women claimed to believe in God, but there the similarity ended. For one, "I" is god, for the other, "We" is (or are?) god! And in between "I" and "We" a thousand gods reside.

How Reasonable Is Reason?

Ayn Rand and Shirley MacLaine reasoned their way into their own conclusions. But brain power can arrive at very different conclusions. Many centuries ago Archbishop Anselm reasoned that if people can imagine "a being than which nothing greater can be conceived," there must be some reality behind their imagining. There must be a super being somewhere. This was called the "ontological argument." Then Thomas Aquinas, developing the "cosmological argument," reasoned that nothing happens without a reason. Behind every effect there is a cause. So the world could not just happen; there must be an original cause for it, a reason behind it. He called this uncaused cause, God. Then along came Voltaire arguing from design. He could not imagine a clock without a clockmaker. No more could he conceive of an intricate world without an intelligent designer. We call his reasoning the "teleological argument." Cosmological, ontological, and teleological are certainly not the kind of words we use every day. But at least they are all logical!

Each of these approaches has merit, but none of them proves conclusively the existence of God. Even if they did, God would be nothing more than a brilliant, powerful, original designer—certainly an accurate but insufficient reflection of who God is. Truth but not the whole truth.

Another line of reasoning called the "moral argument" takes us a little further. Human beings have an inbuilt sense of right and wrong, fairness and unfairness, justice and injustice. This innate sense of right and wrong must come from an ultimate source of morality called God—a moral being who is personal, powerful, and brilliant.

All these arguments are based on human reason. While reason is a gift from God and should therefore be used—there is no excuse for gray matter solidifying in the cranium—like all aspects of our humanity, human reason is fallen. That does not mean it is incapable of reasoning rightly, but it does mean that it cannot reason infallibly. Therefore to gain a right view of God, more than reason is necessary.

Speculation or Revelation?

But this raises enormous questions, such as, "Assuming that behind all things there is at least a brilliant, powerful moral being called God, is it conceivable that he would wish to relate to human beings? And if so, how are we to know him in order to relate to him? If discovery of God is beyond the capability of fallen human reason, how are we to find the information necessary?" This is where revelation comes into play. The Christian believes that knowing who God is cannot and must not be left to guesswork—or speculation. What we need is revelation. Speculation is all about people thinking up their own answers to the question, "Who is God?" Revelation is God leaning out of heaven and saying, "Please be quiet and pay attention, and I'll tell you who I am." Speculation is human guesswork. Revelation is divine handiwork.

More than Instinct

We have seen that humans instinctively react godward in times of extremity or ecstasy. Burke dismissively called this "religious animal" behavior, but the apostle Paul, speaking about human beings, said, "The truth about God is known to them instinctively. God has put this knowledge in their hearts" (Rom. 1:19 NLT).

We marvel at the powerful instincts of animals such as the tiny plover, which migrates from the polar ice cap to Hawaii over thousands of miles of ocean, making landfall where the slightest error would mean a watery grave. Presumably such instincts are a gift of God to the creatures he made. But the instincts that turn a human to God in praise or terror are much greater than the ability to steer unerringly across a trackless ocean. These instincts include the gift of innate knowledge of him. And it has nothing to do with humankind and everything to do with God. It is part of his handiwork. It is part of God's self-revelation.

Seeing the Invisible

But there is much more. Paul elaborated further: "From the time the world was created, people have seen the earth and sky and all that God made. They can clearly see his invisible qualities—his eternal power and divine nature. So they have no excuse whatsoever for not knowing God. Yes, they knew God" (Rom. 1:20–21 NLT).

Paul was making the point that even though this remarkable revelation of God in creation had been made available to all, yet they
had rejected it—they had pushed "the truth away from themselves"
(Rom. 1:18 NLT). Rejected or not, however, the revelation of God's
"invisible qualities" goes on relentlessly day after day in created
things large and small. Do you want a picture of God's awesome
power? Then sit with David in the Judean hills on a dark night and
say with him,

> When I look at the night sky and see
>   the work of your fingers—
>   the moon and the stars you have set in place—
> what are mortals that you should think of us,
>   mere humans that you should care for us? . . .
> O LORD, our Lord, the majesty of your name
>   fills the earth! (Ps. 8:3–4, 9 NLT)

Do you want a sense of God's aesthetic sensibilities? "Consider
the lilies." Or his attention to minute detail? Then "consider the
ants." Wherever we look at the creation, there is evidence of the invisible God; there are indications not only of his existence but hints and
clues to his character. But the pinnacle of divine creation is
humankind. So no study of creation with a view to understanding
the Creator can be complete without a study of the divine master-
piece—humanity! In the study of humanity there are things to be
learned about the realities of deity. Scripture reminds us that "God
created man in his own image, in the image of God he created him;
male and female he created them" (Gen. 1:27).

Whatever it means that humankind is created in the divine
image, it surely means that in the complexity of our humanity
there are traces of the intricacy of the divine being. In the same way
that a work of art tells the insightful observer something of the
artist, so the reverent observer of humanity catches glimpses of the
One who made us—and even made us capable of fellowship with
him. It might be argued that the fallenness of humankind pre-

cludes any accurate reflection of the divine in the human makeup. And there is much about humankind that we would never believe is reflective of God's character. But even a tiny fractured, fragment of an excavated Grecian vase tells something of the skill of the ancient workman. Even flawed humans reveal something of a holy God. Their ability to reason, to love, to create, to choose, to decide—all these point unerringly to the One by whom and for whom they were created.

But Does God Care about Us?

God's self-revelation has gone far beyond what we have discussed so far. For this we should be thankful. Not everybody is philosophically inclined, so it might never occur to them to think about God by logical reasoning. By the same token many people would not make the connection between a blooming flower and a God of beauty. But everybody knows something about relationships, because it is in the relational arena that life is lived. So God has revealed himself as a relational being.

God as Father

When God sent Moses back to Egypt with instructions to demand from Pharoah the release of the children of Israel, he told his reluctant messenger to say, "'Israel is my firstborn son. I commanded you to let him go, so he could worship me. But since you have refused, be warned! I will kill your firstborn son!'" (Exod. 4:22–23 NLT). In referring to the enslaved people as his son, God was speaking of himself as Father.

Much later—after many weary, wasted, wandering years in the wilderness—Moses upbraided the same people and told them,

"Is this the way you repay the Lord,
    you foolish and senseless people?
Isn't he your Father who created you?
    Has he not made you and established you?"
(Deut. 32:6 NLT)

God, years later, spoke through the prophet Hosea, using similar language: "When Israel was a child, I loved him as a son, and I called my son out of Egypt. But the more I called to him, the more he rebelled, offering sacrifices to the images of Baal and burning incense to idols" (Hos. 11:1–2 NLT).

Nevertheless, the Father continued to shower his love and compassion upon his rebellious "son," and the psalmist captured the poignancy of the situation when he wrote, "The LORD is like a father to his children, tender and compassionate to those who fear him" (Ps. 103:13 NLT).

So through his dealings with Israel his adopted son, a picture of a loving, caring, disappointed, but relentlessly faithful Father emerges. God the Father!

The Father and the Son

But it was not until Jesus embarked on his public ministry that the full picture of the Fatherhood of God was revealed. In the Fourth Gospel, John wrote, "No one has ever seen God. But his only Son, who is himself God, is near to the Father's heart; he has told us about him" (John 1:18 NLT).

It is interesting to note that in John's Gospel alone, God is described as Father 122 times. Many of these Scriptures give details of Jesus' teaching about the Father that we do not have space to pursue in this chapter. Nevertheless, time spent on a study of the material would be time well spent. Yet the ministry of Jesus was designed not only to tell people about the Father but also to show the Father in action. When Jesus explained to his troubled disciples that he was about to return to the Father, an interesting exchange between Philip and Jesus ensued.

"Philip said, 'Lord show us the Father and we will be satisfied.' Jesus replied, 'Philip, don't you even yet know who I am, even after all the time I have been with you? Anyone who has seen me has seen the Father! So why are you asking to see him?'" (John 14:8–9 NLT).

The Lord Jesus really said that anyone who had seen him had seen the Father! This powerful statement opens up to us the possibility of being able to put together a picture of the Father in action from the deeds of the Lord Jesus. In fact, Jesus apparently assumed that Philip had insight into the relationship between the Father and the Son when he asked, "Don't you believe that I am in the Father and the Father is in me? The words I say are not my own, but my Father who lives in me does his work through me. Just believe that I am in the Father and the Father is in me. Or at least believe because of what you have seen me do" (John 14:10–11 NLT).

Poor Philip was struggling to understand how Jesus and the Father were so inextricably bound up in each other that when Jesus acted it was actually the Father at work through him. And Jesus understood his problem. That's why, in effect, he said to Philip, "You've seen the remarkable things that I have done. If you can't grasp the relationship I have with the Father, at least grasp this—that what is going on here is a revelation of who the Father is. You've seen what happened—that was the Father at work. You want to know what he is like. Then look at what I have been doing and that's what the Father does. And that's what he is like!"

So when Jesus cried over Jerusalem, those were the Father's tears. When he overturned the tables of the rogues and rascals in the temple, that was the Father's anger. When he forgave the sinful woman, that was Fatherly grace in action. When he lovingly restored the dead-and-buried Lazarus to his grieving sisters, that was the Father's power in evidence. If you've seen Jesus, you've seen the Father. No need for speculation now. Revelation has been made available.

Our Father

But Jesus took the revelation of the Father a step further. He showed the people that while his eternal relationship with the Father was unique, they could be related to him as well—not in precisely the same way but in a deep, living relationship nevertheless. So he talked to them about "my Father" and "your Father." Imagine the wonder in Mary's heart as she knelt before the risen Christ and heard him say, "I am ascending to my Father and your Father, my God and your God" (John 20:17 NLT).

When Jesus referred to God as his Father, he apparently used the Aramaic word *Abba*, which we believe no one before had ever used to address God. *Abba* was used by small children to speak to their fathers, and Jesus' use of this term must have introduced the Jewish people to a way of looking at God in warm, intimate, personal terms—something new to them. We know the early Christians certainly embraced Jesus' way of speaking about and to the Father because the word *Abba* was retained in the Greek New Testament and, in fact, made its way into many English translations too! For instance, Paul wrote, "Because you are sons, God sent the Spirit of his Son into our hearts, the Spirit who calls out, '*Abba*, Father'" (Gal. 4:6).

The Lord Jesus always addressed God as "Father" in prayer—with one exception, when he quoted Psalm 22 on the cross. It is not surprising therefore that when the disciples asked the Lord to teach them to pray, he told them to direct their prayers to "our Father in heaven" (Matt. 6:9). The winsomeness and power of this can be seen in the delightful homely illustration he used to assure his disciples that their prayers would be heard and answered. He asked them, "You fathers—if your children ask for a fish, do you give them a snake instead? Or if they ask for an egg, do you give them a scorpion? Of course not! If you sinful people know how to give good gifts to your children, how much more will your heavenly Father give the Holy Spirit to those who ask him" (Luke 11:11–13 NLT).

Like Father, Like Son

Some people assume that God is everybody's Father. In the sense that he is Creator of all, this may be true. But Jesus was blunt in explaining to some of his contemporaries who were rejecting him that they should not assume that God was their Father in the fullest sense of the word. They should not go glibly through life without any desire for a loving, obedient, trusting relationship with the Father and assume that they were his children anyway and all would be well in the end. In fact, he said to them, "If God were your Father, you would love me, . . . For you are the children of your father the Devil, and you love to do the evil things he does" (John 8:42, 44 NLT).

The evidence that we are his children and he is truly our Father is that we accept what Jesus has said and done to show us the Father's love and that we have submitted ourselves gladly to his saving grace—a submission that is demonstrated by obedience to his instructions.

The followers of Jesus were glad to embrace their relationship with God as Father, and this was reflected in some of their teaching. For example, the writer of the letter to the Hebrews wrote, "Whoever heard of a child who was never disciplined? If God doesn't discipline you as he does all of his children, it means that you are illegitimate and are not really his children after all. Since we respect our earthly fathers who disciplined us, should we not all the more cheerfully submit to the discipline of our heavenly Father and live forever?" (Heb. 12:7–9 NLT).

This dimension of divine fathering is often overlooked—and sometimes resented and denied—for the rather obvious reason that it is more pleasant to dwell on the tender, loving care of a father than to consider the often painful experience of discipline that a loving father must administer. But if we are to really know the Father, we must embrace this side of the relationship as well.

The Father Almighty

We saw earlier that through human reasoning it was possible to come to the conclusion that behind the vast universe stands a powerful Creator. But we have also noted that the best speculation in the world has its limits, and we must therefore turn our attention to revelation. So what do Christians believe about the power of God? The Apostles' Creed states, "I believe in God the Father Almighty, Maker of heaven and earth."

"When Abram was ninety-nine years old, the LORD appeared to him and said, 'I am God Almighty; serve me faithfully and live a blameless life. I will make a covenant with you, by which I will guarantee to make you into a mighty nation'" (Gen. 17:1–2 NLT). It was important for Abram to be told that God was Almighty because what God was promising to do was utterly impossible from a human point of view. God had already promised Abram that his descendants would be so numerous that it would be impossible to count them. They would represent many nations, kings would be among them, and all these people would be descended from a yet unborn child who would be born of Abram's barren wife, Sarai.

Remember, Abram was ninety-nine, and Sarai was ninety and infertile! So when we talk about God being Almighty, we need to remember what an Almighty God looks like! As Paul said years later, "Abraham is the father of all who believe. . . . This happened because Abraham believed in the God who brings the dead back to life and who brings into existence what didn't exist before" (Rom. 4:16–17 NLT).

"Almighty" describes God in his awesome, majestic power ruling over all things, including things that do not exist and even death itself! Now that's Almighty!

It is noteworthy that having introduced himself to Abram, in what we call Genesis (the first book of the Bible) God is praised by the worshiping multitudes in eternity, a fact recorded for us in Revelation (the last book of the Bible)—and the theme is his Almighty–ness:

"Great and marvelous are your actions, Lord God Almighty.
Just and true are all your ways,
    O King of the nations.
Who will not fear, O Lord, and glorify your name?
    For you alone are holy.
All nations will come and worship before you,
    for your righteous deeds have been revealed."
(Rev. 15:3–4 NLT)

So God is revealed in Scripture as both Father and Almighty. And we are right in affirming "I believe in God the Father Almighty" because this statement presents the two balancing aspects of the divine being. The revelation of God as Father speaks of his presence, love, grace, care, and concern in our lives—we call this his immanence.

In the same way, the fact that he is "Almighty, Maker of heaven and earth" reminds us that he is awesome in majesty, creativity, power, and rule. We call this his transcendence. A balanced understanding of these two dimensions of God's self-revelation is imperative if we are to know God correctly. To concentrate only on his immanence can lead to an inappropriate familiarity with God that lacks a sense of awe and reverence. On the other hand, to concentrate exclusively on his transcendence can mean that we never enter into the intimacy of his love and enjoy his presence through the Spirit in our lives. He is truly "the Father Almighty."

This balance is seen beautifully in Job's attitude after he had suffered the devastating loss of his family, his health, and his possessions. Job did not underestimate either the power of the Almighty, the possibility of correction by a father, or the caring compassion of the Almighty Father. He said in response to his unhelpful "friend" Eliphaz, "Consider the joy of those corrected by God! Do not despise the chastening of the Almighty when you sin. For though he wounds, he also bandages. He strikes, but his hands also heal. He will rescue you again and again so that no evil can touch you" (Job 5:17–19 NLT).

Maker of Heaven and Earth

Small children in times of stress often resort to arguments with their peers on the relative power and might of their fathers. "My dad's bigger than your dad!" "My dad'll whip your dad any day." They derive great comfort from the knowledge that they have a father who is not only capable of looking after himself but also of protecting and caring for them against all odds. Believers can also do a little bragging—for their heavenly Father is also the "Maker of heaven and earth." Now that's power!

While philosophers struggle with theories about the meaning of the universe and scientists search for its origins, the Scriptures say very little about the Creation. We are told that "in the beginning" God already existed and that he thought, desired, willed, and brought into being "all things," including us. We also are told that everything that God made was tainted, warped, and corrupted by the Fall, and as a result the whole creation "anticipates the day when it will join God's children in glorious freedom from death and decay" (Rom. 8:21 NLT). When God is good and ready, he will "set the heavens on fire and the elements will melt away in the flames. But we are looking forward to the new heavens and new earth he has promised, a world where everyone is right with God" (2 Pet. 3:12–13 NLT).

God is the one who originates, perpetuates, and terminates. Then he will recreate! My Father is awesome.

My Father, the Maker of Heaven and Earth

So when I say "I believe in God the Father Almighty, Maker of heaven and earth," I affirm that I am convinced that I am not an accident. I was created by an intelligent God for an intelligent purpose. Discovering and experiencing this God is crucial to my existence as a human being. I declare that my own brain power is not sufficient to unveil the mysteries of existence in general and mine in particular but that the God who made me has chosen to reveal himself to me in a knowable and understandable fashion. This revelation comes through creation, through Scripture, and most vividly in the Lord Jesus.

I have discovered that the God so revealed wants me to experience his loving, compassionate, directing, supporting fatherliness while at the same time I remember that he is awesome in his power and control. I realize that even the world we live in exists only through his will. When he is good and ready, he will bring even that to an end and make in its place a completely new, totally awesome new creation in which he will allow me to share. This is possible because I came to him in acknowledgment of my failure as a human being, seeking his merciful and gracious forgiveness made available through the merits of his Son, our Lord Jesus Christ. But that belongs in another chapter.

For now, let us worship the Father Almighty joyfully and humbly, embracing him with heart, mind, and strength and rejoicing that he rules eternally over us and lives incredibly within us.

The Next Step
Scriptures with One-Sentence Contextual Explanation

Genesis 1:1. In these opening words the Bible states without introduction or apology that God exists and that he is the originator of all things.

Genesis 1:27–28. God created man—male and female—uniquely capable of intimate fellowship with God and with responsibilities for the rest of creation.

Genesis 6:5–8. God was deeply grieved and pained by man's evil rebellion and waywardness, but he showed extraordinary grace to those whose hearts were right before him.

Genesis 12:1–3. God determined to reach out in love and grace to the human race, and he chose Abram and his descendants as the channels through whom blessing would ultimately flow to the whole world.

Deuteronomy 32:6. As time went on, the descendants of Abram— a.k.a. the children of Israel—showed little interest in responding positively to God's goodness. Their leaders found it necessary to remind them that this was no way to treat God, their Father.

John 14:10–11. When Jesus came, he referred constantly to God as his Father and even went so far as to say that if people watched him in action they would get a visual portrait of the invisible God at work.

Matthew 6:9–13. When Jesus' disciples asked him to teach them to pray as he prayed, he told them to address their prayers to "Our

Father," thereby including them to a certain degree in the intimate relationship he enjoyed with the Father in heaven.

Luke 11:11–13. Human fathers are sinful, so it is not always possible to use them as examples of the heavenly Father. But in this instance Jesus showed his disciples that if even less-than-perfect fathers know how to be good to their children they could anticipate God giving them all they needed in life.

Hebrews 12:10–11. While fathers should model care and concern to their children, they are also required to discipline them if they are to grow up to be responsible citizens. In the same way, the heavenly Father finds it necessary to discipline his children so they will grow into spiritual maturity.

Hebrews 2:10–12. If Jesus is our Savior, then God is our Father, Jesus is our brother, and his children are our family. It is in this complex of relationships that the believer finds security, support, joy, peace, and purpose.

Books for Further Reading

- *I Believe in the Creator* by James M. Houston (Eerdmans).
- *God—Knowing Our Creator* ("We Believe" series) by Max Anders (Nelson).
- *The Sovereign God* by James Montgomery Boice (InterVarsity Press).
- *Knowing God* by James I. Packer (InterVarsity Press).
- *The Apostles' Creed* by Stuart Briscoe (Harold Shaw).

D. STUART BRISCOE was born in Millom, Cumbria, England, in 1930. He graduated from high school and promptly embarked on a career in banking. At the age of seventeen he started to preach, and for twelve years this and banking kept him fully occupied. In 1959 he left the business world to share in the ministry of the Torchbearers, a youth organization reaching out to the far corners of the world.

In 1970, Elmbrook Church in Brookfield, Wisconsin, USA, asked Stuart to become pastor. The church has since grown to a weekly attendance of more than seven thousand and has planted eight sister churches in the Milwaukee area. Elmbrook's TV and radio ministries, *Telling the Truth,* are broadcast widely while Briscoe's video- and audiotapes and more than forty books extend his ministry.

Briscoe and his wife, Jill, have three children and thirteen grandchildren, at last count. In his spare time, Stuart likes to read, run, garden, and enjoy God's creation.

God the Son, Jesus Christ

what makes Jesus unique?

By Max Lucado

The Son

"And in Jesus Christ His only Son our Lord, who was conceived by the Holy Spirit, born of the Virgin Mary;"

In the beginning was the Word;
and the Word was with God,
and the Word was God.
He was with God in the beginning.
All things were created through Him,
and apart from Him not one thing was created
that has been created.
In Him was life,
and that life was the light of men.
That light shines in the darkness,
yet the darkness did not overcome it.
(John 1:1–5 HCSB)

In those days a decree went out from Caesar Augustus that the whole empire should be registered. This first registration took place while Quirinius was governing Syria. So everyone went to be registered, each to his own town.

And Joseph also went up from the town of Nazareth in Galilee, to Judea, to the city of David, which is called Bethlehem, because he was of the house and family line of David, to be registered along with Mary, who was engaged to him and was pregnant. While they were there, it happened that the days were completed for her to give birth. Then she gave birth to her firstborn Son, and she wrapped Him snugly in cloth and laid Him in a manger—because there was no room for them at the inn. (Luke 2:1–7 HCSB)

God had entered the world as a baby.

Yet, were someone to chance upon the sheep stable on the outskirts of Bethlehem that morning, what a peculiar scene they would behold.

The stable stinks like all stables do. The stench of urine, dung, and sheep reeks pungently in the air. The ground is hard, the hay scarce. Cobwebs cling to the ceiling, and a mouse scurries across the dirt floor.

A more lowly place of birth could not exist.

Off to one side sit a group of shepherds. They sit silently on the floor; perhaps perplexed, perhaps in awe, no doubt in amazement. Their night watch had been interrupted by an explosion of light from heaven and a symphony of angels. God goes to those who have time to hear him—so on this cloudless night he went to simple shepherds.

Near the young mother sits the weary father. If anyone is dozing, he is. He can't remember the last time he sat down. And now that the excitement has subsided a bit, now that Mary and the baby are comfortable, he leans against the wall of the stable and feels his eyes grow heavy. He still hasn't figured it all out. The mystery of the event puzzles him. But he hasn't the energy to wrestle with the questions. What's important is that the baby is fine and that Mary is safe. As

sleep comes he remembers the name the angel told him to use—
Jesus. "We will call him Jesus."

Wide awake is Mary. My, how young she looks! Her head rests on
the soft leather of Joseph's saddle. The pain has been eclipsed by
wonder. She looks into the face of the baby. Her son. Her Lord. His
Majesty. At this point in history, the human being who best understands who God is and what he is doing is a teenage girl in a smelly
stable. She can't take her eyes off him. Somehow Mary knows she is
holding God. So this is he. She remembers the words of the angel.
"His kingdom will have no end" (Luke 1:33 HCSB).

He looks like anything but a king. His face is prunish and red. His
cry, though strong and healthy, is still the helpless and piercing cry of
a baby. And he is absolutely dependent upon Mary for his well-
being.

Majesty in the midst of the mundane. Holiness in the filth of
sheep manure and sweat. Divinity entering the world on the floor of
a stable, through the womb of a teenager, and in the presence of a
carpenter.

She touches the face of the infant-God. How long was your
journey!

This baby had overlooked the universe. These rags keeping him
warm were the robes of eternity. His golden throne room had been
abandoned in favor of a dirty sheep pen. And worshiping angels had
been replaced with kind but bewildered shepherds.

Meanwhile, the city hums. The merchants are unaware that God
has visited their planet. The innkeeper would never believe that he
had just sent God into the cold. And the people would scoff at
anyone who told them the Messiah lay in the arms of a teenager
on the outskirts of their village. They were all too busy to consider
the possibility.

Those who missed His Majesty's arrival that night missed it not
because of evil acts or malice; no, they missed it because they simply
weren't looking.

Little has changed in the last two thousand years, has it not?[1]

When they had completed everything according to the law of the Lord, they returned to Galilee, to their own town of Nazareth. The boy grew up and became strong, filled with wisdom, and God's grace was on Him.

Every year His parents traveled to Jerusalem for the Passover Festival. When He was 12 years old, they went up according to the custom of the festival. After those days were over, as they were returning, the boy Jesus stayed behind in Jerusalem, but His parents did not know it. Assuming He was in the traveling party, they went a day's journey. Then they began looking for Him among their relatives and friends. When they did not find Him, they returned to Jerusalem to search for Him. After three days, they found Him in the temple complex sitting among the teachers, listening to them and asking them questions. And all those who heard Him were astounded at His understanding and His answers. When His parents saw Him, they were astonished, and His mother said to Him, "Son, why have You treated us like this? Your father and I have been anxiously searching for You."

"Why were you searching for Me?" He asked them. "Didn't you know that I must be involved in My Father's interests?" But they did not understand what He said to them. . . .

And Jesus increased in wisdom and stature, and in favor with God and with people. . . .

When all the people were baptized, Jesus also was baptized. As He was praying, heaven opened, and the Holy Spirit descended on Him in a physical appearance like a dove. And a voice came from heaven:

> You are My beloved Son.
> I take delight in You!

As He began His ministry, Jesus was about 30 years old. (Luke 2:39–50, 52; 3:21–23a HCSB)

The heavy door creaked on its hinges as he pushed it open. With a few strides he crossed the silent shop and opened the wooden shutters to a square shaft of sunshine that pierced the darkness, painting a box of daylight on the dirt floor.

He looked around the carpentry shop. He stood a moment in the refuge of the little room that housed so many sweet memories. He balanced the hammer in his hand. He ran his fingers across the sharp teeth of the saw. He stroked the smoothly worn wood of the sawhorse. He had come to say good-bye.

It was time for him to leave. He had heard something that made him know it was time to go. So he came one last time to smell the sawdust and lumber.

Life was peaceful here. Life was so . . . safe.

Here he had spent countless hours of contentment. On this dirt floor he had played as a toddler while his father worked. Here Joseph had taught him how to grip a hammer. And on this workbench he had built his first chair.

I wonder what he thought as he took one last look around the room. Perhaps he stood for a moment at the workbench looking at the tiny shadows cast by the chisel and shavings. Perhaps he listened as voices from the past filled the air.

I wonder if he hesitated. I wonder if his heart was torn. I wonder if he rolled a nail between his thumb and fingers, anticipating the pain.

It was in the carpentry shop that he must have given birth to his thoughts. Here concepts and convictions were woven together to form the fabric of his ministry.

You can almost see the tools of the trade in his words as he spoke. You can see the trueness of a plumb line as he called for moral standards. You can hear the whistle of the plane as he pleads for religion to shave away unnecessary traditions. You can picture the snugness of a dovetail joint as he demands loyalty in relationships. You can imagine him with a pencil and a ledger as he urges honesty.

It was here that his human hands shaped the wood his divine hands had created. And it was here that his body matured while his spirit waited for the right moment, the right day.

And now that day had arrived.

It must have been difficult to leave. After all, life as a carpenter wasn't bad. It wasn't bad at all. Business was good. The future was bright, and his work was enjoyable.

In Nazareth he was known only as Jesus, the son of Joseph. You can be sure he was respected in the community. He was good with his hands. He had many friends. He was a favorite among the children. He could tell a good joke and had a habit of filling the air with contagious laughter.

I wonder if he wanted to stay. "I could do a good job here in Nazareth. Settle down. Raise a family. Be a civic leader."

I wonder because I know he had already read the last chapter. He knew that the feet that would step out of the safe shadow of the carpentry shop would not rest until they had been placed on a Roman cross and pierced.

You see, he didn't have to go. He had a choice. He could have stayed. He could have kept his mouth shut. He could have ignored the call or at least postponed it. And had he chosen to stay, who would have known? Who would have blamed him?

He could have come back as a man in another era when society wasn't so volatile, when religion wasn't so stale, when people would listen better.

He could have come back when crosses were out of style.

But his heart wouldn't let him. If there was hesitation on the part of his humanity, it was overcome by the compassion of his divinity. His divinity heard the voices. His divinity heard the hopeless cries of the poor, the bitter accusations of the abandoned, the dangling despair of those who were trying to save themselves.

And his divinity saw the faces. From the face of Adam to the face of the infant born somewhere in the world as you read these words, he saw them all.

And you can be sure of one thing. Among the voices that found their way into that carpentry shop in Nazareth was your voice. Your silent prayers uttered on tear-stained pillows were heard before they were said. Your deepest questions about death and eternity were answered before they were asked. And your direst need, your need for a Savior, was met before you ever sinned.

And not only did he hear you; he saw you. He saw your face aglow the hour you first knew him. He saw your face in shame the hour you first fell. The same face that looked back at you from this morning's mirror looked at him. And it was enough to kill him.

He left because of you.

He laid his security down with his hammer. He hung tranquility on the peg with his nail apron. He closed the window shutters on the sunshine of his youth and locked the door on the comfort and ease of anonymity.

Since he could bear your sins more easily than he could bear the thought of your hopelessness, he chose to leave.

It wasn't easy.[2]

"And there are also many other things that Jesus did, which, if they were written one by one, I suppose not even the world itself could contain the books that would be written" (John 21:25 HCSB).

The Sacrifice
*"Suffered under Pontius Pilate, was crucified, dead, and buried; He descended into hell;"** *

Pontius Pilate ascends the landing and takes his seat. The accused is brought into the room and placed below him. A covey of robed religious leaders follow, walk over to one side of the room, and stand.

Pilate looks at the lone figure.

"Doesn't look like a Christ," he mutters.

Feet swollen and muddy. Hands. Knuckles lumpy.

Looks more like a laborer than a teacher. Looks even less like a troublemaker.

---

*See editor's note at the end of this chapter.

One eye is black and swollen shut. The other looks at the floor. Lower lip split and scabbed. Hair blood-matted to forehead. Arms and thighs streaked with crimson.

It's obvious what the beating has done.

"Are you the king of the Jews?"

For the first time, Jesus lifts his eyes. He doesn't raise his head, but he lifts his eyes. He peers at the procurator from beneath his brow. Pilate is surprised at the tone in Jesus' voice.

"Those are your words."

Before Pilate can respond, the knot of Jewish leaders mock the accused from the side of the courtroom.

"See, he has no respect."

"He stirs the people!"

"He claims to be king!"

Pilate doesn't hear them. *"Those are your words."* No defense. No explanation. No panic. The Galilean is looking at the floor again.

Pilate looks at the Jewish leaders huddled in the corner across the court. Their insistence angers him. The lashes aren't enough. The mockery inadequate. *Jealous,* he wants to say to their faces, but doesn't. *Jealous buzzards, the whole obstinate lot of you. Killing your own prophets.*

Pilate wants to let Jesus go. *Just give me a reason,* he thinks, almost aloud. *I'll set you free.*

His thoughts are interrupted by a tap on the shoulder. A messenger leans and whispers. Strange. Pilate's wife has sent word for him not to get involved in the case. Something about a dream she had.

How many times has he sat here? How many stories has he heard? How many pleas has he received? How many wide eyes have stared at him, pleading for mercy, begging for acquittal?

But the eyes of this Nazarene are calm, silent. They don't scream. They don't dart. Pilate searches them for anxiety . . . for anger. He doesn't find it. What he finds makes him shift again.

He's not angry with me. He's not afraid . . . he seems to understand.

Pilate is correct in his curiosity. Where, if Jesus is a leader, are his followers? What, if he is the Messiah, does he intend to do? Why, if he is a teacher, are the religious leaders so angry at him?

Pilate is also correct in his question. "What should I do with Jesus, the one called the Christ?" (see Mark 15:12).

Perhaps you, like Pilate, are curious about this one called Jesus. You, like Pilate, are puzzled by his claims and stirred by his passions. You have heard the stories: God descending the stars, cocooning in flesh, placing a stake of truth in the globe. You, like Pilate, have heard the others speak; now you would like for him to speak.

What do you do with a man who claims to be God, yet hates religion? What do you do with a man who calls himself the Savior, yet condemns systems? What do you do with a man who knows the place and time of his death, yet goes there anyway?

Pilate's question is yours.

You have two choices.

You can reject him. That is an option. You can, as have many, decide that the idea of God becoming a carpenter is too bizarre—and walk away.

Or you can accept him. You can journey with him. You can listen for his voice amid the hundreds of voices and follow him.

Pilate could have. He heard many voices that day—he could have heard Christ's. Had Pilate chosen to respond to this bruised Messiah, his story would have been different.

Pilate wavers amid the voices. He steps toward one, then stops, and steps toward the other. Four times he tries to free Jesus, and four times he is swayed otherwise. He tries to give the people Barabbas; but they want Jesus. He sends Jesus to the whipping post; they want him sent to Golgotha. He states he finds nothing against this man; they accuse Pilate of violating the law. Pilate, afraid of who Jesus might be, tries one final time to release him; the Jews accuse him of betraying Caesar.

So many voices. The voice of compromise. The voice of expedience. The voice of politics. The voice of conscience.

And the soft, firm voice of Christ. "The only power you have over me is the power given to you by God" (see John 19:11).

Jesus' voice is distinct. Unique. He doesn't cajole or plead. He just states the case.

Pilate thought he could avoid making a choice. He washed his hands of Jesus. He climbed on the fence and sat down.

But in not making a choice, Pilate made a choice.

Rather than ask for God's grace, he asked for a bowl. Rather than invite Jesus to stay, he sent him away. Rather than hear Christ's voice, he heard the voice of the people.

Legend has it that Pilate's wife became a believer. And legend has it that Pilate's eternal home is a mountain lake where he daily surfaces, still plunging his hands into the water seeking forgiveness. Forever trying to wash away his guilt . . . not for the evil he did, but for the kindness he didn't do.[3]

Then the governor's soldiers took Jesus into headquarters and gathered the whole company around Him. They stripped Him and dressed Him in a scarlet robe. They twisted a crown out of thorns, put it on His head, and placed a reed in His right hand. And they knelt down before Him and mocked Him: "Hail, King of the Jews!" Then they spit at Him, took the reed, and kept hitting Him on the head. When they had mocked him, they stripped Him of the robe, put His clothes on Him, and led Him away to crucify Him.

As they were going out, they found a Cyrenian man named Simon. They forced this man to carry His cross. When they came to a place called *Golgotha* (which means Skull Place), they gave Him wine mixed with gall to drink. But when He tasted it, He would not drink it. After crucifying Him they divided His clothes by casting lots. Then they sat down and were guarding Him there. Above His head they put up the charge against Him in writing:

THIS IS JESUS
THE KING OF THE JEWS

Then two criminals were crucified with Him, one on the right and one on the left. Those who passed by were yelling insults at Him, shaking their heads and saying, "The One who would demolish the sanctuary and rebuild it in three days, save Yourself! If You are the Son of God, come down from the cross!" In the same way the chief priests, with the scribes and elders, mocked Him and said, "He saved others, but He cannot save Himself! He is the King of Israel! Let Him come down now from the cross, and we will believe in Him. He has put His trust in God; let God rescue Him now—if He wants Him! For He said, 'I am God's Son.'" In the same way even the criminals who were crucified with Him kept taunting Him.

From noon until three in the afternoon darkness came over the whole land. At about three in the afternoon Jesus cried out with a loud voice, *"Eli, Eli, lemá sabachtháni?"* that is, "My God, My God, why have You forsaken Me?"

When some of those standing there heard this, they said, "He's calling for Elijah!"

Immediately one of them ran and got a sponge, filled it with sour wine, fixed it on a reed, and offered Him a drink. But the rest said, "Let us see if Elijah comes to save Him!"

Jesus shouted again with a loud voice and gave up His spirit. Suddenly, the curtain of the sanctuary was split in two from top to bottom; the earth quaked and the rocks were split. (Matt. 27:27–51 HCSB)

The Sensational Sunday

"The third day He rose again from the dead;"

Waxy lips open. Wooden fingers lift. Heart valves swish and hinged joints bend.

And, as we envision the moment, we stand in awe.

We stand in awe not just because of what we see, but because of what we know. We know that we, too, will die. We know that we, too, will be buried. Our lungs, like his, will empty. Our hands, like his, will stiffen. But the rising of his body and the rolling of the stone give birth to a mighty belief: "What we believe is this: If we get included in Christ's sin-conquering death, we also get included in his life-saving resurrection. We know that when Jesus was raised from the dead it was a signal of the end of death-as-the-end. Never again will death have the last word. When Jesus died, he took sin down with him, but alive he brings God down to us" (Rom. 6:5–9 The Message).

To the Thessalonians Paul stated: "Since Jesus died and broke loose from the grave, God will most certainly bring to life those who die in Jesus" (1 Thess. 4:14 The Message).

And to the Corinthians he affirms: "All who are related to Christ will rise again. Each, however, in his own turn: Christ rose first; then when Christ comes back, all people will become alive again" (see 1 Cor. 15:22–23 The Message).

For Paul and any follower of Christ, the promise is simply this: The resurrection of Jesus is proof and preview of our own.

But can we trust the promise? Is the resurrection a reality? Are the claims of the empty tomb true? This is not only a good question; it is *the* question. For Paul wrote, "If Christ has not been raised, then your faith has nothing to it; you are still guilty of your sins" (1 Cor. 15:17). In other words, if Christ has been raised, then his followers will join him; but if not, then his followers are fools. The resurrection, then, is the keystone in the arch of the Christian faith. If it be solid, the door-way is trustworthy. Dislodge it and the doorway crumbles.

However, the keystone is not easily budged, for if Jesus is not in the tomb, where is he?

Some speculate he never even died. He was only thought to be dead, but he was actually unconscious. Then he awoke and walked out of the grave. But honestly, how likely is this theory? Jesus endures torturous whippings, thirst and dehydration, nails in his hands and feet, and most of all, a spear in his side. Could he single-handedly roll back a huge rock from the tomb and then overpower Roman guards and escape? Hardly. Dismiss any thought of Jesus not being dead.

Others accuse the disciples of stealing the body in order to fake the resurrection. They say that Jesus' followers—ordinary tax collectors and fishermen—overcame the sophisticated and well-armed Roman soldiers and detained them long enough to roll back the sealed stone and unwrap the body and escape. Hardly seems plausible, but even if it were, even if the disciples did steal the body, how do we explain their martyrdom? Many of them died for the faith. They died for their belief in the resurrected Lord. Would they fake the resurrection and then die for a hoax? I don't think so. We have to agree with John R. Stott, who wrote, "Hypocrites and martyrs are not made of the same stuff."[4]

Some go so far as to claim that the Jews stole the body. Is it possible that Jesus' enemies took the corpse? Perhaps. But why would they? They wanted the body in the tomb. And we ask just as quickly, if they did steal the body, why didn't they produce it? Display it? Place the carpenter's corpse on a funeral bier and parade it through Jerusalem, and the movement of Jesus would have fizzled like a torch in a lake. But they didn't produce the body. Why? Because they didn't have it.

Christ's death was real. The disciples didn't take his body. The Jews didn't take it. So where is it? Well, during the last two thousand years, millions have opted to accept the simple explanation the angel gave Mary Magdalene. When she came to visit the grave and found it empty, she was told: "He is not here. He is risen from the dead as he said he would" (see Matt. 28:6).

For three days Jesus' body decayed. It did not rest, mind you. It decayed. The cheeks sank and the skin paled. But after three days the process was reversed. There was a stirring, a stirring deep within the grave—and the living Christ stepped forth.

And the moment he stepped forth, everything changed. As Paul stated: "When Jesus was raised from the dead it was a signal of the end of death-as-the-end" (Rom. 6:5–6 The Message).

Don't you love that sentence? "It was the signal of the end of death-as-the-end." The resurrection is an exploding flare announcing to all sincere seekers that it is safe to believe. Safe to believe in ultimate justice. Safe to believe in eternal bodies. Safe to believe in heaven as our estate and the earth as its porch. Safe to believe in a time when questions won't keep us awake and pain won't keep us down. Safe to believe in open graves and endless days and genuine praise.

Because we can accept the resurrection story, it is safe to accept the rest of the story.

Because of the resurrection, everything changes.

Death changes. It used to be the end; now it is the beginning.

The cemetery changes. People once went there to say good-bye; now they go to say, "We'll be together again."

Even the coffin changes. The casket is no longer a box where we hide bodies, but rather a cocoon in which the body is kept until God sets it free to fly.

And some day, according to Christ, he will set us free. He will come back. "I will come back and take you to be with me" (see John 14:3). And to prove that he was serious about his promise, the stone was rolled and his body was raised.

For he knows that someday this world will shake again. In the blink of an eye, as fast as the lightning flashes from the east to the west, he will come back. And everyone will see him—you will, I will. Bodies will push back the dirt and break the surface of the sea. The earth will tremble, the sky will roar, and those who do not know him will shudder. But in that hour you will not fear, because you know him.[5]

The Seat

"He ascended into heaven, and sitteth on the right
hand of God the Father Almighty;"

"In My Father's house are many dwelling places; if not, I
would have told you. I am going away to prepare a place for
you." (John 14:2 HCSB)

God took an oath that Christ would always be a priest,
but he never did this for any other priest. Only to Jesus did
he say,

> "The Lord has taken an oath
> and will not break his vow:
> 'You are a priest forever.'"

Because of God's oath, it is Jesus who guarantees the effec-
tiveness of this better covenant.

Another difference is that there were many priests under
the old system. When one priest died, another had to take
his place. But Jesus remains a priest forever; his priesthood
will never end. Therefore he is able, once and forever, to
save everyone who comes to God through him. He lives
forever to plead with God on their behalf. (Heb. 7:20–25
NLT)

Imagine a person standing in front of the White House. Better
still, imagine yourself standing in front of the White House.

That's you on the sidewalk, peering through the fence, over the
lawn, at the residence of the president. That's you—in fine form—
hair in place and shoes shined. That's you turning toward the
entrance. Your pace is brisk and stride sure. It should be. You have
come to meet with the president.

You have a few matters you wish to discuss with him.

First, there is the matter of the fire hydrant in front of your house.
Could they soften the red just a shade? It's too bright.

Then there's the issue of world peace. You are for it—would he
create it?

And lastly, college tuition is too high. Could he call the admis-
sions office of your daughter's school and ask them to lighten up? He
might have some influence.

All worthy issues, correct? Won't take more than a few minutes.
Besides, you brought him some cookies that he can share with the
first lady and the first puppy. So with bag in hand and a smile on

your face, you step up to the gate and announce to the guard, "I'd like to see the president, please."

He asks for your name, and you give it. He looks at you and then at his list and says, "We have no record of your appointment."

"You have to have an appointment?"

"Yes."

"How do I get one?"

"Through his office staff."

"Could I have their number?"

"No, it's restricted."

"Then how can I get in?"

"It's better to wait until they call you."

"But they don't know me!"

The guard shrugs. "Then they probably won't call."

And so you sigh and turn and begin your journey home. Your questions are unanswered and your needs unmet.

And you were so close! Had the president stepped out onto the lawn, you could've waved, and he would've waved back. You were only yards from his front door . . . but you might as well have been miles. The two of you were separated by the fence and the guard.

Then there is the problem of the Secret Service. Had you somehow entered, they would have stopped you. The staff would have done the same. There were too many barriers.

And what about the invisible barriers? Barriers of time (the president's too busy). Barriers of status (you have no clout). Barriers of protocol (you have to go through the right channels). You leave the White House with nothing more than a hard lesson learned. You do not have access to the president. Your chat with the commander-in-chief? It ain't gonna happen. You'll have to take your problem about peace and your question about the fire hydrant with you.

That is, unless he takes the initiative. Unless he, spotting you on the sidewalk, takes pity on your plight and says to his chief of staff, "See that person with the sack of cookies? Go tell him I'd like to talk with him for a minute."

If he gives such a command, all barriers will drop. The oval office will call the head of security. The head of security will call the guard, and the guard will call your name. "Guess what? I can't explain it, but the door to the Oval Office is wide open."

You stop and turn and straighten your shoulders and enter the same door where, only moments before, you were denied access. The guard is the same. The gates are the same. The security personnel are the same. But the situation is not the same. You can now go where you could not before.

And, what's more, you are not the same. You feel special, chosen. Why? Because the man up there saw you down here and made it possible for you to come in.

Yeah, you're right. It's a fanciful story. You and I both know when it comes to the president, don't hold your breath—no invitation will arrive. But when it comes to God, pick up your cookies and walk in, because it already has.

He has spotted you. He has heard you, and he has invited you. What once separated you has been removed: "Now in Christ Jesus, you who were far away from God are brought near" (see Eph. 2:13). Nothing remains between you and God but an open door.

But how could this be? If we can't get in to see the president, how could we be granted an audience with God? What happened? In a word, someone opened the curtain. Someone tore down the veil. Something happened in the death of Christ that opened the door for you and me. And that something is described by the writer of Hebrews: "So, brothers and sisters, we are completely free to enter the Most Holy Place without fear because of the blood of Jesus' death. We can enter through a new and living way that Jesus opened for us. It leads through the curtain—Christ's body" (see Heb. 10:19–20).

To the original readers, those last four words were explosive: "the curtain—Christ's body." According to the writer, the curtain equals Jesus. Hence, whatever happened to the flesh of Jesus happened to the curtain. What happened to his flesh? It was torn. Torn by the whips, torn by the thorns. Torn by the weight of the cross and the points of the nails. But in the horror of his torn flesh, we find the splendor of the open door.

"But Jesus cried out again in a loud voice and died. Then the curtain in the temple was torn into two pieces, from top to the bottom" (see Matt. 27:50–51).

The curtain is nothing short of the curtain of the temple. The veil that hung before the holy of holies.

The holy of holies, you'll remember, was a part of the temple that no one could enter. Jewish worshipers could enter the outer court, but only the priests could enter the holy place. And no one, except the high priest on one day a year, entered the holy of holies. No one. Why? Because the shekinah glory—the glory of God—was present there.

If you were told you were free to enter the Oval Office of the White House, you would likely shake your head and chuckle, "You're one brick short of a load, buddy." Multiply your disbelief by a thousand, and you'll have an idea how a Jew would feel if someone told him he could enter the holy of holies. "Yeah, right. You're one bagel short of a dozen."

No one but the high priest entered the holy of holies. No one. To do so meant death. Two of Aaron's sons died when they entered the holy of holies in order to offer sacrifices to the Lord (see Lev. 10:1–2). In no uncertain terms, the curtain declared: "This far and no farther!"

What did fifteen hundred years of a curtain-draped holy of holies communicate? Simple. God is holy—separate from us and unapproachable. Even Moses was told, "You cannot see my face, for no one may see me and live" (Exod. 33:20). God is holy, and we are sinners, and there is a distance between us.

Isn't this our problem? We know God is good. We know we are not, and we feel far from God. The ancient words of Job are ours, "If only there were a mediator who could bring us together" (Job 9:33 NLT).

Oh, but there is! Jesus hasn't left us with an unapproachable God. Yes, God is holy. Yes, we are sinful. But, yes, yes, yes, Jesus is our mediator. "There is one God and one mediator between God and men, the man Christ Jesus" (1 Tim. 2:5). Is not a mediator one who "goes between"? Wasn't Jesus the curtain between us and God? And wasn't his flesh torn?

What appeared to be the cruelty of man was actually the sovereignty of God. Matthew tells us: "And when Jesus had cried out again in a loud voice, he gave up his spirit. At that moment the curtain of the temple was torn in two from top to bottom" (Matt. 27:50–51).

It's as if the hands of heaven had been gripping the veil, waiting for this moment. Keep in mind the size of the curtain—sixty feet tall and thirty feet wide. One instant it was whole; the next it was ripped in two from top to bottom. No delay. No hesitation.

What did the torn curtain mean? For the Jews it meant no more barrier between them and the holy of holies. No more priests to go between them and God. No more animal sacrifices to atone for their sins.

And for us? What did the torn curtain signify for us?

We are welcome to enter into God's presence—any day, any time. God has removed the barrier that separates us from him. The barrier of sin? Down. He has removed the curtain.

But we have a tendency to put the barrier back up. Though there is no curtain in a temple, there is a curtain in the heart. Like the ticks on the clock are the mistakes of the heart. And sometimes, no, oftentimes, we allow those mistakes to keep us from God.

As a result we hide from our Master.

God isn't angry with you. He has already dealt with your mistake.

Somewhere, sometime, somehow you may get tangled up in garbage, and you may try to avoid God. You'll allow a veil of guilt to come between you and your Father. You'll wonder if you could ever feel close to God again. The message of the torn flesh is you can. God welcomes you. God will not avoid you. God will not resist you. The curtain is down, the door is open, and God invites you in.

Don't trust your conscience. Trust the cross. The blood has been spilt and the veil has been split. You are welcome in God's presence. And you don't even have to bring cookies.[6]

The Sure Return

"From thence He shall come to judge the quick and the dead."

"If I go away and prepare a place for you, I will come back and receive you to Myself, so that where I am you may be also." (John 14:3 HCSB)

How do we know that his return is sure? Jesus told us. According to Matthew, Jesus told us in the last sermon he ever preached.

It may surprise you that Jesus made preparedness the theme of his last sermon. It did me. I would have preached on love or family or the importance of the church. Jesus didn't. Jesus preached on what many today consider to be old-fashioned. He preached on being ready for heaven and staying out of hell.

It's his message when he tells of the wise and the foolish servants (see Matt. 24:45–51). The wise one was ready for the return of the master; the foolish one was not.

It's his message when he tells about the ten bridesmaids. Five were wise and five were foolish (see Matt. 25:1–13). The wise ones were ready when the groom came, and the foolish ones were at the corner store looking for more oil.

It's his message when he tells of the three servants and the bags of gold (see Matt. 25:14–30). Two servants put the money to work and made more money for the master. The third hid his in a hole. The first two were ready and were rewarded when the master returned. The third was unprepared and punished.

Be ready. It's a first step, nonnegotiable, a sure principle.

That is the theme of Jesus' last sermon, "So always be ready, because you don't know the day your Lord will come" (see

Matt. 24:42). He didn't tell when the day of the Lord would be, but he did describe what the day would be like. It's a day no one will miss.

Every person who has ever lived will be present at that final gathering. Every heart that has ever beat. Every mouth that has ever spoken. On that day you will be surrounded by a sea of people. Rich, poor. Famous, unknown. Kings, bums. Brilliant, demented. All will be present. And all will be looking in one direction. All will be looking at him. Every human being.

"The Son of Man will come again in his great glory" (see Matt. 25:31).

You won't look at anyone else. No side glances to see what others are wearing. No whispers about new jewelry or comments about who is present. At this, the greatest gathering in history, you will have eyes for only One—the Son of Man. Wrapped in splendor. Shot through with radiance. Imploded with light and magnetic in power.

Jesus describes this day with certainty.

He leaves no room for doubt. He doesn't say he may return, or might return, but that he will return. By the way, one-twentieth of the New Testament speaks about his return. There are more than three hundred references to his second coming. Twenty-three of the twenty-seven New Testament books speak of it. And they speak of it with confidence.

"You also must be ready, because the Son of Man will come at a time you don't expect him" (see Matt. 24:44).

"Jesus, who has been taken from you into heaven, will come back in the same way you have seen him go into heaven" (Acts 1:11).

"He will come a second time, not to offer himself for sin, but to bring salvation to those who are waiting for him" (see Heb. 9:28).

"The day of the Lord will come like a thief in the night" (1 Thess. 5:2).

His return is certain.

His return is final.

Upon his return "he will separate them into two groups as a shepherd separates the sheep from the goats. The Son of Man will put the sheep on his right and the goats on his left" (see Matt. 25:32–33).

The word *separate* is a sad word. To separate a mother from a daughter, a father from a son, a husband from a wife. To separate people on earth is sorrowful, but to think of it being done for eternity is horrible.

Especially when one group is destined for heaven and the other group is going to hell.

We don't like to talk about hell, do we? In intellectual circles the topic of hell is regarded as primitive and foolish. It's not logical. "A loving God wouldn't send people to hell." So we dismiss it.

But to dismiss it is to dismiss a core teaching of Jesus. The doctrine of hell is not one developed by Paul, Peter, or John. It is taught by Jesus himself.

And to dismiss it is to dismiss much more. It is to dismiss the presence of a loving God and the privilege of a free choice. Let me explain.

We are free to either love God or not. He invites us to love him. He urges us to love him. He came that we might love him. But, in the end, the choice is yours and mine. To take that choice from each of us, for him to force us to love him, would be less than love.

God explains the benefits, outlines the promises, and articulates very clearly the consequences. And then, in the end, he leaves the choice to us.

Hell was not prepared for people. Hell "was prepared for the devil and his angels" (see Matt. 25:41). For a person to go to hell, then, is for a person to go against God's intended destiny. "God has not destined us to the terror of judgment, but to the full attainment of salvation through our Lord Jesus Christ" (see 1 Thess. 5:9). Hell is man's choice, not God's choice.

Consider, then, this explanation of hell: Hell is the chosen place of the person who loves self more than God, who loves sin more than his Savior, who loves this world more than God's world.

Judgment is that moment when God looks at the rebellious and says, "Your choice will be honored."[7]

MAX LUCADO is senior minister at Oak Hills Church of Christ in San Antonio, Texas. He and his wife, Denalyn, have three daughters, Jenna, Andrea, and Sara.

Lucado has a bachelor of arts degree in mass communications and a master's degree in biblical and related studies from Abilene Christian University. Over the years, he has led a radio program and written numerous booklets and books for adults, youth, and children. Many of his works have won awards, including ECPA/CBA Christian Book of the Year for *Just Like Jesus, In the Grip of Grace,* and *When God Whispers Your Name.*

Editor's note: "He descended into hell." What in the world does that mean? Well, we're not completely sure. The text in mind, when this clause of the creed was formulated, was 1 Peter 3:18–19: "He was put to death in the body but made alive by the Spirit, through whom also he went and preached to the spirits in prison who disobeyed long ago when God waited patiently in the days of Noah while the ark was being built." There is considerable debate in Christian circles as to the meaning of this text. Samples of the options include: (1) The spirits are the souls of the faithful in the Old

Testament, and the "prison" is a place they await Christ. (2) The spirits are the souls of those who died in Noah's flood. (3) The spirits are
the fallen angels of Genesis 6:1, and the prison is where they are kept
bound. (4) The spirits are the demons, the offspring of the fallen
angels of Genesis 6:1. This is pretty confusing stuff, isn't it?

This provides for us a teachable moment. The majority of
Scripture is really easy to understand. Mark Twain once said, "It isn't
the parts of the Bible I don't understand that bother me, it is the parts
I do!" Periodically, however, a very difficult passage will present
itself. When this happens, I encourage you to study, grapple, ask, and
inquire. If this work, however, doesn't provide a solution, count
yourself in the growing number of "inquisitive Christians." Make a
mental note of the difficulty, and move on in the text. I have a large
folder of "mental notes" myself. I can't wait to ask Jesus each and
every one. In fact, I picture, in the great hall room of heaven, dozens
of "break out rooms" each with a sign over the door. One says,
"Predestination"; another, "Speaking in tongues"; and a third, "Old
Testament ethics." If you want, I'll meet you in the room with the
sign, "He descended into hell," and we'll learn together.

Whatever we decide about this text, the intent of the credal
writers was to ensure we were completely convinced of the reality
of the death of Christ.

God the Holy Spirit

is he really a ghost?

By Walter C. Kaiser Jr.

"I believe in the Holy Spirit; the holy Christian church,
the Communion of the saints; the forgiveness of sins; the resurrection
of the body; and the life everlasting. Amen."

What do we mean when we say, "I believe in the Holy Spirit"? We mean that he is the third person of the Trinity and that he is fully God. To sin against the Holy Spirit, then, is to sin against God. Thus, when the man and his wife in Acts 5:4 lied to the Holy Spirit, the apostle Peter said, "You have lied . . . to God." He acts as only a person can, for the Holy Spirit hears, speaks, teaches, forbids, helps, and guides throughout Scripture.

The full expression "Holy Spirit" occurs in the Old Testament only three times (Ps. 51:11; Isa. 63:10–11). Yet there are ninety distinct references to his person in the Old Testament with eighteen different words or expressions used to describe him. His works, even in the Old Testament, are numerous and remarkable. For example: (1) The Holy Spirit shared in creating the world (Gen. 1:2; Ps. 104:30). (2) He revealed God's messages to his prophets, who in turn shared them with Israel and with all of us in the Scriptures

(Num. 24:2; Micah 3:8; Zech. 4:6; 7:12). (3) The Holy Spirit gave artistic ability and creative skills in the arts (Exod. 31:1–11). (4) He also elicited faith, repentance, righteousness, and obedience from the hearts of men and women in Old Testament times as well (Ps. 51:10–12; Joel 2:28; Zech. 12:10).

The Holy Spirit is no less real and active in the New Testament, which has more than 260 distinct references to the Holy Spirit with 39 separate title or descriptions of him and his work. Among the things we are taught that he does in the New Testament are these: (1) He unites believers to Jesus so we become sharers in his kingdom (Rom. 14:7) and members of his body, the church, of which he is the head (Eph. 4:3–16). (2) He assures believers that we are his children and heirs of God (Rom. 8:12–17). (3) He transforms believers into the spiritual and moral likeness of Jesus (2 Cor. 3:18). (4) He prays effectively for believers in Christ at times when they are unable to pray for themselves (Rom. 8:26–27). (5) He prompts missionary activity so that the gospel is spread throughout the earth (Acts 8:29). (6) He gives gifts for witnessing and serving so that the body of Christ can be built up (1 Cor. 12). (7) He led the apostles to remember all that Jesus had said to the disciples when he was with them so they could compose the New Testament (John 14:25–26; 15:26–27; 16:12–13).

The Holy Spirit is not an optional spiritual additive or a luxury in the Christian life. It is impossible to be a Christian without the person and work of the Holy Spirit in one's life. So strong is this association that Paul can almost make an equation out of it: Those who have the Spirit of God are the sons and daughters of the living God (Rom. 8:9–14). But if there is no evidence of the Holy Spirit, then no claim can be made of belonging to Christ.

On the other hand, Christians are not to grieve the Holy Spirit (Eph. 4:30–31) or to quench his activity in one's life (1 Thess. 5:19). Instead, they are to be continually filled and permeated with the presence and work of the Holy Spirit in their lives (Eph. 5:18) and to live according to his direction in our hearts and lives (Gal. 5:16).

Among the numerous expressions used in connection with the Holy Spirit are several that call for a brief definition. For example, "drinking the Holy Spirit," much like being "baptized by the Holy Spirit" (see 1 Cor. 12:12–13), marks our initiation into the body of believers. In this act the Holy Spirit incorporates all who ever believed in Jesus as Lord and Savior into one body, regardless of their church affiliation or brand of theology. Another expression is "sealed by the Holy Spirit" (see Eph. 1:13). This phrase emphasizes the fact of the believer's security in Christ; that is, that he or she is owned by God. All who have believed were sealed and kept by the power of God. The "filling of the Holy Spirit" can occur at many different times; hence the New Testament will urge us to keep on being filled with the Holy Spirit (Eph. 5:18). Finally, there is the "communion of the Holy Ghost" (2 Cor. 13:14 KJV) in which we have fellowship and participate with the Holy Spirit in all the good things of God.

The Holy Christian Church

The origin of the church goes back to Jesus himself (Matt. 16:18). Only in Matthew 16:18 and 18:17 does Jesus use the word *church*. This body, which had Old Testament antecedents in the believing "people of God" in Israel's day, was depicted in the New Testament under a myriad of images and concepts. Whether this new body was the "people of God," "the new creation," "the fellowship in faith," or "the body of Christ," they were distinctly the work of God. They were described as the salt of the earth, the branches of the vine, the bride of Christ, a chosen race, sons of God, or the household of faith. All of these concepts were brought together at the Church Councils at Constantinople (A.D. 381), Ephesus (A.D. 431), and Chalcedon (A.D. 451) to affirm that the church was the "one, holy, catholic [= "universal"] and apostolic" body formed and kept by the power of God.

But is the church "one"? With upwards of some 25,000 to 30,000 denominations, do not these numbers easily refute that claim? Jesus prayed in John 17:20–26 that all his followers might be one. And

Paul declared in Galatians 3:27–28 that all indeed are one without distinction of race, gender, or social status. The unity of the church is a top priority for Paul as he warned against divisions and called the church to be united (1 Cor. 1:10–30). Christians are told frankly that they are to make it their business to recognize and maintain the unity of the Spirit that does exist among Christians regardless of their local or denominational affiliation (Eph. 4:1–6).

But can the church be described as holy since the reality of sin was acknowledged even in the New Testament church at Corinth, much less in our own day? Some have claimed that they are the true church since they alone have cast all sin out of their midst. However, 1 John 1:8 shows that is not the truth of the matter, for there is no church that has no sin to confess. So how can the church be holy? Holiness does not mean one is free from sin or is separated from what is common and profane. Instead, to be holy is to be dedicated to God and his service (2 Thess. 2:13; Col. 3:12).

If we are Protestant, how can the church be "catholic"? The answer is that the Greek word *katholikos* means "universal." The church includes believers of all cultures and societies in past and the present. By catholic, then, we mean the entire church of all times and in all the world, which has the same Lord, the same origins, and the same purpose. This is the universal or catholic church.

How, then, we ask finally, is the church "apostolic"? It is apostolic in that it is built on the foundation of the apostles and prophets (Eph. 2:20). The apostles were the eyewitnesses of Jesus, and the prophets were those spokespersons who proclaimed the risen Christ. The claim of apostolicity is not to argue for a direct line of succession through certain individuals, but it is to point to the message and the mission that came through the Scriptures as it was given to the apostles who first received it from our Lord. Thus, "one, holy, catholic, apostolic" church supplies us with enough of the essential doctrine that is needed to describe who and what the church is. But it is not so definitive that it does not allow for differences between churches in ways that allows them to fulfill their mission and ministry.

The Communion of the Saints

This term was used in the creeds of the early church to refer to the fellowship that all believers shared. Originally, the expression referred to the fact that the living and the dead were united in one body in a single church. Often the text in Hebrews 12:1, "we are surrounded by such a great cloud of witnesses," was interpreted to mean that the saints now in heaven were watching those now living on earth to see how they completed their journey.

While later theology tended to modify this concept by redefining what "saint" and "communion" meant, recently the emphasis has been restored to agree with the original intent of the creeds. It is argued that there is a fellowship of Christians in every age, past, present, and future; the dead are included as well as the living in this one great fellowship. In that sense, the present generation must preserve the doctrine and practice that was inherited from the past. Thus, all believers—regardless of their cultures, languages, nationalities, or denominational ties—shared a harmony and partnership in the gospel.

This sharing featured a unity that existed despite all of our diversity. This unity leaves us with a requirement that we owe all believers our love and a bonding in fellowship that transcends all known boundaries that are politically, ethnically, linguistically, or doctrinally motivated.

The Forgiveness of Sin

There are three Old Testament and four New Testament words for forgiveness. They are used both of human and divine forgiveness. But the Bible is unique in that it alone teaches that God can completely forgive sin. In so doing, our Lord removes all guilt and restores us to an intimate relationship with himself.

Especially significant for the doctrine of the forgiveness of sin was the Day of Atonement in the Old Testament (Lev. 16). After two goats were chosen by lot, one was offered as a sin offering after the high priest Aaron confessed over the first goat's head all the wickedness, all the rebellion, and all the sin of all Israel. Then that goat was killed, and its blood was taken into the holy of holies on this one day a year to be placed under the mercy seat where the glory of God dwelt. That goat was the substitute for all who were so deeply in debt for their sin that they should have died. Instead, God graciously accepted a substitute that would point symbolically to his own coming sacrificial substitution on our behalf.

The other goat likewise had the sin of Israel laid on its head and then was taken far out in the wilderness so that it would never again come back into the camp of Israel. Sins were now not only ransomed by a substitute, but really removed from their conscience and from God's recollection.

The dual picture of sin, then, is that sin was forgiven on the basis of a substitute (the first goat) and sins were forgotten and removed as far as the east is from the west (the second goat) (Ps. 103:12). And that is exactly what Christ, the ultimate Lamb of God, did with our sins. He delivered and ransomed us from them by the substitution of his perfect life (of a 100 percent God and 100 percent man) for our lives, and he deliberately refused to call our sins back to his mind as he "remembered them against us no more."

Some have tried to argue that God only forgave certain sins in the Old Testament, i.e., unintentional ones. But in view of the fact that David was forgiven of murder and adultery (Ps. 32, 51) and that all sins were forgiven on the Day of Atonement (i.e., those who really afflicted their souls and grieved inwardly over them), this distinction is not helpful.

All too often in the Bible, God forgave sins of those whom we would have thought could not have been forgiven. David's murder of Uriah (2 Sam. 11), his sin with Bathsheba (2 Sam. 12), Solomon's worship of the god Molech and other gods (1 Kings 11), or King Ahab's complicity in the murder of Naboth—these sins would have finished them as far as God's justice was concerned. However, God forgave them for the sake of his own mercy and grace.

The Resurrection of the Body

While it has become customary to affirm in our day that there is no uniform and sure doctrine of the afterlife in the Old Testament, such a conclusion does not agree with the text of the older testament. For why should the Hebrews, even apart from revelation (which they never were without), be thought to be bankrupt in this area when all over the ancient Near East their writings were so full of life after death?

In fact, from the very start, the mortal Enoch was "taken" bodily to be with God (Gen. 5:24), and mortality entered into the very presence of the immortal God!

But even more convincing is the case of Abraham and his son Isaac. His word to the waiting servants at the foot of Mount Moriah, even as he knew that God had demanded that he offer up his son Isaac on the altar, was this: "We will worship and then we will come back to you" (Gen. 22:5). Hebrews 11:17–19 explained "that God was able to raise [Isaac] up, even from the dead" (KJV).

Job, early in the patriarchal period, asked if a tree is cut down, is there hope for that tree? Yes, he affirmed, for often that cut-off trunk of the tree will sprout or shoot forth again (Job 14:7). But what about a human being? If a person dies, will that one live again? Yes, answered Job, for all our days of hard labor we will wait until our sprouting, release, or shooting forth comes (Job 14:14). But even more clearly stated is Job 19:25–27. He cried out, "I know that my redeemer lives; and that he will at last arise to vindicate me: and after my death and the decomposition of my skin I shall see God" (my translation).

No less certain was David in Psalm 16:10. As he spoke of the coming Messiah, he affirmed, "You will not abandon me to the grave, nor will you let your Holy One (Hebrew: *hasid*) see decay." This accorded with the sons of Korah's Psalm 49:15: "But God will redeem my life from the grave; he will surely take me to himself."

There are many other texts in the Old Testament that declare that mortals can and will be raised bodily in a resurrection at the last day.

But two other key texts must be noted. Isaiah 26:19 said, "Your dead will live; their bodies will rise. You who dwell in the dust, wake up and shout for joy." The other is Daniel 12:2–3: "Multitudes who sleep in the dust of the earth will awake: some to everlasting life, others to shame and everlasting contempt. Those who are wise will shine like the brightness of the heavens, and those who lead many to righteousness, like the stars for ever and ever."

In the New Testament, the greatest text on the resurrection is 1 Corinthians 15. The twenty-second verse assures us that as all men died in Adam, so in Christ all shall be made alive. But Paul did not mean that everyone would be saved. He said, instead, that there would be a certain order in which all were raised.

Yet, some mocked by asking, how shall dead people be made alive? They will come in three platoons or "orders" (Greek: *tagma* is a military term). The first resurrection is the one that occurred on the first Easter Sunday as Christ rose from the dead. The second will occur when all the believers are raised when Christ returns again to this earth. The last group to be raised (apparently, after a period of intervening time; Greek: *epeita . . . eita*, "then . . . then," which always implies a time gap) will be all the unbelievers raised at the end of history to stand at the great white judgment throne (1 Cor. 15:22–28).

Unsatisfied, Paul heard some complain, "Yes, but how are dead people raised up? And with what sort of body do they come back?" (see 1 Cor. 15:35). Paul scoffed, "I am surprised you missed that one. The body you sow is the one you are made alive in. And all this happens by the power of God just as it has been happening in your gardens since the beginning of time" (see 1 Cor. 15:36–49).

If one should ask, "Yes, but what happens immediately after death?" Paul answered that question in 2 Corinthians 5:1–5. Just as life leaves our body here, believers are immediately, personally in the presence of God, yet without their physical bodies. This "naked estate" will be remedied when Christ returns, and our bodies are raised from the graves and joined with those who in the meantime have been enjoying real, personal presence with God.

In summary, just as Christ's body was raised at the resurrection with marks of continuity with his preresurrection body (Matt. 28:9–10; Luke 24:34; John 20:11–17), so, too, the bodies of believers will be raised in that final day (1 Pet. 3:21–22).

And Life Everlasting

Believers are assured of the gift of blessedness in God's presence that endures without end. This life in Christ is such that it has already begun in the quality of life lived with God now, but there is more to be in the age to come. Thus, eternal life relates to both a quality of life in this age and the quality and duration of life in the age to come.

Just as God is eternal (Deut. 33:27; Pss. 10:16; 48:14) and his word is eternal (Ps. 119:89), so is the gift of the quality and duration of life in the ages to come as eternal for all who believe.

Eternal life is a dominant theme of the New Testament. Nicodemus, the teacher of the Jews, sought out Jesus at night to ask how he might attain eternal life. Jesus' answer was that it came as a gift to all who believed (John 3:15–16). Even the adulterous woman at the well could experience "a spring of water welling up" within her "to eternal life" if she should believe (John 4:14, 36). Eternal life was to be found in Christ as imparted in the Scriptures (John 5:39). That is "food that endures to eternal life, which the Son of Man will give you" (John 6:27).

Thus, eternal life is not only the *length of time* that God will give to us in eternity, but it is also *the quality of existence* that we may enjoy immediately upon receiving Christ as our Savior. We do not wait to receive eternal life after the undertaker hangs a crepe on the door to indicate that we have died; it begins as soon as we believe! The hope of eternal life is a fact that is foundational to all of our doctrine and knowledge of God (Titus 1:1–2). And "hope," as Paul used it, is not an uncertainty, but a sure and certain reality, even if we have not as yet realized it in all of its dimensions.

WALTER C. KAISER JR. is the Colman M. Mockler distinguished professor of Old. Testament and president of Gordon-Conwell Theological Seminary in South Hamilton, Massachusetts. He received his A.B. from Wheaton College and a B.D. from Wheaton Graduate School. He has earned both an M.A. and a Ph.D. in Mediterranean studies from Brandeis University. A recipient of the Danforth Teacher Study Grant, Dr. Kaiser is a member of the Wheaton College Scholastic Honor Society and serves on the boards of several Christian organizations.

Dr. Kaiser has contributed to publications such as *Journal for the Study of Old Testament, Journal of the Evangelical Theological Society,* and *Christianity Today.* He also has written more than thirty books, including *Toward an Old Testament Theology, Ecclesiastes: Total Life,* and *Toward an Exegetical Theology: Biblical Exegesis for Preaching and Teaching.*

Residents of South Hamilton, Massachusetts, Dr. Kaiser and his wife, Marge, have three sons, one daughter, four granddaughters, and one grandson.

part 3

Vibrant Christian Living

Introduction to Vibrant Christian Living

By Pete Briscoe

The Christian life is a continuum, not a static event. The process looks like this:

→

Election, Regeneration, Justification, Sanctification, Glorification

Although very mysterious, difficult to understand, and controversial in Christian circles, *election* is the initiative of God to call sinners into a personal relationship with him. The Holy Spirit starts pulling us in, like fish on the end of a line, convicting us of our sin, and creating within us a desire for salvation. *Regeneration* means simply "rebirth." We are born again the moment we trust Christ and Christ alone for salvation. The Bible says at that moment we are a new creation, fully *justified* before God.

Justification means to be declared righteous. God, because we have trusted in the blood of his Son for salvation, declares that our sin will not be counted against us. Jesus has paid our debt, and positionally we are righteous in his sight. *Sanctification* is the process of becoming what we have been declared to be. Our life starts, little by little, to catch up to our righteous position. Sanctification will continue until the day we die. After passing from this world, we will be glorified. *Glorification* is a fancy word used to describe the wonderful event when we, as Christians, will receive our heavenly bodies.

Remember, Paul told Timothy to "watch his *life* and his *doctrine* closely." The previous section outlined Christian doctrine; the remainder of this book deals with sanctification—that span of time between your conversion (another word for regeneration) and your final breath on earth. In other words, the Christian life.

For a sermon I was preaching at my home church one Sunday morning I asked for a three-legged stool to use as an illustration. I hoped to sit on it to show the strength of the three points I wanted to make in my sermon. When I arrived at the church, they handed me a miniature milker's stool no more than eight inches high. Disguising my disappointment, I went to the pulpit. Explaining my dilemma to the crowd, I held up the stool, exclaimed that I now knew what a "stool sample" was, and proceeded to make my point. The size of the stool was irrelevant. As long as there were three, sturdy, well-balanced legs, the stool was capable of holding a lot of weight. The Christian life is not easy. The Bible stops just short of promising that great pressure will come upon you because of your stand in Christ. Your perseverance, depth, and growth will rest squarely on three fundamental legs: grace, holiness, and transformation. Grace is our motivation, holiness is our manner, and transformation is our mode of operation or method of procedure.

Our Motivation: Grace

Grace or "unmerited favor" is anything we receive that we desperately need, don't deserve, and can't repay. When junior gets into a financial bind at college and mom and dad send a check, grace is at work. When a husband forgives a wife for infidelity simply because he loves her, grace trumps sin. When the Creator of all sends his only Son to die a wretched death, grace has burst onto the scene. Scripture teaches us that we are saved by grace, not by works, but grace is also involved in our sanctification.

It is God's grace that enables and motivates us to be "eager to do what is good" (Titus 2:14). As we come to grips with the immense price that Jesus paid, the pathetic indifference we demonstrated, and the persevering tenacity he maintained as he "ran us down," we are humbled and driven to "love him back." We are not trying to be "good Christians" to earn God's favor. We already own God's favor. We walk closely with him out of gratitude for the grace he has already showered upon us.

Our Manner: Holiness

The Hebrew word translated "holiness" means to separate from the ordinary or profane. Thus God is holy, and any person or thing dedicated to him becomes holy as well. Our word *sanctification* comes from the Greek root word for holiness. We are constantly being "set apart" for God's service. Thus in Jesus' great prayer for his disciples in John 17, he prays that they would be "in the world, but not of the world, while they are sent to the world." This passage gives us a tidy summary of holy living. We are to dwell *"in the world because we are sent to the world."* We have no choice; the safe-and-sound "run away to the mountain" lifestyle is not an option for followers of Christ. To separate ourselves from the lost would be negligent self-ishness akin to withholding bread from starving family members.

The reason we don't hold you under when we baptize you and just send you right on up to heaven is because there is still work to be done. The world that God loves needs to hear of his passion, and we are his mouthpiece. However, while we live in the world, we are not to be "of the world." God expects us to be distinctive, different, set apart.

The choices we make, the lifestyles we live, the grace we show, the joy we spread will attract the lost to us and ultimately to him. So in response to God's grace, let us resonate with Paul as he exhorts us to purify ourselves from everything that contaminates body and spirit, perfecting holiness out of reverence for God (see 2 Cor. 7:1).

Our Method of Operation: Transformation

You've heard people say, "I might be interested in God if his people weren't such jerks!" You've seen the car with the metallic fish on the back swerving in and out of traffic. Maybe you've heard the invocation before a sporting event emanate from the mouth of the slimiest business man in town. Often I sit in my office and plead seekers not to judge the King by his subjects. Why are so many Christians poor reflections of their Master? How can you keep from falling into this hypocritical trap? The key is *authenticity*—the inside matching the outside.

A little boy got in trouble in his Sunday school room. The teacher told him to quiet down, but he refused, so she made him sit in the corner. As he plunked down in his undersized chair, he yelled, "I may be sitting on the outside, but inside, I'm still standing up!" The goal of sanctification is not to change outward behavior, but to transform the heart. The heart does not follow behavior; behavior flows from the heart. So our goal is inner life, not outer conformity; morphing, not masquerading. *Metamorphous* is the Greek word translated "transformed" in Romans 12:1–2: "Therefore, I urge you, brothers [and sisters], in view of God's mercy, to offer your bodies as living sacrifices, holy and pleasing to God—this is your spiritual act of worship. Do not conform any longer to the pattern of this world, but be *transformed* by the renewing of your mind" (emphasis added).

Children play with transformer toys that "morph" into different beings. One minute they are a car, the next a space fighter on a dangerous mission. Transformation is a change from the outside that comes from the inside; masquerading is an outward drama staged to convince others of our holiness. True transformation, motivated by grace, occurs as you renew your mind.

The next section will help in starting that process, renewing your mind to the biblical pattern for biblical living: the inner life of Christ flowing through us. Thus the chapters discuss the inner things first, followed by the outer actions that flow from that inner life. Ramesh Richard delineates our inner drives, Ian Thomas our inner abilities, and Jill Briscoe our inner ears. Dr. George McCalep Jr. discusses what affect sin has on the Christian's life.

Then, flowing from that inner life, Joni Eareckson Tada and Steven Estes share a chapter describing how God helps us grow through suffering. Dave Hall discusses flowing worship, Kay Arthur flowing prayer, Brian Kluth flowing stewardship, Henry Blackaby flowing servanthood, Captain John Cheydleur flowing compassion, and Randy Raysbrook flowing evangelism. The book ends with a chapter describing our blessed hope, heaven, courtesy of John Eldredge and Brent Curtis.

As you read these chapters, remember the three legs: the context of grace, holiness, and transformation.

Your Purpose

what is my reason for living?

BY RAMESH RICHARD

A time management expert, business legend goes, impressed high achievers with an unforgettable point. He carefully placed a dozen fist-sized rocks in a wide-mouthed glass jar and asked, "Is the jar full?"

"Yes," they replied.

"Really?" He poured a can of gravel into the jar. As he shook the container, the gravel found spaces to lodge themselves. "Is the jar full now?" he quizzed them.

Having caught on, they answered, "Probably not."

"Good!" he replied. He brought out a bucket of sand and poured some into the jar. The sand went into the spaces between the rocks and the gravel.

Once more he asked, "Is this jar full?"

"No!" the class barked.

Again he said, "Good!" He poured in a mug of water to fill the jar to the brim.

He wanted to drive home the point: "What is the lesson in this illustration?"

One person immediately blurted the obvious: "No matter how

full your schedule is, if you try really hard, you can always fit some more things into it!"

"No," the speaker replied, "that's not the point. The illustration teaches us that if you don't put the big rocks in first, you'll never get them in at all."[1]

That insight holds true for your spiritual life as well.

I want to suggest three big "life rocks" that must be in place in your life so the little rocks can find rightful lodging. Since you've transferred your trust to the Lord Jesus Christ as your only God and Savior, you now possess divine presence and power to prioritize, plan, and place these rocks where they fit. Through the rest of your life, you will need to return constantly to these rocks as the basic three, the first three, the main three rocks of your spiritual life. They comprise a biblical philosophy of spiritual existence.

Life Rock 1: Your Passion

Yesterday I received a catalog from a watch store enticing me "to fulfill a passion" with a one-hundred-dollar gift certificate. I don't know how watches relate to passion yet, but some do pursue expensive watches passionately to justify an exquisite, directly mailed catalog. You'll hear the word *passion* thrown about in a hundred contexts—work, food, automobiles, sports, computers, whatever. The word *passion* seems to generate *emotion*, actually *over-emotion* inside the heart, doesn't it?

The problem with the "emotion" understanding of passion is that both the objects and feelings can change at whim. We over-emote about several objects at the same time and over the same object at different times. Someone remarked about three passions of the American male—first cars, then girls, and back to cars again! If what you feel at a particular moment determines your passion, you easily retreat to a pre-Jesus heart-set. It is very possible to return to "the evil desires you had when you lived in ignorance," says Peter (1 Pet. 1:14).

A second problem with the "over-emotion" understanding of passion is that your nonevil passions vie and tie for first place inside your soul. I asked a prominent Christian businessman in our city about his passions. He listed six in this order: "Work, family, Jesus Christ, two organizations that I serve as a board member" and he added, "to be honest, put money in there as well." I appreciated his honesty, but I was grieved over his choices, priorities, and the implications. By experience I knew that multiple passions tear the soul and destabilize and complicate life. The human heart was not made for multiple passions of life.

In its original sense, "passion" addressed the biblical question, "What have you set your heart upon?" The root meaning actually related to "suffering." That definition forces the real question: "What have you set your heart upon so intensely that you are willing to sacrifice for it?"

The Lord Jesus set his heart upon you so intensely that he was willing to die for you. He is passionate about you, and he would do anything for you. In return, because he first loved us, the believer's passion must be his love for the Lord Jesus. He clearly stated that expectation of you. The first commandment is to "love him with all your heart, soul, mind, and strength" (see Mark 12:30). Simply and straightforwardly, God wants your heart set upon him, whatever it takes. The first "life rock" settles the question of your passion—love him for who he is with all you've got!

At this juncture, a natural question arises about other passions in life. Am I not supposed to be passionate about other stuff in life? Shouldn't a person be passionate about mate and family? An athlete about his sport and team? A business person about work and deals?

Why, of course! Here is the clarification. You can possess many passions *in* life, but only one passion *of* life. Read that line again. When you take any or many of those passions *in* life and turn them into the passion *of* your life, you experience spiritual dysfunction. You fall into idolatry. Even non-Christians who are set on a singular passion are better balanced than Christians who pursue many passions. Focused non-Christians know that principle, but they must evaluate the validity of their singular, passionate object. Believers, instead, must possess one passion of life—the Lord Jesus—to ground, stabilize, and nurture the other passions in the fullest way. If your passions are equally weighted or coexist, they will compete with one another and weaken your spiritual vitality. If they flow from a singular passion—for the Lord Jesus Christ—you will experience his promise of life in all its fullness.

The fact of the matter is simple: You can't love all the other stuff rightly if you don't love Jesus as you should. Let me illustrate that conclusion from marriage. If you are married, you know what I mean. If matters are going smoothly with your spouse, everything else is a little easier. But if they aren't, everything else is affected adversely. Similarly, don't be afraid of loving God as your first love, because then you can love everything else—your family, business, even your car—rightly! But if you don't love God like you should, then everything else carries a cloud over it. Don't be afraid of loving Jesus too much. For when you love him too much, you can love those passions in life, whether persons or things, fully and rightly.

May I suggest a practical strategy in making Jesus your passion, your first love? Get yourself a composition notebook or create a daily note space on your organizer. For a start, write a note of love to your Lord Jesus. I wish I had started this practice earlier. I do it with a cup of hot coffee (passion in life!) as my first and regular act of love *before* I begin the bustle of the business day. This is a heartfelt thank-you to the Lord Jesus, scribbled out in illegible handwriting but indelible ink. You could scrawl a love note in appreciation, or reflect on the Scripture reading of the morning, or even express frustration about his invisibility at any given moment.

Develop your own way of returning your love to him. Be creative, change tactics, get new ideas, so you won't get stuck in legalistic routine or God-controlling formulas. Remember, you are expressing love to him, not attempting to gain merit with him. Some time later, visit that love journal to see how God has been working himself into the passion of your life. Your underlying passion, the passion *of* life, will ground and grow all your passions in life fully and rightly. Make Jesus your first love.

Life Rock 2: Your Mission

The U.S. border patrol watched young Juan push his gleaming new bike every day across the Mexico-U.S. border with a sandbag straddled across his center bar. Concerned about the illegal import of contraband, the agent assigned to Juan stopped him each day to find sand in the sandbags. Spot checking did not help incriminate Juan either.

In desperation one day, unable to find out just what Juan was smuggling in every day, the agent made a deal: "Juan, I'll only ask you this question once. I'll never stop you again from entering the country. I know you are smuggling something very valuable into the country. What is it? Tell me, and I'll never stop you again."

Juan answered, "Bicycles!"

The boy's mission was to smuggle in bicycles. He used the sandbags to accomplish the mission. Too many Christians make hauling sandbags the mission of their lives and confuse those who watch and wonder. Instead, the "sandbags of life"—the dimensions at which we must live—must fulfill our ultimate purpose, our mission.

Your life, like mine, may be divided into three major segments—personal life, family life, and work life. These "sandbags" must straddle the center bar rather than become the mission of our lives.

Your personal life is made up of several aspects—food, drink, exercise, spirituality, sexuality, sleep, education, character, values, clothes, cosmetics, transportation, television, leisure, etc.

Your family life relates to spouse, kids, parents, siblings, relatives, etc.

Your work life connects to home, business, company, and profession. This dimension of your life calls for personal development, performance issues, relationships with colleagues, etc.

Before you became a believer in the Lord Jesus, you may have asked honest questions about the routineness, the repetitiveness, the monotonies of life: "Why should I get up every day to the unwelcome bray of an alarm clock, wash up, sip Starbucks while negotiating clogged freeways, delete voice mail and E-mail intrusions, put up with office walk-ins, be victimized by my digitized to-do, all without being able to please my boss?"

You returned home weary each night after visiting the fitness center, play with the kids, gobble up the evening meal, catch late-night humor monologues, then set your alarm clock to do it all over again and wait for the weekend.

You asked yourself, "Why should I, like Sisyphus, push the stone up the mountain, let it roll down, and push it up again?" And all you get to be is older, hopefully wiser (but that doesn't follow), and definitely more feeble (check the burgeoning medicine kit filled with new prescriptions).

That somewhat bleak, daily scenario harasses our existence unless we have an ultimate purpose that justifies every aspect of human living in its excitements, repetitions, joys, and sorrows. The basic dimensions of life can be pursued daily in the despairing way just described—weighed down by them. Or, the meaningless monotony must be broken. Everyone—Christian and non-Christian—must deliver sandbags. But Christians should not turn them into the mission of life. The Bible gives a powerful answer to the question of mission: "Why do I exist?"

Your new relationship to the Lord Jesus Christ offers the alternative to repetitive despair. The Bible provides the answer to the "why" of life. Jesus lifts the question to a different level and transforms the criterion for your existence.

His mission for your life unifies, focuses, and motivates those dull routines into purposeful excellence. Your mission, according to God's Word, is to glorify him—to make God look great. Before you came to know Jesus, you had no resources to please anybody but yourself. Upon conversion, you have the capacity to pursue a valid mission for life.

The purpose of your existence is to make God look good— whether in the basics of eating and drinking or in whatever you do (1 Cor. 10:31). You exist to glorify God. That's your mission. Missions *in* life—personal, family, and work life—are hung on the center bar of God's glory—the mission *of* your life.

The concept of "glory" in the Bible derives from the word *weight.* We still use phrases like "he throws around his weight" or "he carries clout" to refer to influence and power. Consequently, I ask two questions that I want you to process slowly, think deeply about, and act upon soon: (1) In which segment of your life—personal, family, work—is God a lightweight at present? Is it in your food habits, your use of money, your marriage, your integrity at work? (2) In which aspect of your life should he increase his weight?

Identify a couple of these areas, write them in the margins, and strategize to increase God's weight in those areas. Then go on to make God look good with specific goals and action plans. For example, "By January 31, research the options for investing _____ % of my income in God's work. By April 30, I will invest half of that sum in appropriate places to increase God's work in my county (_____), country, (_____), and in the following regions of the world (_____)."

The brilliant composer Johannes Sebastian Bach initialed each of his compositions: S.D.G. He dedicated each of his incredible works to the glory of God alone *(Soli Deo Gloria).* I desire that kind of unifying, ulterior orientation for all my activities.

As I write this chapter, I ask if I can place S.D.G. as a footer on each page. I invite you to turn the glory of God into the mission of your life so you can sign every one of life's segments, subsegments, and sub-subsegments with S.D.G.

God is after his reputation; he pursues cosmic recognition; he has staked his glory on the way you live your life. Make God look great in all the dimensions of your life.

Life Rock 3: Your Vision

The most distinguished astronomer at the turn of the nineteenth century, Sir Percival Lowell, was particularly known for his expertise on the red planet, Mars. He theorized that Mars featured water canals and channels. In 1877, an Italian colleague saw lines crisscrossing the planet, which Lowell claimed proved his theory. Lowell was so eminent in his field that no one dared question his conclusion.

NASA scientists know Mars much better than Lowell ever hoped to know. They send sophisticated probes to map the planet like the back of our hands and haven't found a single water canal or channel. Ophthalmology has also advanced in the knowledge of the human eye since 1900. Lowell thought he was studying Mars when he was actually mapping the blood vessels in his own eyeballs. An eye disease has actually been named after him. Lowell suffered from "Lowell's Syndrome."

That "vision" problem afflicts all of us. We equate vision with the things nearest to us, demands urgent to us, stresses pressing in on us in the personal, family, and work aspects of our lives. We construct solid goals for these three areas and think we are looking at God's purposes for us. Without good eyes we can't see at all. A good pair of spiritual eyes became a reality at your conversion. These areas of life must be restructured to make God look good. But our daily mission is not to be our life vision. We can easily develop a spiritual eye disease that equates the near with the far and substitutes mission for vision, replacing the ultimate with penultimate.

Instead, God's vision for the whole world, for all people, and for all history and geography beckons us to lift our eyes and not map our own eyeballs. If the mission of God is to bring glory to himself, the vision of God is to bring people to himself. Bringing people to himself is not one of God's new thoughts that became a reality when you trusted the Lord Jesus. His vision of bringing people to himself runs from eternity to eternity. Let me excerpt from God's global vision from the Old Testament:

In Genesis 1–11 God creates humanity, judges sin, and provides for all humanity to come to him in primal pattern, whether in Adam, Abel, or Noah.

In Genesis 12 God covenants with Abraham with a vision of blessing for all the families of the earth through his chosen people.

In Exodus 19:6 Israel is chartered to be a kingdom of priests. The whole nation functions as a priest to the whole world.

In the second book of the Psalms (42–72) the psalmist prefers the "global" rather than the "national" name for the God who relates to the nations.

The climax of Isaiah (60–66) invites the ends of the earth to turn to God and be saved.

We could add "the salvation of non-Jews" theme throughout the Old Testament—Abraham, Melchizedek, Rahab, Naaman, Nebuchadnezzar, and Nineveh—to prove God's global vision. Unfortunately, the nation of Israel only occasionally implemented God's vision. God's heart is not reflected in Israel's activity.

The New Testament, of course, unleashes the Great Commission of Jesus through his disciples and the church. Peter, Paul, and the apostles sensed a calling to participate in God's vision for the whole world. God's vision climaxes with uncountable multitudes from across the world's political, ethnic, racial, and linguistic landscape emerging from the great tribulation around God's throne (Rev. 7:9–11).

Israel's and Lowell's eye disease, a tendency to focus on the self rather than the world while thinking we are looking far away, plagues believers today. You could tell them to get off your planet. But right from the beginning of your new spiritual journey, God calls you to look outward to his vision of making Jesus known throughout the world.

In late 1999 the world crossed the six billion mark in population. Six billion people is a rather large number. Only one billion minutes have passed since the earthly ministry of Jesus until now. The earth's population quadrupled in only one hundred years, with the last billion added in a little more than four thousand days. But we have not topped it off yet. It's six billion and increasing! Population is increasing in places where knowledge of Jesus is least accessible and understood.

That's where you come in. As one who has experienced new life in the Lord Jesus Christ, you are called to participate in God's vision for the whole world. People, someone noted, are controlled by the *strengths* of the vision they see. I think, however, that people are governed by the *weaknesses* of their visions. You and I, if left to our eye diseases, will carry too weak a vision. We are often ruled by quantity and quality of immediate life issues—what car we drive, what clothes we wear, what power we wield, how comfortably we will live at retirement. These are tiny, weak issues that we create for ourselves as our visions for the future. Instead, God calls us to "make Jesus well known"—to implement his vision for the world. There are no weaknesses to this vision—only costs. Every vision carries a cost, and we ought to evaluate the validity of the vision regularly by its costs. In God's vision, it cost him the life of his Son. He doesn't call you to participate in anything that hasn't cost him everything already.

How can you find your specific part in God's vision for the world? For a start, draw the following three columns on a sheet of paper with an attitude of expectant prayer, asking for God's direction in your participation in his vision. You are about to reflect deeply on your life.

1. *List Resources:* In this column, list all your gifts, talents, and resources. Human relations, administrative gifts, social, intellectual, and financial resources, whatever. Take some time to do it. You will be amazed at what God has given you. Thank God for these provisions.

2. *Understand Experiences:* Especially your sufferings. Write out the ways in which God has broken you. Where has suffering touched you deeply? Write about times when God got your attention, when he put you through the fire to mature you. Think about your entire life, from its very early years and experiences in suffering. Where do you still show scars from the pain of the past? You will notice that your sensitivity to particular kinds of needs arises from your past brokenness.

3. *Discern Needs:* Discernment goes beyond listing and understanding. Begin with all the needs you see around you. Make an unending list of human needs, because human needs are unending. You have to train your mind to see needs. Now train your memory to discern opportunities. Not all needs are opportunities

for your involvement. Some are, and you need to discover them. Look especially for needs with which you identify. These would match your own experiences with other similar needs. Your suffering tenderized you enough to empathize with a particular cluster of needs.

Pray over these three lists. The columns may extend into several pages. Come back later—a second and a third time—as you remember to add more. Ask God to help you to detect connections (1) between your giftedness and your brokenness; (2) between your suffering and human needs; and (3) between giftedness and human needs. Are themes emerging for your serious consideration in your involvement in God's vision to make Jesus well known? From this blend of resources, experiences, and needs arrive at a dominant but tentative personal vision in making Jesus well known, starting now right where you are. Then offer your present understanding of your part to God. Let him add, delete, change, replace at will, because you are really after his vision for your life.

A young lady doing this reflective exercise suddenly noticed strong connections between her talents, experiences, and identifiable needs. She was raised in a difficult home, having called six men "Dad" before she was nineteen. Now happily married with two children, she could have lived for herself. Instead, she became involved in making Jesus well known by initiating a ministry to children from shattered families in her church. Sensitized to their needs because of her own experience, having identified her gifts of administration and leadership, she addressed the needs of others.

Having discovered the outlines of your vision in life, strategize for your participation in God's vision. Then work the strategy. Working the strategy means you will be adding a fourth segment to your "missions in life." In addition to taking responsibility and action in terms of your personal, family, and work life, you add "ministry life" to that mix as a major dimension. There are two levels at which you may be involved in ministry life—a leadership role or a support role. Actually, you can lead one part of God's vision and support other parts of his vision, depending on a number of factors, especially time, talent, energy, and money that you listed among your resources. Also take your season of life into consideration in identifying your specific roles and responsibilities. God's vision will grow on you as you mature. It will demand increasing involvement, so be ready to lend support or lead actively in whatever role God gives you in implementing his vision for the world.

Passion relates to the person of God, mission to the purpose of God, and vision to the program of God. When you put these life rocks in place—*passion, mission, vision*—the lesser ones—responsibilities, activities, hobbies, etc.—will find their right places in your life. The passion of your life would be to make Jesus the first love of your life. The mission of your life would be to make Jesus look good in your life. The vision of your life would be to make Jesus well known through your life. I welcome you to the most effective and fruitful life that has ever been offered to the human race.

On the Intentional Life

1. The Lord Jesus looked back at his life to declare to his Father, "I have glorified You on the earth. I have finished the work which You have given Me" (John 17:4 NKJV). If you had twenty-four hours to live, what would be the final statement you would make about your life?

2. Paul was conscious of the course God had marked for his life (Acts 20:24; 2 Tim. 4:7–8). Do you think God has a personal course for you to finish in life?

On Passion

1. The first of the Ten Commandments begins with the love of God (Deut. 6:5). Why is love of God more important than any other aspect of our relationship with God?

2. In Mark 12:29–30, the Lord Jesus "adds" *the mind* to the Old Testament facets of loving God with heart, soul, and strength. What should we make of this addition?

On Mission

1. Psalm 8 argues that all creation, especially humans, were created "to make God look good." Where is God looking good in your life?

2. The word *glory*, we said, means "weight." We ought to glorify God in everything, from mundane activities of eating and drinking to anything we do (1 Cor. 10:31). In which of your activities is God a lightweight?

On Vision

1. Psalm 67:1–2 tells us why God has blessed us—that the ends of the earth may know of his salvation. Are your blessings translating into bringing the Good News to the world, beginning with your unbelieving neighbors?

2. Matthew 9:35–38 tells us the results of what Jesus saw. Filled with compassion, he commissioned his disciples to pray and participate in the ready harvest. Does God's vision for humanity grip you?

RAMESH RICHARD is a professor at Dallas Theological Seminary, where he teaches in three academic departments. He is also the founder and president of *RREACH* (Ramesh Richard Evangelism and Church Helps) International, a global proclamation ministry. Dr. Richard frequently travels throughout the world, clarifying the message of the Bible through lectures and preaching, and training thousands of church leaders to preach, lead, and think biblically. He, his wife Bonnie, and their children—Ryan, Robby, and Sitara—live in the Dallas area.

Walking with God

can I live the Christian life?

By Major W. Ian Thomas

W hat do you think we are? Cannibals?"
That, in all probability, would have been the response of my
family to anybody who had suggested that we were not Christians!
Born in England, white-faced, comfortably middle-class, and
respectable members in good standing of a local church—what more
could reasonably have been expected of us?

We were indeed "Christianized," but pathetically less than
Christian—bearing only that thin veneer of churchmanship that
passes muster in a wayward, godless society for true religion. A society in which songs were still sung with fervor about the "Faith of Our
Fathers," but in which men and women neither knew their God nor
the inspiration of their faith.

In spite of this, even before I reached my teens, there was an
unspoken quest and an indefinable urge within my heart: a longing after God. I can remember talking to him about the trivial
things that loom so large in the world of a small boy, but my
words echoed into space! God was "somewhere out there," but I
did not know where to find him and I did not know how to get
his attention.

It was a boy my own age who provided the link. Kenneth had found a good thing, and as my friend he wanted to share with me what he had discovered.

It was not to get "converted," however, that I accompanied my young friend to that summer camp, for the simple reason that I did not know what it meant to be converted! This was an entirely new language to me. "Conversion," "redemption," the idea that I could be "saved" through receiving Christ as my Savior because he had died in my place upon the cross, that I could be "born again" and receive "eternal life"—to all this I was a total stranger.

I did not find it difficult to listen to Mr. Lawrence Head, the camp chaplain, when he spoke to us. For one thing, he frothed at the mouth when he spoke and was, therefore, affectionately known as "Bubbly Head." It was fun watching the bubbles, wondering on which side of his mouth they would burst first! "Bubbly" was a businessman with a lovely way of communicating the truth of the gospel, and in a way even a small boy could understand.

I learned from the tenth chapter of John's Gospel about the Good Shepherd who lay down his life for the sheep. I understood clearly that Christ had died in my place that I might be forgiven, and that if only I would ask him, he would come into my life as my Savior and give me eternal life. Forgiven, I would become a child of God and never perish.

There was a quiet moment at the end of the meeting during which any boy could speak to the Lord Jesus in his heart, thankfully claim forgiveness, and receive him as Savior. I told nobody then of what had happened in the silence, but that evening life for me took on an entirely new dimension. There were to be consequences far beyond my wildest dreams, calculated completely to change the course of my life. I had been redeemed!

That, however, was not my most significant encounter with God. I had entered consciously only into the good of what Christ had done through his redeeming death, in reconciling me to God. I had not come to understand the purpose for which that reconciliation had been effected, nor the solid substance of that spiritual regeneration that had taken place—though still unknown to me—by the coming of the Holy Spirit to live within me.

To have testified then as I did that "Christ lived in my heart" was simply another way of saying that I had been converted; that Christ was my Savior, that my sins had been forgiven, and that I was on my way to heaven. That Jesus Christ as my God and Creator had actually come to dwell within me through his Holy Spirit to share his life with me was something the significance of which had not yet begun to dawn upon my soul. I just did not know how wealthy I had become!

"Jesus living in my heart" was not an unmeaningful expression in terms of my redemption, but it represented to me only a sentimental attachment, a sense of gratitude rather than a working relationship between man and God in spiritual union. My gratitude to Christ for dying in my place motivated me to work for him and represent his cause with genuine sincerity, but he remained external to my endeavors. Though the honored *object* of these activities, Christ had not yet become in me the *origin* of those activities.

I took real delight in reading my Bible and enjoyed best the company of those who loved my Savior. At the age of fifteen I assumed the leadership of the Christian group at my high school. It was at that age that I first dedicated my life to missionary service, with my eyes on Africa, and began preaching in the open in a public park.

Convinced that I would be more useful on the mission field in Africa as a doctor, at seventeen I enrolled at London University to study medicine. Already an assistant leader in the Bible class through which I had been converted, I assumed additional responsibilities in the Inter-Varsity Christian Union at Saint Bartholomew's Hospital where I was studying and at the same time established a Christian club for underprivileged boys in the heart of London. My vacations, summer and winter, were now wholly dedicated to evangelistic crusades, Bible camps, Christian sailing cruises, seaside missions, and other forms of missionary outreach.

In my zeal I had joined the rat race!

I began to feel like the Mississippi steamboat that stopped every time it blew its whistle. There was enough steam to make a noise, but not enough power to drive the pistons! I could "rev" the engine and sound impressive but somehow could not get the power from under the hood into the wheels on the road. I wanted to shift gears but could not find the gear shift. That can be frustrating!

It was not that I differed from the rest, because I saw no evidence in others that there was any better quality of life to be expected. I learned from those who had done the same before me. We all ran by the same rules, but for me the race was nearly over. I was a very, very tired rat!

In spite of my noblest endeavors, I was baffled at my inability to bring others to the point of accepting Christ as their Savior, nor was there any evidence that the words on my lips were actually being translated into the reality of other people's lives.

Coupled with this increasing sense of futility in all I attempted to do was the increasing consciousness of personal failure and defeat in my sincere desire to honor Christ by reflecting his likeness in my life. All this brought despair, and I knew that I would be as useless in Africa as I had been in England. Crossing an ocean would not make me a saint, nor could carving my way through the scrub with a bush knife in one hand and a Bible in the other turn a spiritual pygmy into a spiritual giant! I wanted so much to be a man of God, but I was desperately tired and very, very discouraged.

What a relief it is to discover that you have never been a bigger failure than God always expected you to be! I unburdened my soul to a loving, understanding Savior. I told him how utterly discouraged I had become, that I could look back only upon seven years of barrenness and that any further effort now seemed futile.

God knows, I thought to myself, *how hard I have tried; desperately hard, and yet to no avail.* All hope within my heart had been abandoned. Noble longings and strivings after godliness had withered at the roots, and in deep despair I prayed: "Lord Jesus, I love you with all my heart, and I shall never cease to be thankful that you died for me upon the cross. I know you are my Redeemer: I know my sins are forgiven! I know I am on my way to heaven! I have cherished only one ambition: to be used in your service to bring others to yourself and to bring glory to your name. But I am beaten! I just don't have what it takes, and I am on my back. I'm sorry, but I quit!"

I thought the Lord Jesus Christ would be greatly disappointed, but I almost heard him sigh with relief! It was as though he said to me: "Thank you! I have been waiting for this for seven years. All that time, with great sincerity but with misguided dedication, you have been trying to live for me a life that only I can live through you. At last I am in business!"

Yes, indeed he was! He was in business: the glorious business of demonstrating the overwhelming adequacy of an indwelling Savior to meet every last need of those who will let him be God, and who will give him the opportunity of proving that he is big enough for the job!

In a moment of revelation I graduated out of bankruptcy. Out of the bitterness of despair I discovered my true wealth, that "treasure" that God, as the seal of our redemption, is pleased to place within the earthen vessels of our frail humanity: Christ himself.

I did not receive one thing more at that moment than had already been mine throughout the whole seven years of my previous Christian life. I simply discovered that the spiritual poverty in which I had been living stemmed from my ignorance of the true content of the Christian life. "For if, when we were God's enemies, we were reconciled to him through the death of his Son, how much more, having been reconciled, *shall we be saved through his life*" (Rom. 5:10, emphasis added).

I had long been reconciled to God by the death of the Lord Jesus, but I had wholly failed to grasp the fact that his death *for me*, in reconciling me to God, was designed to put his life *in me*, so that I might be "saved through his life"—deriving from him every moment of every day the divine dynamic that makes life essentially miraculous.

"For to me, to live is Christ and to die is gain" (Phil. 1:21). "I have been crucified with Christ and I no longer live, but *Christ lives in me.* The life I live in the body, I live by faith in the Son of God, who loved me and gave himself for me" (Gal. 2:20, emphasis added). "When Christ, who is your life, appears, then you also will appear with him in glory" (Col. 3:4).

These were the familiar Scriptures that suddenly leaped into life as my soul was flooded with life. My spirit was released, and I experienced a profound sense of peace and quiet confidence. My heart overflowed with unspeakable joy.

Jesus Christ himself, alive, and living in me!

How long and how wearily I had hoped, begged, and prayed for what was already mine. At last I could see it! All that he was, I had. I could not have more, and needed never to enjoy less. I simply have to take, and say, "Thank You!"

How gloriously simple! Christ does not *give* us strength; he *is* our strength. He does not *give* us victory; he *is* our victory. He is all that we could ever need at any time in any circumstance! That, without a doubt, was my most memorable encounter with God. For I had learned to relate every new situation to the person of the Lord Jesus Christ whose life I shared, and who waited only for my availability to demonstrate his marvelous all-sufficiency.

To share the life of Jesus Christ is to live miraculously. Why settle for less?

There are so very many who, with no little sincerity, try to live the Christian life and fail miserably, weary of the struggle. Perhaps you are numbered among them, as I was, and are as bewildered as the rest.

Nearly always it is for one of two reasons: either *trying to live a life you do not have,* or *having a life you do not live.* To understand the first reason, you need to understand what happened to Adam and the whole human race when Adam fell.

Adam became a living soul in the day that God breathed into him the Spirit of life, and he became a "spiritual being"—one to whom the indwelling presence of the Creator was indispensable if man was to be functional in revealing his likeness, character, and glory, and so fulfill the purpose for which he was made.

When God created all the other forms of animal life, he built into them an instinctive thrust that would give to each its own distinctive behavior patterns. However, man's behavior was not to be governed that way. God himself would be, in man, the origin of his own image; the source in man of his own activity; the dynamic in man of his own demands; and at all times, the sole cause in man of his own effect—teaching man's mind, controlling his emotions, directing his will, and governing his behavior, so that the Scripture would be fulfilled: "Then God said, 'Let us make man in our image, in our likeness.' . . . So God created man in his own image, in the image of God he created him; male and female he created them" (Gen. 1:26–27).

What went wrong?

Satan deceived man into believing that he could be independent of God and therefore could afford to be disobedient to God, without incurring any adverse consequences. "And the LORD God commanded the man, 'You are free to eat from any tree in the garden; but you must not eat from the tree of the knowledge of good and evil, for when you eat of it you will surely die'" (Gen. 2:16–17). "'You will not surely die,' the serpent said to the woman. 'For God knows that when you eat of it your eyes will be opened, and you will be like God, knowing good and evil.' . . . She took some and ate it. She also gave some to her husband, who was with her, and he ate it" (Gen. 3:4–6).

Did they die that day, as God said they would? Yes, but not physically, for that did not happen for more than nine hundred years. But God withdrew from their human spirit, and from that day on, every boy, girl, man, and woman has been born spiritually aborted—physically alive, but spiritually "dead in your transgressions and sins" (Eph. 2:1). The consequences of the fall of man must not be relegated only to the future at the final judgment, for "the wages of sin is death" (Rom. 6:23), and that is in the present tense, in the "here and now," not just in the "then and there!"

Having died to restore guilty sinners to right standing before a holy God, Christ can now restore life to the dead. This spiritual re-creation or new birth takes place in response to genuine repentance and to the obedience of faith, instantly restoring to forgiven sinners the life of Christ, whose indwelling and controlling presence alone can restore a person to normality and make him functional. "So it is written: 'The first man Adam became a living being'; the last Adam, a life-giving spirit. . . . The first man was of the dust of the earth, the second man from heaven" (1 Cor. 15:45, 47).

This is the missing factor in the gospel as it is so often preached today. That is why so many come to Jesus quite sincerely for *what he did*, without receiving him for *who he is!* Christ suffered a death like ours, so we might enjoy a resurrection like his! The Lord Jesus laid down his life for us so that he might give his life to us and live his life through us!

There is something worse than pushing a car with an empty tank! And that is going to church, attending seminars, or going to a theo-logical college to learn how to push a car with a full tank! That is the state of the vast majority of Christians: they are indeed born again, but they have never by faith appropriated the indwelling, resurrec-tion life of the only One capable of living the Christian life—because he alone *is* the Christian life.

How would you define a miracle?

Maybe the simplest way to describe a miracle would be to say, "It is something that happens, for which there is no possible explana-tion but God." The life of the Lord Jesus Christ was therefore a mir-acle, for he himself said: "By myself [without my Father] I can do nothing" (John 5:30).

The Lord Jesus was, is, and always will be our God and Creator. But while on earth for our sake, he gave us those attributes of deity that would have been incompatible with his humanity. Though never ever less than God, while in this world Christ chose to behave as though he were never ever more than man. As man, he could do what he never could have done as God. He was seen, though "no one has ever seen God" (John 1:18). He was tempted, though "God cannot be tempted by evil" (James 1:13). He "became obedient to death—even death on a cross" (Phil. 2:8), though God obeys nobody. He died that we might be forgiven, though God cannot die; he "alone is immortal" and is not subject to any form of death (1 Tim. 6:16).

The Lord Jesus lived in a disposition toward the Father of utter dependence on him and of total obedience to him, and he refused to allow there to be any possible explanation for anything he did, said, or was apart from the Father. That is why his life is rightly described as a miracle. As a result, God could again be seen in a man: "Don't you believe that I am in the Father, and that the Father is in me? The words I say to you are not just my own. Rather, it is the Father, living in me, who is doing his work" (John 14:10).

Christ was not being a "superman," but man in normality, as he himself created man to be. That is why the Lord Jesus said, "As the Father has sent me, I am sending you" (John 20:21), and "If a man remains in me and I in him, he will bear much fruit; apart from me you can do nothing" (John 15:5). In other words, *it takes God to be a man,* and *Christ in the Christian puts God back into the man.* God never created people to be functional apart from his indwelling presence. It takes Christ himself to be a Christian; not just what he did when he died to redeem us, nor just the beautiful life that he lived then to inspire us. We need his indwelling life every moment of every day to be what he created us and redeemed us to be. *Christ came not just to get people out of hell and into heaven. He came to get himself out of heaven and into people!*

Where are you? Are you trying to live a life you don't have? If so, then "you must be born again" (John 3:7). You must go to the one and only Savior and trust in him, the One who died in your place upon the cross to reconcile you to a holy God, and receive the gift of eternal life.

On the other hand, are you failing to live a life you already have? Are you trying to do the impossible? Are you trying to produce by your own sweat and steam a life that only Christ can live in and through you? Remember, it was the Lord Jesus who said: "Come to me, all you who are weary and burdened, and I will give you rest. Take my yoke upon you and learn from me, for I am gentle and humble in heart, and you will find rest for your souls. For my yoke is easy and my burden is light" (Matt. 11:28–30).

If you were digging a hole and I wanted to give you a rest, you would have to drop your spade and get out—vacate! The only way the Lord Jesus can give you a rest is for you to drop your spade and get out, one step at a time. "So then, just as you received Christ Jesus as Lord, continue to live in him" (Col. 2:6). For every situation into which each new step takes you, *vacate*, and let Christ *occupy*. He will handle every situation magnificently.

So just say "Thank you, Lord" and stop pushing a car with a full tank. Get on board, put your foot on the gas, and go for a ride! Remember that faith always says "Thank You," both for what Christ has done and for who he is. Then you will always be on vacation, and Christ will always be in business!

MAJOR W. IAN THOMAS was born in London, England, of middle-class parents and was converted at the age of twelve in a boy's camp. With the intention of becoming a missionary in Africa, he studied medicine at London University for two years. As a student, in deep discouragement about his Christian life, he discovered the life-transforming secret of the indwelling life of the living Christ in the life of the believer. This discovery led him into an evangelistic and Bible-teaching ministry that has spread around the world.

Through this ministry, a Young Peoples Christian Conference Center and Bible School were founded at Capernwray Hall, Carnforth, in northwest England. From this beginning sprang the Capernwray Missionary Fellowship of Torchbearers, of which Major Thomas is the founder and general director. There are now conference centers and Bible schools beyond the British Isles in Germany, Austria, Switzerland, Spain, Sweden, Canada, the U.S.A., Australia, New Zealand, India, Indonesia, Japan, Costa Rica, and additional headquarters established in the Sudan, Micronesia, Malaysia, and the Philippines Books by Major Thomas include *The Saving Life of Christ, Saving Life of Christ and the Mystery of Godliness,* and *If I Perish, I Perish!*

Obeying God's Voice

how does God talk to me?

By Jill Briscoe

I was lying in a hospital bed talking to the girl who had just led me to the Lord. Janet was a nurse who, out of sheer obedience, had explained the gospel to her captive audience. If Janet had not listened to God and been obedient, I would not be writing this chapter. In fact, my son Pete would not have asked me to write it as he would not even be here! The repercussions of being obedient are incredible!

I learned to listen to God and do what he told me to do as soon as I accepted Christ. One of the things I learned was that God expects us to tell others how they can become Christians. Almost as soon as I read this in Romans 10:14–15, I was given a chance to apply it.

I had been invited to spend an evening at a yacht club by a young businessman who drank too much and had no particular interest in things of eternal worth. His philosophy followed a biblical example (the only biblical thing about him): "Take life easy; eat, drink and be merry" (Luke 12:19). Being a few months old in Christ, I accepted his invitation and went.

I was not prepared for my reaction. This was the first time I had been back to my old haunt since becoming a Christian. Everything sounded jaded and off key. Why had I never thought about our empty conversation before? I realized that just like my friends I had spent a large part of my eighteen years rushing around my world speaking from the depths of my considerable ignorance about nothing very much! Suddenly I had some peace and assurance in my life, and I wanted to tell everyone what had happened to me in the hospital.

I longed to share the secret I had just been let into, how the risen Christ had brought substance and relevance to my life. But what would my companion think about it? I said to my date, "Would you mind very much if I got up on a table and told everyone about my conversion?" He looked startled but hastily recovered and said he would mind very much indeed. My immediate reaction was to forget it, but I found myself praying instead. A verse of Scripture popped into my head, "How can they hear without someone preaching to them?" (Rom. 10:14). The answer to Paul's rhetorical question was obviously, "They won't!" I found myself listening to God. This passage was his voice, his Word. This is one way he speaks to us.

I couldn't see a preacher in sight, nor had I ever seen one in that particular bar, so I reasoned they would have to settle for me until one turned up. I was about to lose the only friends I had at the time, not to mention my promising date. I was not the first to mount the table top to propound some idea or philosophy in that place, and I would not be the last. But in obedience to the Word of my God that told me to go into all the world (and this was my piece of it) and preach the gospel to those who had never heard (and as far as I knew these crazy friends of mine had never heard), I obeyed. They heard!

They did not hear a fluent, erudite speaker; neither did they hear a convincing argument as to why they should follow Christ. In fact, they didn't even allow me to finish or to respond to their ribald comments, but they heard the voice of "obedience" perhaps for the first time in their lives. Obedience to the Christ I already loved to distraction, my friend, my Savior, my everything.

Forty-five years later I bumped into one of those old friends! Shyly she asked me if I would send her one of my books. She told me her search for God began that memorable night long ago, when a new believer just couldn't shut up about a Jesus she had fallen in love with. Obedience casts a long shadow, and it always pays off in the end. So what is obedience, and how do we learn it?

Obedience to the Living Christ

The first question to ask is, Obedience to what? A creed? Religious philosophy? Dogma? A new idea? I am talking about being obedient to the living Christ. To what he says. The obvious question that comes next is, What does he say and how does he say it? How do we learn to listen to God and do what he tells us to do?

Listening to God

The Holy Spirit will guide us into all truth by "prompting" us to right action. I remember as a young believer asking God to protect me from error. I had no biblical background whatsoever, and I was concerned about my ability to discern the voice of God. I also had a vivid imagination and was skeptical of the "voices" I heard and the ideas that came to me. God answered that particular prayer, guiding me by the Spirit and training me in the Word. He guarded my mind until I knew enough and grew enough to recognize counterfeit thinking.

Listening to God through His Word

Listening to God follows the same general rules as listening to anyone else. First, you need to spend time with the one you are listening to. This means you have to have a plan of attack. If you are going to sit at the same table in a restaurant with someone, you make arrangements. You block the time off on your calendar. Similarly, we need to reserve some time each day to meet with Jesus. Choose the time that will be most convenient every day and mark it down. Any time will work for God, but your schedule may be so hectic that you need to enter a different time every day.

Then show up. You know how disappointed you get if you make arrangements to have lunch with someone and they don't turn up? They must have a very good reason, you think, trying to help yourself not to feel too disappointed. Imagine how hurt you would be to find out they just chose to eat lunch with someone else and never even bothered to let you know! We must take our scheduled time with God very seriously if we are to learn to recognize his voice and obey it.

After you show up, what happens next? Calm your heart and listen. *What am I listening for?* you may wonder. *Will I hear a humanlike voice in my head?* Maybe, maybe not. The safest way to be sure you are hearing God's voice is to read the Bible. Start with ten minutes. Read systematically. Choose a book and read twenty or so verses. Then think about these verses in silence. This will focus you on him. When you read the Bible, you will be able to distinguish between God's voice and Satan's deception. When an idea pops into your mind, which can be one way God speaks to you, check it out with Scripture. At first, as you are getting familiar with the Scripture, you may not hear the difference between his voice and other voices.

My husband was a bank inspector. The bank he worked for trained their employees by giving them thousands of notes and slipping a few counterfeit ones among them. After counting thousands and thousands of the real things, it was easy to recognize a counterfeit note.

I once had a young married woman tell me that she had fallen in love with a married man. She informed me she had prayed about it and God had told her he wanted her to be happy—so this was the answer to her prayers. "God is love," the woman said. "It says so in the Bible, so if he has given me a love for this man it must be right." This reasoning totally contradicted the clear teaching of the very Bible she was quoting! My husband says that if we take a text out of context we end up with a *con*, and this was clearly the case here. The devil, who is the arch deceiver, had conned her into twisting Scripture to suit her purposes. We don't change Scripture to match our lives; we match our lives to Scripture! As we keep close to God and practice listening to him, we will begin to know instinctively what he wants us to do; what is right and what is wrong.

Listening to God through Others

Another way we can hear the voice of God is through godly counsel. God speaks through godly men and women who are a little further along the way than we are. In the late 1960s we prayed long and hard about the invitation we had received to leave our native England to pastor a church in Milwaukee, Wisconsin. Asking God to speak to us clearly, we spent a lot of time in prayer and shared what we were thinking as the situation developed.

Then we involved respected people, fully expecting to hear the voice of God through them. The Bible gives the example of the priest Hilkiah and religious leaders of Israel coming to Hulda the prophetess to give them some insight into the will of God revealed in the Word of God (2 Kings 22:14). Stuart and I turned to some godly men and women we could trust to give us insight.

After each conversation we compared notes and prayed. We prayed about the pros and cons, the fears and barriers to such a huge step of faith. We searched the Scriptures apart and together and once more compared what each read and the guidance we felt we were being given. God's voice, at first faint, began to get louder! The almost unanimous approval from this group of counselors, the clear direction we discerned through Scripture, and the peace gained from hours in prayer confirmed our decision to immigrate.

So we can listen to God in our thoughts, and we can hear his voice through counselors. We can also hear the voice of God in circumstances.

Listening to God through Circumstances

C. S. Lewis says, "God whispers to us in our pleasures, speaks to us in our sorrows and shouts to us in our pain." "What is God saying?" is an appropriate response when either painful or joyful circumstances happen. Particularly when trouble comes, the shout of his assurance can be heard above the wind and waves as Peter heard it when he was swamped in the boat on Galilee. "It is I. Don't be afraid," said Jesus (Matt. 14:27). But you have to be listening.

As difficult things have happened in my life, the voice of God has been heard. Sickness tells me I am not immortal. A lack of money says I need to depend more on God than on myself. Old age shows me "this world is not my home; I'm just passing through," and each birthday reminds me he has numbered my days; they are given to please him and not myself. God has had things to say to me in trouble of all kinds. My ear must be tuned to listen.

One time God told me what to do simply through circumstances. I was teaching in Liverpool, England, and found myself struggling with a tough class of kids. Try as I might, I could not keep order in the classroom. Then I realized these children were starved for love and attention. One day after asking God to guide me, one of my kids told me his big brother was in trouble with the police. I was concerned for the boy, as this particular brother seemed to be the caregiver for the younger siblings. What was God saying?

Circumstances took me to the streets of Liverpool one night to look for that boy. I found him in the most dangerous situation. It was not difficult to hear the voice of God even though I heard no voice and no Scripture directed me. The confrontation of need spoke to my heart, and that incident began a youth outreach to kids on the streets that continues today.

Listening to God through Creation

The Book of Romans teaches that there is enough evidence of God's majesty and glory in the things he has made to convince the most skeptical person of his existence (Rom. 1:20). There is some truth in the old adage, "One is nearer God's heart in a garden than anywhere else on earth." God can, if he wishes, use a bug, a flower, or even a donkey to communicate his truth! But the creation is fallen, and the creatures he made are as well. The safest way to listen to God is to read his written Word and to study the life of Jesus, the Living Word. Spend time with him in silence and in prayer and meditation. Walk in the grand world he has made and learn his genius, care, and creativity in all things great and small. And keep tuned to circumstances that may be God's way of alerting you to something he wants to tell you.

The point of hearing God's voice is to respond to it. The Bible says that a person who looks at himself in the glass and sees his true reflection and then goes away and does nothing about the things he has seen in the mirror is a foolish person (James 1:23–24). The Bible is like a mirror showing us the things that need to be changed.

One day I was baby-sitting one of our grandchildren. He loved looking at the baby in the mirror. My daughter said he was too small to realize the baby was he! So often we read the Bible that speaks to us about our true condition, but we do not see ourselves mirrored in the Word. We think the reflection is another baby. How can we grow to the point where we obey what we've heard?

Obedience—Finding His Will

We can know the will of God by looking in the Word of God. It is the Word that reveals the will. If we really want to know the answers to our dilemmas, then the secret is locked in the will of God. The Bible is the key that unlocks those secrets.

There was a time in my life when I was dating an unbeliever. As a new Christian, I was unfamiliar with Scripture. My conscience (another way God speaks to us) was alerting me to something being out of kilter. *Could it be God's will for me to marry this young man?* I wondered. I started to read the Bible, telling God I would read until I found an answer. It wasn't long until I came across 2 Corinthians 6:14: "Do not be yoked together with unbelievers." Well, that was pretty straightforward! The Word of God reveals the will of God, and once it does, we do well to obey! I didn't need to pray about knowing what to do anymore, as I would have been wasting my breath.

Being Honest

When you are asking God to tell you what to do in a given circumstance, try questioning yourself along these lines. "Do I genuinely want to know the answer to my question?" You will not hear his answer if you are playing games. Years ago, shortly after coming to Christ, I was struggling to be ready to stay single if God wanted me to. One day I caught myself praying fervently, "Lord, I am willing to be single." This sounded quite impressive but wasn't really true. I was honest enough to catch myself and say, "Actually, Lord, I was hoping you would be so impressed with my prayer you would give me a husband anyway!" Praying Psalm 139:23–24 can prepare your heart to hear and obey: "Search me, O God, and know my heart; test me and know my anxious thoughts. See if there is any offensive way in me, and lead me in the way everlasting." It is quite permissible to add, "And may I mean it."

Second, don't be afraid to tell God your feelings about anything and everything. Sometimes we act as if God doesn't know us very well. We pray as if we are trying to impress a stranger. That's why many of us just keep talking and don't want to listen when we pray. We are afraid if we pause God will get a word in edgewise and tell us he knows what we are really like and what we are really feeling.

Third, always remember there is nothing you can do to make God love you more or less; he already loves you perfectly! Whenever my daughter Judy has to reprimand her youngest child, Stephen, she calls him to her. He comes but hangs his head low and refuses to look at her. She kneels down to get on his level and grips his little face in her two hands. "Look at me, Stephen," she says gently. His eyes roll to the right, then they roll to the left, and then right into the back of his head! Judy keeps at it, saying determinedly, "Look at me, Stephen," until his eyes focus on his mother's face. The first thing Judy always says is, "I love you, Stephen!" Then she tells him what she needs to tell him. Remember, whatever you have done, "He loves you." So with a start like this you will in all likelihood hear the voice of God. The challenge lies in doing something about what you hear.

Giving Up Control

So what's so hard about doing what you hear? We are essentially selfish creatures, creatures of habit, and control freaks! For all these reasons and more, we don't want to do the will and work of God. So it is unlikely that we will be honest and vulnerable in our prayer times. The idea of prayer is to make us God-centered and not self-centered. The purpose of prayer is to bring us into touch with the power of God in order to break habits that have us by the throat. The joy of prayer is found in letting him have control and giving up the necessity of being in control of our lives.

Tania Rich is the young wife of one of the New Tribes missionaries taken hostage by Colombian guerrillas in the early 1990s. She told me how her prayer life has developed since the nightmare began. Now she doesn't plead, cajole, or bargain with God for the safe release of her husband. Still not knowing whether the three men are dead or alive, she says she is at peace whatever the outcome. She prays accordingly. She has also quit putting a time limit on her prayers. It is enough to know he knows and to rest in his timetable. She is certain that God's clocks keep perfect time. When you can't praise him for what he allows, you can praise him for who he is in the midst of what he allows. Tania has not come to this without many tears, but here is a woman who hears the voice of God and obeys.

It was Hannah who praised the Lord in the middle of hard times by saying, "My heart rejoices in the LORD" (1 Sam. 2:1). She could have said, "My heart rejoices in the Lord and not my circumstances." So we can learn to obey him not only in our worries but also in our woes. As the Word reveals his will, whether we are celebrating or suffering, prayer is a refuge. A place to listen to God and respond.

Let Love Drive Obedience

The bottom line is love. Jesus said, "If you love me you'll obey me!" (see John 14:15). Love makes spiritual discipline easy. I once heard an interview on TV. It was the story of a World War II couple who were separated for the duration of the war but who corresponded the entire time. At the end of the war more than three thousand letters had been sent. The couple was interviewed on a talk show about the book of letters that had just been published. The host expressed amazement at the letters. "Why should you be surprised," asked the husband. "We loved each other and had to be in communication." "That was an awful lot of responsibility for a pen and a little piece of paper," added the wife. "Can you imagine how much two people in love had to say to each other?"

Love must be in touch with the beloved all the time. The word *discipline* is a foreign concept to lovers who are trying to stay in touch. No one breathes down their necks, threatens, or cajoles. There is only planning and scheming to be in touch at the next possible moment. Fall in love with Jesus, and the desire to listen and obey will grow within you.

Scripture Passages Relating to Obedience

Be wholehearted. (Deut. 26:16)
Obedience is better than sacrifice. (1 Sam. 15:22)
Obedience to God rather than man. (Acts 5:29)

Examples of Obedience

Christ (Heb. 5:8)
Joshua (Josh. 11:15)
Joseph and Mary (Luke 2:39)
Paul (Acts 26:19)

Promises for Obedience

Exodus 19:5
Deuteronomy 5:29
Jesus said: "If you obey my commands, you will remain in my love, just as I have obeyed my Father's commands and remain in his love" (John 15:10).

Other Resources

Books
A Long Obedience in the Same Direction by Eugene Peterson
Following Christ by Joseph Stowell

Spiritual Disciplines for the Christian Life by A. Donald Whitney
How to Listen to God by Charles Stanley
Experiencing God by Henry T. Blackaby and Claude V. King

Tapes
"Prayer that Works" by Jill Briscoe at www.tellingthetruth.org

Sermon Information
www.sermoncentral.com

JILL BRISCOE has an active speaking and writing ministry that has taken her to many countries. She has written more than forty books, including study guides, devotional material, poetry, and children's books.

Jill is executive editor of *Just Between Us*, a magazine of encouragement for ministry wives and women in leadership. She serves on the board of World Relief and Christianity Today, Inc.

A native of Liverpool, England, Jill launched into youth evangelism after becoming a Christian at age eighteen. She married her husband, Stuart, in 1958, and since then they have ministered together through Telling the Truth media ministries at conferences and mission organizations around the world. They reside in suburban Milwaukee, Wisconsin, where Stuart has been senior pastor of Elmbrook Church since 1970. They have three children—David, Judy, and Peter—and enjoy the blessing of thirteen grandchildren.

Sin

what is sin and what can I do about it?

By George O. McCalep Jr.

B ased on the biblical interpretation of sin, the purpose of this chapter is to (1) simplify, clarify, and summarize an understanding of sin, (2) to assure those that are in Christ that their sins are forgiven, and (3) to help Christians understand what effect sin can have on their lives and their relationship with God. Unfortunately, and to the Christian believer's detriment, the concept of sin has been complicated, deviated, and polluted by secular humanism. Secular humanism is defined as leaning on your own understanding as if God did not exist rather than depending on biblical truth. Also, in today's society sin has found shelter and acceptance under the disguised umbrella of religious theology.

The correct biblical understanding of sin is essential for living out the Christian life to the fullest. Sin cannot be defined or interpreted based on human philosophy, but only by the Word of God. God alone can define sin just as God alone can pardon sin.

The Meaning of Sin

As mentioned, God's Word is the best source from which to develop a working definition of sin. The biblical definition of sin can be summarized as "missing the mark." Actually, the Bible uses a wide-ranging vocabulary when speaking of the concept or definition of sin. Neither the Hebrew nor Greek languages confine their concept of sin to any one word. The Hebrew language builds word pictures more than root meanings. For example, the most frequently used Hebrew root word for sin, *hata,* used more than 580 times in the Bible, is a word borrowed from archery. This undergirds the New Testament where again the most frequently used word is *ha martia,* which basically means the same thing: missing the mark.[1]

William Dyrness offers an orderly classification for the biblical vocabulary that refers to sin. Dyrness's system is divided into three categories. First, the *sin* words usually translate *iniquity* and *perversion,* and belong to a word group in which sin is represented as a deviation from a right way. The essence of sin can be understood in the sense of straying away from a pre-set standard. Second, there is a word group that represents sin as "guilt" before God, words like *guilty, ungodly,* and *wicked* belong in this group. In this category sin is no longer simply abstract but personal; both require an answer and bear accountability. Third, Dyrness identifies a category of rebellion often translated as *trespass.* This language is often employed by the Prophets as the accusation against the people of God who have rebelled against him.[2] Regardless of whether we have strayed or demonstrated wicked ungodliness and/or rebellion, we have all "missed the mark." Only the unmerited grace of God is sufficient to save us from our sins. "For the wages of sin is death, but the gift of God is eternal life in Christ Jesus our Lord" (Rom. 6:23 HCSB).

The Nature of Sin

Sin is real. Sin is devastating. The nonbelieving world often implies that sin is just a prohibition against fun and pleasure. Sin is no laughing matter, nor should we scoff at it. The Bible has much to say about the devastating and perilous nature of sin for the nonbeliever and for the Christian. Note the difference as you review the following in your Bible:

- Sin darkens our minds and hearts (Rom. 1:21).
- Sin causes us to behave in ways that are ugly (Rom. 1:29–31).
- Sin binds and enslaves us so that we do things we do not want to do (Rom. 7:15).
- Sin keeps us from pleasing God (Rom. 8:7–8).
- Sin distorts all our relationships (Gal. 5:19–21).
- Sin is lawlessness (1 John 3:4).
- Sin is all unrighteousness (1 John 5:17).

In addition to sin's devastating and perilous nature, the Bible also teaches us that "there is no one righteous, not even one" (Rom. 3:10), and "all have sinned and fall short of the glory of God" (Rom. 3:23). Believers are in constant spiritual warfare against sin. The perilous and devastating nature of sin is no myth or illusion.

The Presence of Sin

We must be confronted with the truth that even though believers' past, present, and future sins are forgiven, the presence of sin is still with us and we still behave in sinful ways. Sins such as carnal thinking and Christian apathy are a reality, and cleansing solutions can come only from the cleansing Word of God (1 John 1:7–10).

Many Christians make the mistake of thinking that because they no longer engage or participate in fornication, adultery, or other major sin, they are free from the presence of all sin. However, we are sinful by nature as well as by choice, and we are sinful by what we fail to do as well as by what we do. According to God's Word, any time we stray from God's will, way, or purpose, we have "missed the mark" and have sinned. Though for the Christian this cannot result in eternal separation from God, it does bear a price.

Forgiveness of Sin—the Central Foundational Truth

In the construction of any building, it is absolutely necessary that the foundation be flawless, lest whatever you build eventually comes tumbling down. Likewise, when building a spiritual assertion, the foundation is crucial. It is essential that the Christian know that there is no sentence of doom for those who believe in the name of Jesus, and have put their trust and faith in him. "Therefore, no condemnation now exists for those in Christ Jesus, because the Spirit's law of life in Christ Jesus has set you free from the law of sin and of death. What the law could not do since it was limited by the flesh, God did. He condemned sin in the flesh by sending His own Son in flesh like ours under sin's domain, and as a sin offering, in order that the law's requirement would be accomplished in us who do not walk according to the flesh but according to the Spirit" (Rom. 8:1–4 HCSB).

Nothing need be added—no "ifs" and no "buts." Often misunderstanding follows when believers are falsely influenced and persuaded that they have some power or authority to save themselves from the penalty of sin. We are pardoned from the penalty of sin by the shed blood of Jesus, *plus nothing!*

Sin is devastating, but God's forgiveness is more powerful. The Bible has three views of forgiveness: (1) forgiveness is viewed as "lifted off" or "let go," (2) forgiveness is viewed as a "cover," like a lid on top of something, and (3) forgiveness is viewed as erased, canceled, purged, or cleansed. God's provision for our forgiveness is strong enough to overcome all concepts and views of sin. God has promised that "if we confess our sins, He is faithful and righteous to forgive us our sins and to cleanse us from all unrighteousness" (1 John 1:9 HCSB).

When King David was confronted with his sin by the prophet Nathan (2 Sam. 12), he sat down and wrote Psalm 51, a magnificent confessional that provides a model for our prayer of contrition today. Then he wrote Psalm 32, which is designed to help us learn how to find freedom from the guilt of our sin through confession. To confess means to agree, to say to God, "I agree that what I just did was wrong. I know it has caused you great grief, and I'm truly sorry that I've hurt you. Thank you for covering that sin with your blood."

Ten Biblical Revelations

The biblical truth of sin can be told through the following revelations of the unfolding truth concerning sin.

Revelation 1. The world created by God was originally perfect. Sin did not exist in this perfect world because of the complete and special relationship between God and man.

Revelation 2. As a result of one act of disobedience, sin entered the human race. Adam, the first man, is a representation of all humankind because all humanity was "in him." Adam's sin, therefore, became our sin.

Revelation 3. The entering of sin into the human race caused an immediate response from God that resulted in man being separated from God. A state of war was declared, and without Jesus, to this day, there is no peace.

Revelation 4. Grace was woven into God's Word, extending a hope for deliverance and reconciliation, asserting that forgiveness of man's sin rests upon the grace, mercy, and activity of God alone.

Revelation 5. God chose a people to be his people, the *ecclesia*, which means "called out." Abraham was called out by faith to go and look for a city or country, not knowing where he was going. The nation of Israel became God's called-out people and was given the laws of Moses in which sin was codified and the prohibitions laid down in the Ten Commandments. There was finally a law or standard by which sin could be judged and punishment justified.

Revelation 6. The Old Testament prophets and their ministries gave the demands of God's standards to the chosen people of God. As these demands revealed their sins, it became more and more apparent that salvation's hope rested on God's covenant mercy and grace.

Revelation 7. The writers of the Psalms identified and related the personal individual need and responsibility to reveal sin. Sure, all have sinned and fallen short of God's glory, but according to the Psalms, led by David, it is clearly stated: "I" have sinned. The writers of the Psalms reveal to us that, without question, the issue of personal sin remains and a personal debt must be paid before a holy God.

Revelation 8. The advent of the Second Adam, in Christ, represents the fulfillment of the promise of a coming Savior. With his coming, death, and resurrection, humankind was provided a provision to be reconciled to God. Christ is God in flesh (incarnate). He is the God against whom humankind transgressed and rebelled, and from whom we have strayed. He is the mark that humankind missed. He is holy, yet he was made to be sin on the cross so that sin could be punished and our sin debt could be pardoned.

Revelation 9. The New Testament Epistles are commentaries on the gospel written to the churches of that day and to us. Once again they explain the universality of sin and the individuality of sin, with an emphasis on the terrible consequences of sin—unless we repent, confess, and put our faith and trust in him who has already died for our sins and was raised for our justification.

Revelation 10. The Gospels and the Epistles of the New Testament teach us that although the provision of the unfolding redemption plan for forgiveness of sin was finished on Calvary, the Book of Revelation shows us the finality of sin.

The Effects of Sin

The ultimate effect of sin is death (Rom. 6:23). Spiritual death is defined as that which separates us from God. And if not for the grace of God, it would result in eternal damnation (hell). The effects of sin are characterized by darkness, alienation, depravity, and death, affecting the mind, will, and soul. Sin produces an aversion to God and a desire for the things that are not spiritual but antagonistic to God.

For the believer—saved from the penalty of sin, secure in our eternal relationship with God—sin has been defeated. Yet, the presence and power of sin remains and must, therefore, be guarded against. Sin affects believers by hindering fellowship with God and making them weary of commitment and dependence on God as well as weak in the demonstration of their faith and practice of devotion and worship. Sin affects the mind, and thoughts become the parents of our deeds, so believers must safeguard and protect the engagement of all the senses. Participation in sinful acts always leads to pain and hurt. To protect against the effects of sin, the believer should starve the senses of sinful things and feed the senses on spiritual things.

Sin, however, still creeps into our lives. We detest it, struggle against it, and long to be free of it. For the time before we get to heaven, Jesus has provided a path to victory.

At the last, there will be a world with no sin. Not only will heaven's residents be freed from the penalty and power of sin; they will also be freed from the presence of sin. Sin will be dealt a final death blow. There will be, once again, no more sin, death, or curse. Paradise was lost; now paradise will be restored—never to be lost again. Praise God!

GEORGE MCCALEP JR. was called to pastor Greenforest Community Baptist Church in Decatur, Georgia, in 1979. Under his leadership over the past twenty-one years, the congregation has grown from twenty-five members to more than six thousand active members, with an average Sunday school attendance of fifteen hundred.

Pastor McCalep is a former athlete, owner/manager of a registered investment company, and a retired university professor. He recently accepted an adjunct professorship to teach church growth and evangelism at Luther Rice Seminary in Atlanta. He is the author of six books: *Breaking the Huddle*, *Faithful over a Few Things*, *Growing Up to the Head*, *Stir Up the Gifts*, *Sin in the House*, and *Praising the Hell Out of Yourself*.

Suffering

why do bad things happen to God's people?

By Joni Eareckson Tada with Steven Estes

I'm hurting bad . . . to be healed of suffering is to be happy.

*T*his line of thinking is the path I took not long after the diving accident in which I became paralyzed in 1967. Lying on my back in a Stryker frame with my head immobilized in steel tongs, I could look only up. A natural position for talking to God. I tried to imagine what he was thinking. If God were God—I was convinced he was all-powerful and all-loving—he had to be as anxious to relieve my pain as I was. A heavenly Father had to weep over me as my daddy often did, standing by my bedside, white-knuckling the guardrail. I was one of God's children, and God would never do anything to harm one of his own. Didn't Jesus say, "Which of you fathers, if your son asks for a fish, will give him a snake instead? Or if he asks for an egg, will give him a scorpion? If you then . . . know how to give good gifts to your children, how much more will your Father in heaven!" (Luke 11:11–13).

A God this good is worth pursuing. And so, when I was released from the hospital, my friends would drive me to Washington, D.C., so I could be first in line at the door whenever the famous faith healer Kathryn Kuhlman came to town. Miss Kuhlman breezed onto the stage in her white gown, and my heart raced as I prayed, *Lord, the Bible says you heal all our diseases. I'm ready for you to get me out of this wheelchair. Please, would you?*

God answered: I never walked away from my chair. The last time I wheeled away from a Kathryn Kuhlman crusade, I was number fifteen in a line of thirty wheelchair users waiting to exit at the stadium elevator, all of us trying to make a fast escape ahead of the people on crutches. I remember glancing around at all the disappointed and confused people, thinking, *Something's wrong with this picture. Is this the only way to deal with suffering? Trying desperately to remove it?*

When I looked in the mirror after I got home, I saw their sullen expression staring back. I was just as perplexed as the people near the elevator. *OK, let me get this straight: God is good. God is love. He is all-powerful. Plus, when he walked on earth, he bent over backward to relieve the sufferings of people, everyone from the hemorrhaging woman to the centurion's servant. So why does my five-year-old niece, Kelly, have brain cancer? Why did my brother-in-law abandon my sister and their family? Why does Daddy's arthritis not respond to medication?*

Good questions.

As answers elude us, as God's ways stymie us, the fire of suffering is stoked. We feel the heat of wanting what we don't have and having what we don't want. God appears unmoved. Happiness escapes us. We are discontented and restless.

I wonder how many of those sullen-faced people at the elevator after the healing crusade still believe in God? That was almost thirty years ago. Are they still waiting in line? Still hoping? "Hope deferred makes the heart sick," and a heart can break only so many times.

If God is a God who dangles hope like a carrot only to snatch it back, little wonder our appetite for him—our confidence in him—wanes.

We Are Weak but He Is Strong

Second Corinthians 12:9–10 plainly states: "Therefore I will boast all the more gladly about my weaknesses, so that Christ's power may rest on me. . . . I delight in weaknesses, in insults, in hardships, in persecutions, in difficulties. For when I am weak, then I am strong."

Hardships press up against God. It's a universal truth we all learned in the old Sunday school song, "We are weak but he is strong."

God always seems bigger to those who need him the most. And suffering is the tool he uses to help us need him more.

Know God better through suffering? That's a quaint thought. Then again, there's that high school buddy who never *did* take God seriously until trouble hit. Bagging a football scholarship to a Big Ten university consumed all his attention, but in his sophomore year at Michigan, he got slammed on the five-yard line. Two surgeries and three sidelined seasons later, he had done some serious thinking: life was short; where were his priorities? Today he is still into sports (he coaches the Tiny Tornadoes after work), but his priorities are straighter. Bible study and prayer get their chunk of time in his schedule.

Closer to God through trials? Another curiosity. Then there's the couple down the street who tend to be just a tad materialistic. But then last year when he lost his job, they prayed harder, got by with less, and learned some lessons. They found that family means more than possessions, that community college wasn't so bad for their Princeton-bound daughter, and that God took care of them while they climbed back to their feet.

Discover God's hand in heartbreak? One more peculiarity. But then there's the twenty-six-year-old man whose girlfriend had returned the engagement ring. He let it sit on his dresser for months as a monument to his failed love life. He dealt with the grief by pouring his energies into the life of a troubled kid who lived two doors down and had never known a father. He took him to the stables on weekends and taught him to horseback ride. It made him grow up. He learned that his problems were super-small.

Two years later the man ducked into a bookstore to buy a present and spied a honey-blonde girl with a knockout smile flipping through a calendar of palomino horses. They got to talking and discovered they had more in common than just equines. He took her riding the next weekend, joined the singles group at her church, and not long afterward, she said a big yes when he popped the question on her front porch swing. Today, he shudders to think that he could have missed her.

When we are weak, God is strong? Sure, we'll buy that.

So why do we squirm when we feel the crunch? Why do we keep asking why? A clue is hidden in the questions we ask: "Will I ever be happy again?" and "How is this fitting together for my good?" The questions themselves are technical and me-focused. Even when we hit upon good reasons why—like the Michigan football player who got his priorities straightened or the materialistic couple who learned to get by with less or the guy whose pain led him to Miss Perfect—even good reasons can be me-focused:

"Suffering sure has helped me get my spiritual act together."

"I see how this trial is improving my character and prayer life."

"Think what I would have missed had it not been for that heartbreak."

"This tribulation has really strengthened my marriage."

Notice all the me's.

God notices too.

Who Is This God?

Long, long ago before matter existed, when there was nothing— God had already lived forever. He had been *contented* forever. And whatever God was, he still is and always will be.

An odd thought for us moderns. Who says God is contented? Assuming it's true, is it good news? After all, the entire human race is trudging through pain. Maybe the notion of a satisfied, untroubled Creator disturbs you. But it shouldn't. For if God is to rescue anyone from heartache, he had best not be bleeding himself.

Few people today believe in a contented God. The God discussed in Moses' books might appear worried, unsure, petty, jealous, even vindictive. But the Bible calls him "the blessed God." Not a threatened, pacing deity starved for attention but "the blessed and only Ruler, the King of kings and Lord of lords, who alone is immortal" (1 Tim. 6:15–16). One translation actually reads "the blissful God."

What's God so happy about? He lacks for nothing. He once reminded some worshipers who thought they were doing him a favor,

> "I have no need of a bull from your stall
>
>   or of goats from your pens,
>
> for every animal of the forest is mine,
>
>   and the cattle on a thousand hills." (Ps. 50:9–10)

If you were God, where would you go to be impressed? After all, you have created everyone and everything. It's all wonderful, doubtless, but lesser than you. Conversation with any of your creatures, even the grandest, costs an infinite lowering of yourself. What could truly entertain your limitless mind? What idea would intrigue you? Whose company would charm you? Whose character and accomplishments take you aback? Where could you find beauty and grace enough to ravish *you*?

There is only one answer. Nothing can satisfy an infinite being but an infinite being. For God, the real intoxication comes as he stares in the mirror.

Where is this mirror?

It's in the Trinity.

To fathom this you would have to be one of the Three.

Does this blow your mind? It should. But how does it help the cancer patient coughing up blood? Or the prisoner sitting on death row?

Okay, so God likes being God. He's enjoying himself. But does he care about us? We know his Son.

A leper throws himself on the ground. "Lord, if you are willing, you can make me clean." Breaking all protocol and natural revulsion, Jesus reaches forward: "I am willing." Not for a very long time has the man been touched. Sickly white skin blushes, and a neighbor can return home (Luke 5:12–13).

As the sun dips, many sick people feel perky again, many deaf folks are hearing a day's gossip for the first time, and everyone's soul is filled. But their stomachs are empty. "Send them away to buy supper," Jesus' disciples urge him. But he says, "This is a lonely place; where would they go? What food can you find?" Some kid's mom has packed him a lunch he didn't eat. Jesus looks in the basket, they have a prayer, and five thousand people need a good stretch and a belly rub before heading home.

Who does Jesus do all this for? Polite society? Most of them get upset and leave after they hear a thing or two he says. It's the everyday people who really take to him. Jesus goes out of his way for folks carrying just a little too much baggage.

Condemned criminals, half-breeds, short guys with too much money, women whose homes you visited only after dark—these were the people he went after. He saved his anger for the self-important, or for his followers when they tried to shoo kids away, or for when they got to talking about "calling fire down from heaven" on folks who weren't buying the message.

"Very impressive of Jesus," we say. "But what about the Father? There's a little too much Old Testament in him for my taste—all that lightning and thunder on Mount Sinai. He's in heaven enjoying himself. But does he care about us?"

Listen to the eye-opening words of the Son of God: "I tell you the truth, the Son can do nothing by himself; he can do only what he sees his Father doing, because whatever the Father does the Son also does" (John 5:19).

Does the Father care?

As a father has compassion on his children,
    so the LORD has compassion on those who fear him;
for he knows how we are formed,
    he remembers that we are dust. (Ps. 103:13–14)

The Lamb of God turned his cheek to the smiters and pled clemency for his murderers—but we read of Jehovah:

The LORD is compassionate and gracious,
    slow to anger, abounding in love.
He will not always accuse,
    nor will he harbor his anger forever;
he does not treat us as our sins deserve
    or repay us according to our iniquities. (Ps. 103:8–10)

Yet he also says, "It has been granted to you on behalf of Christ not only to believe on him, but also to suffer for him" (Phil. 1:29).

Our call to suffer comes from a God who is tender beyond description. If we do not cling to this through life's worst, we will misread everything and grow to hate him.

But now to something about him even more profound.

The Suffering God

By the flicker of oil lamps he looked up from dinner and studied the faces around the room. Twelve familiar expressions. They were his friends, all but one. The miles they had walked together! Yet how could they fathom his thoughts tonight? Can the child ever really understand his father? Solomon was right: "Each heart knows its own bitterness." These were the ones he had come for—natives of this sad planet who had never tasted what had delighted him in that other place—so slow to learn—so dull in the most urgent of matters—always scrapping about who deserved top honors in a coming world they couldn't possibly grasp. But he loved them.

He sensed that familiar presence he had met in the wilderness— the time was close.

For the next few hours, the most distilled evil in the universe would operate personally through the body of a disciple of Jesus.

The Master spoke quietly to them a final time. What would become of these friends, his only earthly support in this hour? Satan already had the twelfth one by the throat—soon he'd be swinging under a tree limb, gasping and white, facing much worse after his breathing stopped. Prophecy-fulfilled was at the doorstep: "Strike the shepherd, and the sheep will be scattered" (Zech. 13:7).

Stay awake "with me."

For the only time in his life the Shepherd was asking for something from them. *He wanted human comfort that night.*

Now the Son of God dropped to the dirt in an olive grove and vomited in his soul at the prospect before him. Eleven men who would later change world history—some accustomed to working all night on fishing boats—could not keep awake for the scene. Yet sixty feet away their eternal destinies were being fought over.

"It's time to get up," he quietly told the eleven.

The torches arrived. The sheep fled. The Shepherd stood. The hurricane struck.

The Savior was now thrown to men quite different from the eleven. The face that Moses had begged to see was slapped bloody. The thorns that God had sent to curse the earth's rebellion now twisted around his own brow. His back, buttocks, and the rear of his legs felt the whip. By the time the spitting is through there is more saliva on him than in him. No longer can he be recognized. One raises a mallet to sink in the spike.

But these pains are a mere warm-up to his other and growing dread. He begins to feel a foreign sensation. He *feels* dirty. Human wickedness starts to crawl upon his spotless being—the living excrement from our souls.

His Father! He must face his Father like this!

From heaven the Father now arouses himself like a lion disturbed, shakes his mane, and roars against the shriveling remnant of a man hanging on a cross. *Never* has the Son seen the Father look at him so, never felt even the least of his hot breath. But the roar shakes the unseen world and darkens the visible sky. The Son does not recognize these eyes.

"Son of Man! Why have you behaved so? You have cheated, lusted, stolen, gossiped—murdered, envied, hated, lied." The crucified Son is held captive to the ongoing litany of our sin that is now his indictment.

"I hate, I *loathe* these things in you! Disgust for everything about you consumes me! Can you not feel my wrath?"

Of course, the Son is innocent. He is blamelessness itself. The Father knows this. But the divine pair have an agreement, and the unthinkable must now take place. Jesus will be treated as if personally responsible for every sin ever committed.

"Father! Father! Why have you forsaken me?"

The Trinity had planned it. The Son endured it. The Spirit enabled him. The Father rejected the Son whom he loved. Jesus, the God-man from Nazareth, perished. The Father accepted his sacrifice for sin and was satisfied. The rescue was accomplished.

God set down his saw.

This is who asks us to trust him when he calls on us to suffer.

Does He Really Expect Me to Suffer?

"Those who suffer *according to God's will* should commit themselves to their faithful Creator and continue to do good" (1 Pet. 4:19, emphasis added).

Surely you can't mean that God himself actually makes humans suffer. The Bible says God is love—but if the trials I'm facing come from him, we must be using different dictionaries to define love. A God who actually decrees rape, murder, earthquakes, and heart disease is not the God I worship.

"How can this possibly be?" someone asks.

Welcome to the world of finite humans pondering an infinite God.

Unless the Bible is wrong, *nothing* happens outside of God's decree. Nothing good, nothing bad, nothing pleasant, nothing tragic. We may not fathom God's reasons, we may not agree with his thinking, we may love him for it, we may hate him for it. But in simple language, God runs the world. "The LORD works out everything for his own ends—even the wicked." "Our God is in heaven; he does whatever pleases him" (Prov. 16:4; Ps. 115:3).

A Few Reasons Why

The Power of Example

No man is an island. We are all connected. "For none of us lives to himself alone and none of us dies to himself alone" (Rom. 14:7). The purpose of life is to live for others. Jesus showed us that. Especially the "others" whom 1 Corinthians 1:27–28 talks about: "For God chose the foolish things of the world to shame the wise; God chose the weak things of the world to shame the strong. He chose the lowly things of this world and the despised things—and the things that are not—to nullify the things that are, so that no one may boast before him."

For the Sake of Others

We sacrifice comfort but fall back on the cushion of God's arms. We forfeit earthly pleasure but rise to euphoria that is out of this world. We empty ourselves and get fat and sassy on the grace of God.

"We are . . . heirs of God and co-heirs with Christ, if indeed we share in his sufferings in order that we may also share in his glory" (Rom. 8:17). Astounding! We suffer with Christ—that we may share in Christ's *highest glory.* "I consider that our present sufferings are not worth comparing with the glory that will be revealed in us" (Rom. 8:18). For as dark and pernicious as it is, God will squash suffering like a grapefruit in the face of the devil, turning it inside out into something sweet. If suffering can't be avoided, God is going to redeem it to usher us into the highest echelons of heaven.

For the Glory of God

A sacrifice of praise brightens God's glory. It demonstrates the enormously high value we attach to him. Such praise costs us our logic, pride, and preferences. But it's worth it. "Worthy is the Lamb, who was slain, to receive power and wealth and wisdom and strength and honor and glory and praise!" (Rev. 5:12–13).

Suffering fashions us into a "holy and blameless" image of Christ (Eph. 1:4), much like a figure sculpted out of marble. God continues to chisel, chipping more away. "To keep me from becoming conceited . . . there was given me a thorn in my flesh" (2 Cor. 12:7). God works deeper, carefully fashioning every hidden crevice, even our temperament: "Your attitude should be the same as that of Christ Jesus: Who . . . made himself nothing. . . . He humbled himself and became obedient to death—even death on a cross!" (Phil. 2:5–8).

Will this sculpture last the weathering of more storms and trials? "We also rejoice in our sufferings, because we know that suffering produces perseverance; perseverance, character; and character, hope" (Rom. 5:3–4). It's an image of rock-solid hope.

God uses suffering to purge sin from our lives, strengthen our commitment to him, force us to depend on grace, bind us together with other believers, produce discernment, foster sensitivity, discipline our minds, spend our time wisely, stretch our hope, cause us to know Christ better, make us long for truth, lead us to repentance of sin, teach us to give thanks in time of sorrow, increase faith, and strengthen character. It is a *beautiful* image!

I cannot afford to focus on the hammer and chisel. I cannot look around me and bemoan what God is chipping away. Believing in suffering is a dead end. Believing in the Sculptor is living hope.

We must never distance the Bible's answers from God. The problem of suffering is not about some *thing*, but *Someone*. It follows that the answer must not be some thing, but Someone. "Knowing our Lord Jesus Christ" is keeping your eye on the Sculptor—not on the suffering, or even suffering's benefits.

God, like a father, doesn't just give advice. He gives himself. He becomes the husband to the grieving widow (Isa. 54:5). He becomes the comforter to the barren woman (Isa. 54:1). He becomes the father of the orphaned (Ps. 10:14). He becomes the bridegroom to the single person (Isa. 62:5). He is the healer to the sick (Exod. 15:26). He is the wonderful counselor to the confused and depressed (Isa. 9:6).

This is what you do when someone you love is in anguish: you respond to the plea of their heart by giving them your heart. If you are the One at the center of the universe, holding it together, if everything moves, breathes, and has its being in you, you can do no more than give yourself (Acts 17:28).

It's the only answer that ultimately matters.

Making Sense of Suffering

Suffering has no meaning in itself. Left to its own, it is a frustrating and bewildering burden. But given the context of *relationship*, suffering suddenly has meaning.

Study methods and worship techniques are helpful in getting introduced to God (we have to start somewhere), but they easily become flat and mechanical when cultivating a personal relationship. Even Jesus was astounded that people could devote their entire lives to studying Scripture and yet fail to know the One to whom Scripture was pointing (John 5:39–40). Focusing on regiment and routines will do for business executives, army sergeants, and Pharisees, but not for God. You might scratch the surface with him, but it's more—much more. He is not a missing piece of a life that, once found, can be bolted into place so our spiritual lives run efficiently and smoothly.

Personal relationships don't work that way. Certainly not when it comes to God. If we want to grow closer to someone—God or anybody—it means pressing hearts together. Talking, discussing likes and dislikes. Finding joy in one another.

Such things make for intimacy, yet intimacy can't be regimented. Disciplining myself to spend regular time with someone can be regulated but not the intimacy itself.

One experience in particular does it. You wouldn't choose it. It's not tidy. You can't deal with it methodically. It's ugly, messy, painful, and risky because it can draw you closer to God or drive you away. But once you muddle through, you wouldn't trade the sweetness of your intimacy with God for anything. It knits your heart together with his like nothing else.

It's shared suffering. When you're in the trenches, handing bullets to your buddy and fighting a common enemy, hearts can't help but be pressed together. Your knowledge of each other is unique and intimate to you. To you both.

The *esprit de corps* among fellow sufferers is deep.

Suffering shared with God is deeper.

The Fellowship of Sharing His Sufferings

This is the best part: He delights in identifying with us in our suffering.

When the apostle Paul was on the road to Damascus, the risen Lord didn't say, "Saul, why are you persecuting my people?" God said, "Why are you persecuting *me?*" (see Acts 9:4). He considers our sufferings his sufferings. He feels the sting in his chest when you hurt. He takes it personally. "If the world hates you, keep in mind that it hated me first," he said in John 15:18. This is intimacy described from Jesus' perspective.

The Power of His Resurrection

You can't rise above your circumstances without power. Can't push through your pain without a force on your side. Can't even grasp a brighter perspective, a happier hope, without strength from somewhere. But why does Paul say "the power of his *resurrection*"?

First, there is help just by knowing Jesus empathizes. For Jesus to be resurrected, he first had to die. To die, he first had to become human (without ever surrendering his deity). So the resurrected Jesus once walked in our shoes and felt the pain of this earthly life. Even though he is now in heaven, he has a "divinely" good memory that recalls his days upon the earth.

Second, the "power of his resurrection" helps us because we are earmarked as recipients of the Spirit whom the resurrected Jesus won the right to pour out on us. This means immediate access to incredible power.

But wait. There's no gain without pain; remember, Jesus had to conquer sin and death in order to pour out that power. Access to this power will cost us something, like "an eye gouged" or "if your right hand causes you to sin, cut it off and throw it away. It is better for you to lose one part of your body than for your whole body to go into hell" (Matt. 5:29–30). Jesus becomes one with us in our suffering; we, in turn, become one with him in his. He takes on our flesh; we take on his holiness.

If Jesus died *for* sin, we die *to* sin. This doesn't mean we must die as Christ did, paying sin's penalty, but if we are to experience life-changing, suffering-shaking power in our lives, "We always carry the death of Jesus in our body" (2 Cor. 4:10 HCSB).

The Cross

By itself, suffering does no good. But when we see it as the thing *between* God and us, it has meaning. Wedged in the crux—the cross—suffering becomes a transaction. The cross is the place of transaction. "The cross is . . . the power of God" (1 Cor. 1:18). It is the place where power happens *between* God and us.

It's where *relationship* is given birth and depth. The cross was, first, a transaction between the Father and the Son. Because of what transpired there—the work of salvation—the cross has meaning. Not only between the Father and the Son, but between the Son and us. For our salvation, yes, but also for our suffering. The cross is the center of our relationship with Jesus. Something literal happened there two thousand years ago. It is where we were given spiritual birth.

A miraculous exchange happens at the cross. When suffering forces us to our knees at the foot of Calvary, we die to self. We cannot kneel there for long without releasing our pride and anger, unclasping our dreams and desires—this is what "coming to the cross" is all about. In exchange, God imparts power and implants new and lasting hope. We rise, renewed. His yoke becomes easy; his burden, light. But just when we begin to get a tad self-sufficient, suffering presses harder. And so, we seek the cross again, mortifying the martyr in us, destroying the self-display. The transaction then is able to continue. God reveals more of his love, more of his power and peace as we hold fast the cross of suffering.

Stay away from it and . . . no power.

The Love of God Constrains Us

Suffering makes for this marvelous transaction, this *between* God and us. And when something marvelous happens between God and us, his cross no longer seems just a symbol of death. Another miraculous exchange occurs: the cross becomes a symbol of life.

We no longer go to the cross to get something, even something so sweet as "peace like a river." We don't "go" to the cross at all. We are drawn to it. Compelled.

Power in Suffering

It happens by sharing in the fellowship of Christ's sufferings.

It's poignant that when the Son of Man walked on earth, he had the comfort of his Father, but none from his friends. No fellowship of suffering on this planet for him. He only had the blind insensitivity of his disciples. No joy in carrying his cross—he bore it "for the joy that was set before him." He went without comfort so that you might be comforted. He went without joy so that you might have it. He willingly chose isolation so that you and I might never be alone. Most wonderfully, he bore God's wrath so that you wouldn't have to. God has no anger for you; only forgiveness, mercy, and grace.

If "God's kindness leads you toward repentance" (Rom. 2:4), then there's only one response to love like this: beat the breast and "submit yourselves, then, to God. . . . Come near to God . . . . Wash your hands, you sinners, and purify your hearts, . . . Grieve, mourn and wail" (James 4:7–9).

Sound morbid? Maybe. But this is where real power kicks in—not primarily to overcome suffering. That's putting the cart before the horse. Resurrection power is meant to uproot sin out of our lives.

Then we, with holy hearts, experience a greater degree of his love. It is in Christ's love that we become more than conquerors.

Hell Explains Why Christians Suffer

Someone objects: "But the sins of Christians are paid for by Christ's death. They will never experience hell. What does hell-on-earth have to do with them?"

Plenty. Human suffering in this life is merely the splashover from hell. Yes, you would think Christians would be exempt. But this whole section has tried to show why God allows the splashover anyway. God's plan for us in this life is to give us the benefits of heaven only gradually. By letting us struggle with the remnants of a sinful nature, and by letting us know pain, he reminds us of the hell we are being saved from.

If we had an easy life, we would soon forget that we are eternal creatures. But hell's splashover won't allow that. It persistently reminds us that something immense and cosmic is at stake—a heaven to be reached, a hell to be avoided. Human souls are the battleground on which massive spiritual battles are being waged. The stakes are enormous. The winner takes all and the loser loses everything. Every day of our short lives has eternal consequences for good or ill. Eternity is being affected. Right now counts forever. Thus, it is only fitting that God should give us some sense of the stakes involved, some sense of the war's magnitude. He does this by giving us foretastes of heaven in the joys we experience, and foretastes of hell in our suffering.

If we are thinking clearly, each taste of hell that we have drives us to reach out toward our unbelieving friends and neighbors. Perhaps we have cancer. Our bodies are racked with pain. The Christian should think to himself, "How horrible that our sins should bring such suffering to a world that God made perfect! But how wonderful that I am going to heaven and will be rescued from the horrible pain I deserve. Yet my neighbor down the street, whom I very much like, does not believe in Jesus. He is headed for eternal pains far worse

than I am experiencing now. Lord, give me the courage, tact, and wisdom to reach out to him with the truth of the gospel."

All the while that we are experiencing such pain, these trials are
making us more like Christ. They are refining our character and,
thus, winning us eternal rewards. As Paul says, "Our light and
momentary troubles are achieving for us an eternal glory that far
outweighs them all" (2 Cor. 4:17). In other words, by tasting a
small bit of hell now, our heaven is becoming more heavenly. Our
neighbors and friends are more likely to join us there. And our gratitude for our salvation overflows. "I deserve to go to hell," we
admit, "but I'm going to heaven anyway—no one has more reason
to rejoice than I!"

Coming Full Circle

Remember when we peered into the heavenly whirlwind of joy
and pleasure between the Father, Son, and Holy Spirit? Theirs was—
or is—a river of joy splashing over heaven's walls onto us. And
remember how suffering sandblasts us to the core, removing sin and
impurities so that intimacy with Jesus is possible? Do you recall the
suffering and the sacrifice Jesus offered that we might know this intimacy and his joy? It was the Savior's mission: "I have told you this so
that my joy may be in you" (John 15:11).

Misery may love company, but joy craves a crowd. The Father,
Son, and Holy Spirit's plan to rescue humans was not only for man's
sake. It is for God's sake. The Father is gathering a crowd—and inher-
itance, pure and blameless—to worship his Son in the joy of the
Holy Spirit. God is love, and the wish of love is to drench with
delight those for whom God has suffered.

Soon the Father, Son, and Holy Spirit will get their wish.

Soon, perhaps sooner than we think, "the day of our Lord Jesus
Christ" will arrive and "all who have longed for his appearing" will
be stripped of the last vestige of sin. God will close the curtain on sin,
Satan, and suffering, and we will step into the waterfall of the joy and
pleasure that is the Trinity.

Better yet, we will become part of a Niagara Falls of thunderous joy as "God is all and in all" for "when he appears we shall be like him for we shall see him as he is." God in us and we in him.

Our hope is not a "what" but a "Who." The hope we wait for, our *only* hope, is the "blessed hope—the glorious appearing of our great God and Savior, Jesus Christ" (Titus 2:13). Heaven is not a place we are waiting to see; we wait for a Person. It is Jesus we've travailed through all this suffering for. Our hope is for the desire of the nations, the healer of broken hearts, the friend of sinners. True, we are waiting for the party. But more accurately, we are waiting for the Person who will make it a party.

JONI EARECKSON TADA is the author of more than twenty books, including *Diamonds in the Dust, More Precious Than Silver,* the Platinum Award-winning *Joni,* and *When God Weeps* with Steven Estes. She is the founder and president of Joni and Friends, a Christian organization that advances Christ's kingdom among the world's 550 million people with disabilities. She and her husband, Ken, reside in Calabasas, California.

Worship

do I have to be in church to worship?

BY DAVE HALL

Worship, according to Bernard E. Meland, is "turning from the periphery of life to the core of existence . . . as if one entered into the scheme of things." This chapter will help you, as a new believer, turn from the periphery of life to the core of existence, real worship. First, we'll define worship, then we'll explore worship both as a lifestyle and an event, including the worship events of baptism and Communion.

What do we mean when we use the word *worship?* Our word *worship* actually comes from the old English word *worthship.* In worship, we are giving worth or value to the one we are worshiping. Before we met Jesus we worshiped ourselves, our relationships, our favorite addictions, horoscopes, possessions, music, sports, talents, careers, appointment calendars, man-made religions, our children . . . the list is endless. Now, however, you will want to apply the words of Jesus when he said, "You must worship the Lord your God; serve only him" (see Matt. 4:10b). As we leave behind us all these false "gods" not worthy of our worship and begin to explore the breadth and depth of real worship, let us use the following definition.

Real worship is both a lifestyle and an event in which believers, by grace, center their mind's attention and their heart's affection on the Lord, humbly glorifying God in response to his greatness, his mighty acts, and his Word. Even more simply put, "Worship is the occupation of the heart with God himself."

It is true that God desires us to live our lives in such a way that others come to a saving knowledge of Jesus. But it is important that we understand that this is not God's *primary* purpose in saving us. Imagine for a moment that Sarah and I rounded up our children each morning just after breakfast and said, "Children, now remember why we had you. It's so you can share the gospel with your friends. Let's hope and pray that some of them will be saved. Now run along and have a wonderful day!" What's wrong with this picture? What's missing? Only love! Primary in the heart of God is his love for us as his children. We must know him before we can make him known. Real worship is the language we use to express our love for God. His passionate desire is that we know what it means to live real worship as a lifestyle and experience real worship as an event.

Focus on Internals, not Externals

In John chapter 4 we find a surprising encounter between Jesus and a woman from a region known as Samaria. In this divine appointment, Jesus shares the most important words we have recorded in the four Gospels on the subject of worship. "But the time is coming and is already here when true worshipers will worship the Father in spirit and in truth. The Father is looking for anyone who will worship him that way" (John 4:23 NLT). God invented want ads. Read John 4:23 again: "WANTED: WORSHIPERS!" Astonishing isn't it? The God who is majestic in holiness, high and lofty, the God who lives and reigns supremely in eternal splendor, Creator of all we see, desires to know us and draw us into a loving relationship with himself.

In Luke 15 Jesus tells three stories to emphasize the depth of God's passion to have every person come to worship him. The Father loves lost people so much he's searching for them. More than people seek riches, God is seeking real worshipers. More than people seek to recover lost possessions or heal broken relationships, the Father seeks real worshipers. The search is not for those who know how to lead others in worship, leaders who have memorized all the Greek words in the New Testament, translated "worship," or even people who love to sing about God. His search centers on those willing not to *do* something, but *be* something. We need to remember that God made us human *beings*, not human *doings*.

Before we do or accomplish anything, we are worshipers. We are worshipers first, sons and daughters second; worshipers first, husbands and wives, moms and dads, employees, pastors, bakers and candlestick makers second. Like the Samaritan woman, we can cloud worship by focusing on the externals—things like whom we should worship with (and whom we shouldn't) and when and where we should worship. Jesus responds to the "who," "where," and "when" questions with a blunt, "Believe me, the time is coming when it will no longer matter whether you worship the Father here or in Jerusalem" (John 4:21 NLT). Eugene Peterson's paraphrasing of this verse reads, "what you're called will not matter and where you go to worship will not matter. It's who you are and the way you live that count before God" (The Message).

Jesus revolutionized the concept of worship by freeing it from the restraints of time and geographical location. No longer was it a matter of "when and where should I worship" but "when and where is it possible *not* to worship?" Before Christ, one had to go to the temple to be in God's presence; now *we* are the temple of the Holy Spirit. Where we go, the Spirit of Jesus goes; and where Jesus goes, worship goes. In God's divine economy, real worship is always internals first, externals second. Russell Shedd concludes, "The New Testament projects a vision of worship that infuses all of life with the presence and glory of God."

Worship God with Integrity

Jesus pulled no punches with the Samaritan woman. He forced her to take a hard look at her sinful lifestyle, offered her the solution to her sin problem (himself), then told her those who have had their sins washed by his living water will worship "the Father in spirit and in truth" (John 4:23 NLT). This phrase, "spirit and truth," implies that we are to worship God in a truly spiritual manner. All of us are tempted to make others think we're more spiritual than we really are.

Even great Bible characters like Moses succumbed to this temptation. After Moses had his talks with God, he put a veil over his face so he wouldn't blind others with the residual effects of God's glory. Problem was, he kept the veil in place after the glory was long gone. Paul tells us that Moses would "put a veil over his face so the people of Israel would not see the glory fading away" (see 2 Cor. 3:7–13). Worshiping in "spirit and truth" is taking off the masks that used to be such an important part of our wardrobe and just being real before God and others.

Living real worship with integrity is getting our lives and our lips in sync. It's being honest with our employers, our spouses and children, our friends, and our tax accountant. It's making decisions based on principles that are grounded in God's Word and the counsel of godly spiritual leaders and friends. It's working up to our potential, not the status quo. It's finding a brother or sister in Christ who will hold us accountable to living with integrity for his glory.

Worship God with Intensity

It had been several weeks since the day Jesus gave Mary and Martha the most precious of gifts. Lazarus. Once dead, rotting, silent as the tomb they had laid him in. Now alive, laughing, sitting across the table next to Jesus. Mary had a fondness of being at Jesus' feet, the adoring follower, listening closely in order not to miss any word that passed her Master's lips. This evening was no different. But Mary had a surprise in store for her Lord this night. The candle of Mary's faith in Jesus had been lit long before, but now—since Jesus had uttered those three powerful words, "Lazarus, come out!"— now it was a blazing bonfire! How could she show Jesus the depth of her gratitude, the enormity of her love? Yes, hers would be a very extravagant gesture. Perhaps even her own brother and sister would ridicule her, but another chance may never come.

All evening Mary waited expectantly for just the right moment. Now! She could feel her pulse quicken as she rose from the table and gently lifted the bottle from behind the window curtain. Carefully she lifted the cork. Immediately the sweet fragrance of exquisite perfume permeated the room. Standing behind Jesus, she began to pour. First, his head, then down onto his beard and robe. Even this seemed not enough for Mary, and so with the last bit remaining she anointed his feet with the precious, costly liquid. Silence, except for Mary's gentle weeping there at Jesus feet (see John 12).

Judas was the first to speak. And speak he did! His words lashed out, ripping at the fabric of Mary's love. "This perfume is worth a small fortune! An entire year's income poured from a single bottle. What a waste! Why, it could have been sold and the money given to the poor!" One can just imagine Judas thinking to himself as Mary brought out the bottle of expensive perfume, *Oh how nice. What a thoughtful gesture!* Soon, however, his eyes opened wider and wider, his jaw dropped lower and lower as Mary poured, and poured, and poured until the very last drop was spent on Jesus.

Many people today would speak for Judas: "Sure, that's great you have Jesus. Just don't get carried away. Incorporate Jesus into your life and values, not vice versa." The cost of the gift, the ridicule she knew would follow, the risk of her actions being misinterpreted—Mary was willing to pay each price and more. Whatever the cost, she would live real worship in such a way that Jesus knew of the immense, overflowing love she had for him. He was all that mattered.

Who are you most like in this story, Judas or Mary? Do you love Jesus so much that you would risk embarrassment and ridicule, even physical suffering in order to show him the depth of your love? Are you longing for a few more moments at Jesus' feet? Do you thirst for a fresh cup of the water from the hand of the Savior? As we worship God with integrity and intensity, he will gain even greater glory as we become more like him. In possibly the greatest passage on the lifestyle of worship, the apostle Paul said, "Therefore, I urge you, brothers, in view of God's mercy, to offer your bodies as living sacrifices, holy and pleasing to God—this is your spiritual act of worship" (Rom. 12:1). Worship is little more than giving everything you are, everything you have, and everything you ever hope to be to Jesus.

Nurture a Passion to See All Peoples Live for the Glory of God

It is no mere coincidence that Jesus' most important words about worship occur in a Samaritan village. Jesus shared these thoughts about worship with a woman in Samaria to teach us an important lesson: Real worship is about having a growing passion to see all people everywhere worship the same Jesus that we know and love.

The way most Jews saw it, Samaritans were half-breeds, descendants of Jews who had intermarried with other races. They were traitors to both their race and their religion, a people to be despised and avoided. Not only was this woman a Samaritan, but she was, well . . . a woman. Women in Jesus' day were treated more like a commodity to be possessed than persons to be cherished. Many a Jewish man rose early every morning and prayed this prayer, "I thank thee, O God, that I am neither a Gentile (non-Jew) nor a woman." Jesus shattered stereotypes and ignored cultural conventions to bring the good news about himself and real worship to a woman in great need.

It has always been God's intention that the all the nations would worship him. "The whole earth will acknowledge the Lord and return to him. People from every nation will bow down before him" (Ps. 22:27 NLT). Israel as a nation was called of God to be a city on a hill, a lighthouse of God's redeeming love to all the nations of the earth. But Israel had ignored God's desire for the nations to worship him. So Jesus, zealous for the glory of God, "cleaned house" in the temple. He reminded all those present that "the Scriptures declare, 'My Temple will be called a place of prayer for *all nations*,' but you have turned it into a den of thieves" (Mark 11:17; see also Isa. 56:7 NLT, emphasis added).

The result of real worship in the life of the Samaritan woman was more worshipers. Jesus told his disciples, who were aghast at the fact that he was even speaking with this Gentile woman, that there were vast fields of souls that were ripe for the harvest and that they would be the ones to "gather the harvest" (see John 4:38–42 NLT).

Experience Worship by Gathering Regularly with Other Believers

Worship is experienced as an event during worship services, gatherings, baptism, and the regular partaking of Communion.

Gathered worship is ultimately for God. During a worship service we tend to think the musicians are the performers, the congregation is the audience, and the worship leader is the prompter. In actuality, the people in the pews are the performers, the worship leader is the prompter, and God is the audience. It's not about me (my tastes, preferences, opinions, musical style, etc.); it's all about God.

Gathered worship is essential to your spiritual growth. The author of Hebrews reminded us to "not give up meeting together, as some are in the habit of doing" (Heb. 10:25). When we do "give up meeting together," the new believer is like a burning coal that pops out of the fire. She or he cools quickly, and in a short time the flame of real worship is extinguished.

Gathered worship should ignite in us a desire to serve God throughout the week. Soon after you begin to worship regularly with God's people, you will discover that God has given you gifts that he wants you to use for his glory. God desires for you to use these gifts not just on Sunday but every day. When you attend church, prepare your heart before you arrive through prayer and reading of God's Word—pray for all who will take part in the service. Come early, enter in—don't be a spectator. Bring your Bible and take notes. Listen for the Lord's voice and the prompting of the Holy Spirit throughout the service—respond in faith and obedience. Reach out to those around you with a smile and a word of encouragement. Be proactive in getting to know someone after the service.

Experience Real Worship through Baptism

Matthew tells us that Jesus was baptized by John the Baptist in the Jordan River (Matt. 3:13). The fact that all believers should follow Christ in baptism is clearly inferred in Jesus' final words to his disciples. He commanded them to "go and make disciples of all nations, baptizing them in the name of the Father and of the Son and of the Holy Spirit" (Matt. 28:19).

Baptism initiates us into the church by identifying us with Christ in his death (our death to sin) and his resurrection (our power over sin and hope of eternal life). Romans 6:4–5 teaches us that "we died and were buried with Christ by baptism. And just as Christ was raised from the dead by the glorious power of the Father, now we also may live new lives. Since we have been united with him in his death, we will also be raised as he was" (NLT). Thus, when new believers are lowered into the water and raised out again, they demonstrate what has happened in their hearts. Baptism is an outward manifestation of an inward reality.

What Does Baptism Mean?

Baptism is an outward manifestation of an inward change. A drama, powerfully depicting the saving event that has taken place within one's heart. Baptism is seen as an ordinance, that is, one of the things Jesus ordained his followers to do in obedience to God (Matt. 28:18–19). Emphasis is placed on being identified with Christ's death and resurrection (Rom. 6:3–4). Baptism is also seen as a testimony encouraging us to live and "to do what is right for the glory of God" (see Rom. 6:11–14 NLT).

What Method of Baptism Should Be Used?

Three primary methods of baptism have been used throughout the history of the church. They are immersion (dipping or plunging), effusion (pouring), and aspersion (sprinkling). Immersion was commonly used in the early church. Those that prefer this method point to Romans 6:1–4 as grounds for this mode of baptism. Special attention is given to the Greek word, *baptizo*, translated as "baptize." It means "to dip repeatedly, to immerse, to submerge (of vessels sunk)."

The second method, effusion or pouring, was also known to be used in the early church. It has a biblical foundation in Acts 10:44–48 where the Holy Spirit was poured out upon new believers and they were baptized immediately afterwards. The third method is called aspersion (sprinkling), which is symbolic of what it means to be sprinkled and cleansed of sin inwardly by the blood of Christ.

Who Should Be Baptized?

Maybe you've seen the popular bracelet with WWJD printed on it? WWJD stands for "What Would Jesus Do?" As a follower of Jesus, we want to do as Jesus did. If you're a believer and you haven't been baptized, ask yourself, "What would Jesus do?" The answer is clear. All disciples of Jesus should follow Jesus' example and be baptized.

Guard yourself against extremes by knowing what you and your church believe about baptism and why. Some would desire to lead you astray from the whole counsel of God's Word by emphasizing certain parts of Scripture to the exclusion of others. Some teach that you are saved as a direct consequence of your baptism. In other words, the act of being baptized saves you rather than the finished work of Jesus at the cross. Others would teach that you are not truly saved until you've been baptized (just another way of making our salvation dependent upon us, rather than upon Christ).

My pastor once gave me some great advice about this when he said, "Baptisms that are 'mechanical' or 'magical' should be resisted." Most importantly, be sure that what is being taught and what you believe regarding baptism is firmly grounded in the teaching of Scripture.

You may be wondering why we've included this section on baptism in a chapter on worship. It's a good question and deserves some explanation.

Just last week I was speaking with a missionary friend working in an Eastern European country. He was recently in a home looking through a family photo album when he noted that in many pictures one of the faces had been blacked out. When he inquired, he was simply told, "That child doesn't exist any longer." The child wasn't dead; rather, she had been baptized as a new believer in Jesus Christ. In many cultures baptism signifies the crossing from a previous faith system to Christ. Baptism draws a line in the sand that makes a dramatic statement both publicly and spiritually that I belong to Jesus and he belongs to me. It is, therefore, the most fundamental and significant act of worship for a new believer—in any culture.

Experience Real Worship through Communion

Just before his death, Jesus gathered with his disciples in an upper room in Jerusalem for a final time of worship, fellowship, and instruction. After celebrating the Passover meal together, he instituted what has become known as the Lord's Supper or Communion: "Then he took a cup of wine, and when he had given thanks for it, he said, 'Take this and share it among yourselves. For I will not drink wine again until the Kingdom of God has come.' Then he took a loaf of bread; and when he had thanked God for it, he broke it in pieces and gave it to the disciples, saying, 'This is my body, given for you. Do this in remembrance of me'" (Luke 22:17–19 NLT).

In Acts 2 we are told that the church "worshiped together at the Temple each day, met in homes for the Lord's Supper, and shared their meals with great joy and generosity" (Acts 2:46 NLT). The apostle Paul was teaching believers to observe Communion early on in the church's development. His instruction from the Lord was to "do this in remembrance of me as often as you drink it" (1 Cor. 11:24–25 NLT). Paul goes on to say that Communion is not only a remembrance but a proclamation: "every time you eat this bread and drink this cup, you are announcing the Lord's death until he comes again" (1 Cor. 11:26 NLT). Spiritual blessing and growth also result as the bread and the cup refocus us on the foundation of our faith. Millard Eareckson writes, "All Christians who participate in the Lord's Supper see it as conferring a spiritual benefit upon them. In this sense, all agree that the Lord's Supper is *sacramental*. It can be a means, or at least an occasion, of spiritual growth in the Lord."

The early church recognized that Communion reunites us not only with our heavenly Father but was intended to restore broken fellowship among believers. For centuries the passing of the elements in preparation for Communion has been a means used to reconcile any unforgiveness or bitterness that might exist between believers. Worship as you participate by taking Paul's instruction to heart when he writes, "You should examine yourself before eating the bread and drinking from the cup" (1 Cor. 11:28 NLT). Meditate on the whole of Psalm 51. Reflect on where you might be without Jesus. Thank him for the miracle of grace and your spiritual rebirth.

Living and experiencing real worship is a lifelong journey. It is not something that happens easily or quickly. It's a process. But make no mistake, whatever else you may be in this world, you are and will be through all eternity a worshiper of Jesus.

Going Further
The Top Ten Things to Know about Real Worship

1. Real worship is the believer's highest calling (John 4:23; Matt. 6:33; Rom. 12:1–2; 1 Cor. 8:6, 10:31).

2. Real worshipers are real people with real problems (John 4:16–17).

3. Real worshipers don't ride on the coattails of their parent's faith (John 4:20).

4. Real worship is about being thirsty for more of Jesus (John 4:10–15).

5. Real worship will result in a growing passion to pack heaven with more worshipers (John 4:39; 1 Pet. 2:9, 12).

6. Real worship is a global phenomenon that will involve all peoples from all nations (Isa. 61:11; Rev. 5:9–14, 7:9–12, 15:4).

7. Real worship is the atmosphere of heaven (Rev. 4:10, 14:6–7; Isa. 6:1–4).

8. The gathered worship event is not practice for heaven; it is literally a foretaste of heaven—entering into the presence of him who sits on the throne (Heb. 12:18–24).

9. Real worship is always founded upon the character of God (Ps. 95:3–7; John 4:22).

10. We become like that which we worship (Ps. 115:8).

Books That Will Help You Understand and Live Real Worship

Ablaze for God by Wesley L. Duewel (Grand Rapids: Zondervan, 1989).

Devotional Classics by Richard J. Foster and James Bryan Smith (New York: HarperCollins, 1993).

Let the Nations Be Glad by John Piper (Grand Rapids: Baker Book House, 1993).

The Worship and Praise Bible, edited by Robert Webber (*Holy Bible, New Living Translation,* Tyndale House Publishers, Inc., 1997).

DAVE HALL majored in voice at the University of Wisconsin, Madison, and graduated in 1978. In 1990, he graduated with an M.Div from Trinity International University and is now pursuing a doctor of missiology degree in ethnodoxology (the study of how and why people of diverse cultures worship the true and living God).

Over the years, Dave has served God as a Campus Life director, music/drama director, and special representative with Youth for Christ; singles intern pastor and senior high youth pastor for Elmbrook Church in Milwaukee, Wisconsin; and part-time worship leader and pastor of worship and missions at Harvest Bible Chapel in Chicago. Also, Dave and his wife, Sarah, traveled as a music and speaking ministerial team and released two recordings.

In January 1995 the Halls joined Pioneers and began a ministry called Worship From the Nations (WFN). The purpose of WFN is to spread a passion for the glory of God among all peoples. Three years later, Dave and Sarah were invited to bring WFN under the International Coordinating Team of Pioneers. They intend to base their ministry out of Budapest, Hungary, where Pioneers has a mobilization base. They are involved in planting the church through training nationals and church planters in worship and the arts.

The Halls live in Budapest with their three boys—Benjamin David, Caleb Christopher, and Micah Colin—and two adopted daughters Elisabeth Charis and Hannah Tavia. Dave also hosts worship and missions (WAM!) seminars, serves on the executive committee of the International Worship and Arts Network, and consults with and writes for those interested in worship/arts ministry among the unreached.

Prayer

how can I do something
I don't understand?

BY KAY ARTHUR

*T*hen the Twelve summoned the whole company of the disciples and said, 'It would not be right for us to give up preaching about God to wait on tables. Therefore, brothers, select from among you seven men of good reputation, full of the Spirit and wisdom, whom we can appoint to this duty. But we will devote ourselves to prayer and to the preaching ministry'" (Acts 6:2–4 HCSB).

When the apostles of the early church suddenly found themselves embroiled in a controversy that consumed both their time and energy, they had enough spiritual presence of mind to know that something had to be done. They were in danger of missing the priority of their calling—the Word of God and prayer! Thus they called a meeting to keep the birth of the New Testament church on track, and in the process set an immutable precedent for all Christians.

This is where each child of God should be the strongest: in the Word of God and in prayer.

Yet Christianity is more than merely believing and obeying commands and promises. Christianity is not a religion; it is a relationship.

And a relationship requires communication. Prayer is essential because it is through prayer that you and I communicate with our heavenly Father. There are countless decisions to be made, wisdom to be sought, resources that are needed, transgressions to be mended, love and appreciation to be communicated. Thus, we are told to pray without ceasing. The aspects of our daily living may be found in the Word of God in principle but not necessarily in practical detail. Therefore, we need to talk with and listen to our heavenly Father. This is prayer.

The disciples had to be careful lest they become so occupied with serving God that they neglected the Word, which is knowing God, and prayer, which is communicating with him.

What I intend in this writing is to help you dig into the Word of God for yourself and learn in greater depth the Lord's way to pray. The prayer that Jesus uses will teach you to pray "according to His will," and his words on prayer will remain in you. Jesus said, "If you remain in Me and My words remain in you, ask whatever you want and it will be done for you" (John 15:7 HCSB).

When Jesus was with the disciples on earth, they saw the place of prayer in his life and they heard his teaching on the importance of the persistence of prayer. Thus, realizing that they had to know how to pray, they said, "Lord, teach us to pray" (Luke 11:1).

So here it is: not another opinion on prayer, but a study of Jesus' response to his disciples, which began with him saying, "Therefore, you should pray like this:

Our Father in heaven,
Your name be honored as holy.
Your kingdom come.
Your will be done
on earth as it is in heaven.
Give us today our daily bread.
And forgive us our debts,
as we also have forgiven our debtors.
And do not bring us into temptation,
but deliver us from the evil one.

[For Yours is the kingdom
   and the power
   and the glory forever,
   Amen.]"
(Matt. 6:9–13 HCSB)

Let's look at this pattern for prayer sentence by sentence. As we look at it one precept at a time, I am going to take you to other Scriptures that will amplify, illuminate, illustrate, or substantiate each particular precept.

This chart will help us see what percepts go into praying the way God wants us to.

Topic	Index Sentence	Title
Worship	*Our Father in heaven,* *Your name* *be honored as holy.*	Worship of the Father
Allegiance	*Your kingdom come.*	Allegiance to God's sovereignty
Submission	*Your will be done* *on earth as it is in heaven.*	Submission to his will
Petition and Intercession	*Give us today our daily bread.*	Asking for his provision
Confession	*And forgive us our debts,* *as we also have forgiven our* *debtors.*	Confession and forgiveness
Deliverance	*And do not bring us into* *temptation, but deliver us* *from the evil one.*	Watchfulness and deliverance
Worship	*For Yours is the kingdom and* *the power and the glory* *forever, Amen.*	Worship

Worship

In the first index sentence, "Our Father in heaven, Your name be honored as holy," Jesus lays out two imperatives for prayer. The first is that prayer begins with worship of the Father.

To worship someone is to acknowledge his worth, to give him the honor and reverence due him. Thus, Jesus begins by reminding us of the supremacy of God, the one who lives in the third heaven and who controls all the affairs of the universe (see Dan. 4:34–35). His name is to be regarded as holy, to be reverenced above all others.

Why? Because our Father is totally set apart from man. He is other than man, more than man. He is God. Thus, when you come to God in prayer, you are coming to One greater and mightier than yourself. Worship of that mighty One is the first imperative of prayer.

Now, let's look at the second imperative for prayer: the fatherhood of God.

According to God's Word, no man, woman, or child can call God "Father" apart from Jesus; for until we are born again, God is not our Father.

But to all who did receive Him [Jesus Christ],
He gave them the right to be children of God,
to those who believe in His name,
who were born,
not of blood,
or of the will of the flesh,
or of the will of man,
but of God."
(John 1:12–13 HCSB)

Oh, beloved, do you realize what all this means? It means prayer is a privilege reserved for those who are truly the children of God. Prayer is not for the masses. Prayer is only for those who can say with Jesus, "Our Father . . ."

Allegiance

"Your kingdom come," the second index sentence, is potent in its brevity. What does it mean? Why is it a topic for prayer? Why is it separate from "Your will be done, on earth as it is in heaven"?

"Your kingdom come" is a confirmation in prayer of our allegiance to the sovereign rule of the kingdom of God above all else. Prayer is simply communication with God, talking with the sovereign Ruler of all the universe. His name, of course, reveals his person! Then we are to move to allegiance.

Allegiance? Aren't worship and allegiance synonymous? You tell me. Do you know people who acknowledge the "worthship" of God yet who are not fully aligned with his Kingdom and its preeminence? I know people who say, "I know I should study God's Word more," or "I know I should witness," or "I know I should be more involved in his work but . . ." But! But what? What they are actually saying is, "But my first allegiance is not to God." Think about it.

Submission

Now for the third topic for prayer: submission to the will of God.

According to the Lord's Prayer, true prayer is submission to the will of the Father: "Your will be done on earth as it is in heaven." Is that merely a prayer to be fulfilled only when Jesus returns *and* "the sovereignty, the dominion, and the greatness of all the kingdoms under the whole heaven will be given to the people of the saints of the Highest One"—when "all the dominions will serve and obey Him"? (Dan. 7:27 NASB).

No, beloved. "Your will be done" is not simply a prayer to pray as we wait for the coming Kingdom; it is also a heart attitude of the *present* sovereignty and will of the Father.

The will of the Father is that you believe on the Son, the Lord Jesus Christ, God incarnate (John 6:40). *Incarnate* means "in the flesh." In other words, the Father's will is that you believe Jesus Christ is God come in the flesh. Not to believe this truth is to die in your sins (John 8:24).

Submission to God is an integral part of salvation. To believe that Jesus is God is to acknowledge his position and rights as God. To recognize him as Savior is to see that only this God-man can save you from your sins. And what is the root of all sin? Is it not independence? Is it not self having its own way?

Submission to God is also an integral part of prayer. Have you ever been embarrassed or even afraid to pray for things in a definite way for fear God wouldn't answer your prayer? I have. I have thought, "Father, what if you don't answer this prayer? It's going to look like prayer doesn't work!"

Think on it. Pray about it. The will of God is a key to solving many mysteries regarding prayer. What have you been asking God for? Did you ask him first if it was his will? If not, then why don't you spend time in prayer and his Word asking him to show you his will?

Petition and Intercession

We must move on to our fourth index sentence, "Give us today our daily bread." Did you note the word *us?* Remember, when we pray we are not praying for ourselves alone, but rather for the whole body of Christ living in every nook and cranny in this world.

Prayer shows your total dependence upon God because you are to go to him asking for the supply of your daily needs. We are coming to our Father who is in heaven. "Every generous act and every perfect gift is from above, coming down from the Father" (James 1:17 HCSB).

Thus, a major precept of prayer is asking. You may not like that. You may feel it is not right. You may think you ought to get what you need on your own. But, beloved, you are wrong. God has promised to "supply all your needs according to His riches in glory in Christ Jesus" (Phil. 4:19 HCSB).

"But" you may say, "those who do not know Jesus supply their own needs and they survive!" Yes, but how do they survive? Don't they live in constant concern about their material possessions—

having them or keeping them? They are struggling all the time. They do not realize it is only because of who God is that they have what they have, "for He causes His sun to rise on the evil and the good, and sends rain on the righteous and the unrighteous" (Matt. 5:45 HCSB). "Who among all these does not know that the hand of the Lord has done this, in whose hand is the life of every living thing, and breath of all mankind?" (Job 12:9–10 NASB).

Oh, can you not see why we need to pray, "Give us today our daily bread"?

How dependent are you upon God? Do you trust in God or in man?

Confession

The fifth index sentence in the Lord's Prayer has to do with confession and forgiveness: "And forgive us our debts, as we also have forgiven our debtors." That is a loaded index sentence!

As you look on the order of these index sentences, you realize that Jesus must have had a purpose in the way he gave them. Yet, do you wonder why he waited so long to mention the subject of sin and forgiveness? I did, and I meditated upon it.

It seemed to me if I were to confess sin and to seek to forgive my brother before I did anything else in prayer, it might be a superficial cleansing and would probably make forgiveness more difficult—because immediately my focus is on me! However, when I begin in worship, long for his Kingdom, desire his will, and come to him seeking his provision for my needs, then confession must follow!

How can I genuinely worship God, tell him I desire his will, ask him to supply my needs, and not be smitten with my sin, with my need of his favor in forgiveness? And knowing his forgiveness, how can I withhold the same pardon, the same grace, from those who have trespassed against me? I must have his forgiveness because I have wounded our Father. I must forgive as he has forgiven me because to fail to do so is to wound the Lamb of Calvary.

There is one thing God cannot do. He cannot overlook sin. He is holy and, therefore, sin must always be dealt with. It cannot be covered.

Although sin was paid for in full at Calvary, sin unconfessed before the throne of God puts a barrier between God and his child. Why?

Think about it in the light of his character.

There is a principle that applies to saved and lost alike regarding forgiveness: God will not forgive those who will not forgive others. You can argue it, debate it, but it is there in black and white to be believed for what it says. Read Matthew 18:21–35.

When Jesus said, "And forgive us our debts," the debts he was talking about were our moral debts, our sins. We owe God absolute righteousness. To sin is to be in debt!

Have you settled your debts through confessing and forsaking them?

Deliverance

The final index sentence of our Lord's Prayer, "And do not bring us into temptation, but deliver us from the evil one," has been hard for some to understand. James says, "No one undergoing a trial should say, 'I am being tempted by God.' For God is not tempted by evil, and He Himself doesn't tempt anyone" (James 1:13 HCSB).

On the surface, this index sentence of the Lord's Prayer seems to contradict the admonition from James. However, we know that because all Scripture is inspired by God (2 Tim. 3:16), one Scripture cannot deny another Scripture, nor can it state a contradictory truth—because then it would not be truth! Therefore, the question becomes, "Why did Jesus tell us to pray this way if God does not tempt us to do evil? Why this type of prayer?" I want to answer this carefully, but let me warn you that you need to read what I write thoughtfully because it is loaded.

Let's take apart the phrase "do not bring us into temptation." Then we'll dig out the answers to the questions. Follow me carefully. Don't get bogged down.

Lead in the Greek is *eispheró*, which means "to bring to." It is an aorist active subjunctive verb. The aorist tense denotes punctiliar action, occurring at one particular time. The active voice indicates that the subject produces the action of the verb. Therefore, it is God who brings or does not bring us into temptation. The subjunctive mood is a mood of probability and expresses an action that may or should happen but which is not necessarily true at present. Therefore, the statement "do not bring us into temptation" is saying, in essence, "God, I am asking you not to bring us into temptation at any point in time."

Hang in there! The good part is coming. You're growing. Can't you tell by your growing pains? Now, let's look at temptation. Then we will put it together in a practical way.

The Greek word for *temptation* is *peirasmos* and is used for trials of varied character: trials, testings, temptations. Thus, the word *peirasmos* must be interpreted according to its context. For instance, in James 1:2,12 *peirasmos* describes a trial we are to rejoice in, while in James 1:13–14 the same root word is used in connection with sin and, therefore, a temptation to be avoided.

What then is Matthew 6:13 saying? Well, we know it is not saying, "God, don't lead me into sin," because that is contrary to the character of God. It also contradicts James 1:13.

What then is Jesus calling us to cover in prayer? I believe that this index sentence is a reminder or a call to vigilance in "preventive" prayer. When you come to this final topic of prayer, you are letting God know that your heart is set on righteousness, that you do not want to fail, to fall. When you find yourself in a trial (*peirasmos*), if you do not do what James 1:2 says and count it all joy, you are often tempted to give way to your flesh. If you do not realize that "the testing of your faith produces endurance" and you do not "let endurance have its perfect result, that you may be perfect and complete, lacking in nothing" (James 1:3–4 NASB), then you are liable to respond improperly in that trial, fall prey to the seducer, and yield to temptation.

This petition for deliverance is an acknowledgment of the reality of war. Aware that Satan desires to sift us as wheat, even as he did Peter (Luke 22:31), we are telling God we realize that we cannot handle Satan alone. We are willing to stand in righteousness, but God must do the delivering. Oh, how we need to see this truth! Jesus will not have us pray a prayer that God will not answer! Therefore, deliverance is *always* available for those who truly want it. No Christian can ever say, "The devil made me do it!"

We have the promises of 1 Corinthians 10:13: "No temptation has overtaken you except what is common to humanity. God is faithful and He will not allow you to be tempted beyond what you are able, but with the temptation He will provide the way of escape, so that you are able to bear it" (HCSB).

Our final prayer is a prayer for deliverance. It is a cry to God out of poverty of spirit (Matt. 5:3), out of grief at falling short of his standard of holiness (Matt. 5:4), out of meekness (Matt. 5:5), out of a hunger and thirst for righteousness (Matt. 5:6), and out of purity of heart (Matt. 5:8). It is a cry that in its praying says, "Spare me, O Father, from needless trials or testings in which I find myself tempted." It is a cry of awareness that acknowledges the reality of the evil one and of the Christian's warfare. It is an acknowledgment that the flesh is weak. It is heeding our Lord's admonishment to "stay awake and pray, so that you won't enter into temptation. The spirit is willing, but the flesh is weak" (Matt. 26:41 HCSB).

To pray this way, beloved, is to pray our way to victory because this prayer says, "I know *we*—my brothers and sisters and I—are in warfare, and we want to, we will to, we choose to win." Surely those who pray this way are "on the alert with all perseverance and petition for all the saints" and for themselves (Eph. 6:18 NASB).

Although the last sentence, "For Yours is the kingdom and the power and glory forever. Amen," is not in the earliest manuscripts, (that's why it's in brackets), is it any wonder that it was added as a hallelujah of triumph, of worship? It makes the seventh index sentence, and seven is the number of perfection.

Oh, beloved, pause a minute. Hush! Listen! Can you not hear the hallelujahs from heaven? Thanks be to God who always causes us to triumph in Christ Jesus (2 Cor. 2:14)! Here we have the perfect way to pray, taught to us by the One who ever lives to make intercession for the children of God.

So, beloved, we know how to pray! We know what to pray! Now we need to pray . . .[1]

A Final Thought

Intimacy with God and holiness come when you make God your priority, when you get into his Word *and* when you spend time with him, praying and waiting on him to speak to you. Waiting until in the inner man you know he is saying, "This is the way; walk in it."

It is there—waiting before him in prayer—that you will gain great confidence in God and in his will for you each day of your life. Because your goal is not simply to know his Word, but to know the God of the Word intimately, you cannot neglect prayer.

Don't you want to know him so intimately that your heart touches his, until your hearts beat as one? Then you must learn to do more than pray, "Bless . . . bless . . . bless . . . give me . . . help me." You must be still enough to hear his voice. Prayer is searching for the heart of God.

And once you find it, you will know that your sins are covered and your frailties do not matter. In prayer, through his grace, your impotence is filled with his power.

And remember that though a quiet, secluded place and time for prayer is good, you need not bow your head and close your eyes to pray. Prayer should be a constant attitude of the heart. You can and should pray while driving, working, and at most anytime you can think.

God is looking for men, women, teens, and children who tremble at his Word—for those who seek to be holy even as he is holy. You cannot get there without prayer.[2]

KAY ARTHUR and her husband, Jack, are the founders of Precept Ministries. This ministry reaches hundreds of thousands of people internationally through "Precept upon Precept" Bible studies and Kay's radio and television program *Precepts with Kay Arthur*. Kay is the best-selling author of numerous books, including *His Imprint, My Expression; Beloved;* and *How to Study Your Bible.* She is also the active spokeswoman for The International Inductive Study Bible.

Giving

is money really important to God?

BY BRIAN KLUTH

*T*he God who created us knows full well the trials and temptations that the pursuit of money and possessions can have on our lives. That's why he gave us his owner's manual, the Bible. The Bible is filled with his insights and wisdom when it comes to money matters. A friend of mine purchased a new Bible a number of years ago and highlighted in yellow every verse in the Bible that dealt with money and material possessions. When he was finished, he discovered he had highlighted 2,350 verses on financial subjects, including wealth, generosity, borrowing, investing, financial planning, business, inheritances, taxes, purchases, and possessions.

Hundreds of years ago, Martin Luther, one of the great leaders of the Protestant Reformation, said: "People go through three conversions: their head, their heart, and their pocketbook. Unfortunately, not all at the same time."

Throughout this chapter, I would like to share with you some proven biblical and practical principles, practices, and resources that can assist you in your spiritual financial conversion.

God's Ownership

One of the most significant truths a person must come to grips with is that God is the true owner of all we currently have or ever will have. This side of heaven, we are not owners, but merely "temporary possessors" (managers, trustees) of the money, skills, materials, and things that God chooses to entrust to us. Matthew 25:14–30 teaches us that the Lord will ask us some day to give an accounting of how well we used what he entrusted to us during the life he allowed us to live on this earth.

Let me explain it this way. Suppose I fly into a city to conduct business. After getting off the plane, I pick up a rental car that I reserved in advance. They give me the keys to the car, and off I go. The car is "mine" in that I am the temporary possessor of the car and the keys, and I can take it wherever I want. But is the car really mine? No. At the end of my trip, the owners (Hertz, Alamo, Avis, or whoever) will inspect the car to see if I used it properly and returned it in good condition. Once, I accidentally ran my rental car into a metal pole at a gas station. When they inspected the car, the real owners (Alamo) charged me six hundred dollars to repair the damage. We also tend to think that we are the owners of any house we purchase. But are we really the owners? If we miss four or five payments, guess what? The real owners (the bank or mortgage company) will come and take the house back.

When my son, Jeremy, was two, he would grab things away from other people and yell, "Mine!" Some adults still hold the same perspective as my toddler son. Many people will think or sometimes even say aloud, "It's *my* money! It's *my* house! It's *my* car! No one is going to tell me what to do! I earned it. It's *mine*! I'll do with it what I want!" But in Deuteronomy 8:17–18 the Bible cautions us not to have this type of attitude: "You may say to yourself, 'My power and the strength of my hands have produced this wealth for me.' But remember the LORD your God, for it is he who gives you the ability to produce wealth."

When it comes to a list of what God owns, here is a partial list from a variety of Bible passages:

- Every animal and bird and creature (Ps. 50)
- All the silver and all the gold (Hag. 2:8)
- All the land (Lev. 25)
- The wealth of the nations (Hag. 2)
- The wealth of the sinner (Prov. 13:22; Eccles. 2:26)
- Everything in heaven and earth (1 Chron. 29)
- All who live in the world (Ps. 24)
- Riches and honor, enduring wealth and prosperity (Prov. 8)
- Wisdom, power, and counsel (Job 12)
- The sun and the stars in the heavens (Gen. 1)
- All things (Col. 1:16–17)
- Treasures of darkness and secret riches (Isa. 45:3)
- Advancements and promotions (Ps. 75:6–7; Ps. 113:7–8; Dan. 2:21)
- Wealth, honor, strength, and power (1 Chron. 29:12)

Over the years, my wife and I have hosted a number of Crown Ministries twelve-week financial Bible studies in our home. One of the most meaningful exercises in this study is to make a list of everything you "own" and then symbolically "sign it all over" to God. This is not a weird cultlike activity. It is actually a legitimate recognition of the owner of everything we have. Once you go through with this action, you can then live a more liberated life as you seek to look to God and his direction for how he wants you use what he's given you.

A single woman in her fifties told me one day that all her life she had worried about money—how *she* was going to provide for and take care of *herself*. Once she came to understand from the Bible that God was the owner and she was the manager and trustee of what he had given her, she said she had victory over the financial worries that had troubled her for many years. She said she now saw God as her provider and protector.

If you want to know God's complete peace and freedom in financial matters, it will be vital for you to make a spiritual, emotional, and financial decision to recognize God as the true owner and provider of all you have or ever will have. With this foundation firmly in place, you can then move on to discover God's principles of generosity and financial management that will influence your life in a positive way.

Generosity: God's Pathway to Joy and Freedom

Over the years, I have done financial and debt counseling with many people in the midst of financial hardships. As strange and as unlikely as it seems, I have discovered the surest long-term path to get out of debt and financial troubles is to make a decision to give 10 percent of your income to God first, right "off the top" of whatever he gives you.

Ten percent is used here as an example. Although the Bible has many references to this percentage, don't get too hung up on that particular number. As with anything taken to extreme, taking 10 percent as a legal demand of God will prevent you from experiencing God's abundant grace in your finances. As with all of the Christian life, the substance of our obedience should flow from our love for our Creator and his work, not from rigidly meeting legal mandates.

In my counseling sessions I have dealt with people who looked at their situation and said there was no way they could give to God first. I frequently shared with them that it was going to take "all the help of heaven" to get them out of the deep financial pit they were in. I would tell them that honoring God from the first part of their income was vital to their long-term stability and financial freedom. Those who heeded God's counsel grew in their trust and understanding of God's firm grip concerning financial concerns.

In order to help you understand the importance of biblical generosity in your life, I would like to share six principles that might help you govern your giving to God and his work.

Give to God First

After preaching a sermon on the importance of generosity, I had an older man tell me how fifty years earlier, he and his wife made a commitment to give God the first portion of their income. As a young married couple, they studied their budget to see how they could cut expenses. But they found there was no way to do this and still meet the needs of their growing family.

Praying over their decision, they began giving to God first anyway, even knowing that by the end of the third week of every month they would be out of money. God provided faithfully, month after month and year after year. He cared for their family creatively through odd jobs, leading others to share clothing or homegrown vegetables, a bonus or overtime pay from work, close-out-priced items in stores—and the list went on.

By making giving to the Lord's work their first financial priority, they learned more about the love, care, and reality of God as their heavenly Father than through any other spiritual discipline.

There is a story in 1 Kings about a widow and her son who were about to eat their last meal and die because of a severe famine in the land. She gave to God's servant Elijah first before caring for her own needs. God worked miraculously so that her "jar of flour was not used up and the jug of oil did not run dry" (1 Kings 17:16).

When we give to God first, regardless of our needs, we see how big God can be in our lives. If we withhold from the Lord, we miss the many blessings and provisions the Lord is longing to shower on us.

Give to God Systematically

When leading a Sunday school lesson on giving, I encouraged eight-year-old Alex to set up three jars: one marked "God's money," the second "savings," and the third "spending money." Whenever Alex was given money, he could put the first portion in "God's jar" and the second and third portions in the "savings" and "spending" jars.

A few months later when my wife and I were preparing for a five-week ministry trip to India, Alex came to me and pushed three crumpled dollar bills into my hand. He said, "Do you remember the time you taught us about the three jars? Well, I went home and did that. Now you're going to India to do God's work, and God wants me to give you some of his money."

Alex acknowledged that everything he had came from God's hand, and he implemented a practical way to lay aside regularly for God what he received. He then gave from those stored resources as the Lord directed him.

Some people have opened an additional bank account to separate their giving from their household expenses. Others track their finances with bookkeeping accounts and regularly make certain they are "caught up" with their giving. Some Christians in India set aside the first of their rice and eggs for their pastor's family.

Christians who don't have a regular way of laying aside the first of what they receive for the Lord often feel pressed and confused when it comes to giving. Many people making comfortable incomes experience no joy in giving because they haven't determined how they will give.

Give to God Cheerfully

Second Corinthians 9:7 tells us, "God loves a cheerful giver." When Nancy was abandoned by her husband and left to support their three children on the twenty-five dollars a week he sent for groceries, she was excited that she could finally give to the Lord's work, since her husband had never allowed it before.

Out of her grocery money she gave to God, though the small amount she had could never cover her family's living expenses. But God provided Nancy with a job as an assistant to a photographer of cookbooks. When the photo sessions were over, the photographer gave Nancy all the food. Her cupboards were full with the provisions God provided for her family.

R. G. LeTourneau, a Christian businessman, once said, "I shovel out and God shovels in—but God's shovel is always bigger." We should never "give to get," but we can trust that as we give, our God will meet our needs, sometimes in very special ways. Instances arise when it makes no financial sense to give to the Lord. Yet, God wants us to give at times with the realization that we are totally dependent on him to meet our basic needs and desires.

Give to God Eternally

I visited with an elderly couple who had supported a Christian camp financially for more than forty years. The wife expressed feelings of failure over not being used by God during her lifetime. She hadn't led anyone to the Lord, and as a result, she feared her life was a waste. She never realized that her family's giving had been used by God to reach thousands of people. The Bible teaches that those who stay with the supplies and send the supplies will share equally with those who are on the front lines of ministry.

First Timothy 6:18–19 says, "Command them [those who are rich] to do good, to be rich in good deeds, and to be generous and willing to share. In this way they will lay up treasure for themselves as a firm foundation for the coming age." From an investor's perspective, giving to the Lord's work is the safest and wisest investment we can ever make. Our giving will pay heavenly dividends throughout all eternity.

God promises we will share in the reward: "For God is not unfair. He will not forget . . . how you have shown your love to him by caring for other Christians" (Heb. 6:10 NLT).

Managing Your Finances

Once you have learned to recognize God as the owner of all you have and you are honoring him with the first part of your income, it is important to go on and learn additional financial principles that will help you in life.

Manage What You Have vs. Wishing for More

Most people think that the real answer for their financial future is "more money." The desire to always have more can lead people into dishonesty at work, credit card debt, gambling, long work weeks, foolish investments, get-rich-quick schemes, and much worse.

The Bible actually teaches that managing what you have is more important than getting more. Luke 16:10 tells us: "Unless you are faithful in small matters, you won't be faithful in large ones" (NLT).

Over the years I have counseled with many people in deep financial problems. The ultimate answer for their problems was seldom "more money." Usually it was more careful, thoughtful, and prayerful management of what they already had.

Ecclesiastes 5:10–11 tells us: "Those who love money will never have enough. How absurd to think that wealth brings true happiness! The more you have, the more people come to help you spend it. So what is the advantage of wealth—except perhaps to watch it run through your fingers!" (NLT).

Have a Written Plan

Most people have a vague understanding of where their money is really going. Once, I counseled with a couple whose income had increased 400 percent in five years. And although they lived in the same house for the entire time, they always lived from paycheck to paycheck with no real plan for how they were going to spend their money. Regardless of how much their income grew, the money seemed to flow through their hands like water. Haggai 1:6 says, "This is what the LORD Almighty says: 'Your wages disappear as though you were putting them in pockets filled with holes!'" (NLT).

It will be vital to your financial future that you record in detail for thirty to sixty days where your money is going. Once you have tallied this information, you can then sit down and determine the best use of the money God has entrusted to you. You will then be able to move toward telling your money where to go instead of asking where it's gone.

The Bible says in Proverbs 27:23, "Riches can disappear fast. . . . Watch your business interests closely. Know the state of your flocks and your herds" (TLB). In other words, know in specific detail the condition of your income, expenses, debts, and investments. Have a written plan to manage what God has entrusted to you.

Trust Christ More Than Credit

In our world, there are easy credit terms and options everywhere we turn. Almost anyone in America can have multiple credit cards, easy car loans, huge house mortgages, and furniture and electronics products with no money down and no interest for ninety days!

No longer does America save for anything. Today, we borrow and charge to get what we want, when we want it. But in Luke 12:15 Jesus said, "Beware! Don't be greedy for what you don't have. Real life is not measured by how much we own" (NLT).

Jesus knows we need certain things to live in this world. Most people end up paying to their MasterCard to have things they don't really need, with money they don't really have, to impress people they don't really like! There was a time in my life when I had more month than money. I then learned I could pray to the Master (instead of paying to the MasterCard) to meet my real needs. Over the years, I have seen God guide and provide his answers to my prayers for housing, employment, transportation, clothing, recreation, and so much more.

Recently I discovered that if you have three thousand dollars on a credit card and you are only making minimum payments, it will take you more than thirty years to pay off the full amount! No wonder the Bible cautions us about growing indebtedness when it tells us that "the borrower becomes the lender's slave" (see Prov. 22:7).

Regardless of how much of a mountain of debt some people find themselves under, I have discovered that with God's help, most people can become debt-free of all their short-term indebtedness within one to five years. I have seen many people even go on to become mortgage-free within five to ten years. With God's help, you could be completely debt- and mortgage-free in the years to come.

Study God's Blueprint for Finances

Howard Dayton, the founder of Crown Ministries who discovered the 2,350 verses in the Bible on finances and material possessions, summarized all these verses into eight primary principles that every Christian should seek to understand and follow:

- Avoid debt.
- Seek counsel.
- Practice honesty.
- Give generously.
- Spend wisely.
- Work hard.
- Save consistently.
- Train your children.

Advice on Christian Giving

Here is some practical advice from years of teaching and counseling people concerning personal finances, debt, and giving. I hope you will find this helpful in your walk with Christ.

If You Are Not a Christian

Don't worry about giving to God—but realize and accept what God wants to give to you: complete forgiveness, eternal life, and a brand-new start.

For All Christians

Always give to your church first. After your faithful church support, then give special gifts and offerings to other Christian causes that you feel are important.

If You Want to Begin to Give to God First

Whenever you get any money, lay aside the first part in a special place to give to the Lord as he directs you, or whenever you put a deposit in your checkbook, write out a check for the percentage you want to be giving to the Lord's work. If you track your income and expenses, set up a category for your church giving and another category for giving to other Christian causes. Review these accounts regularly and give to the Lord based on the percentage or amounts you decided on.

If You Are Married to a Christian but Are Still Not in Agreement about Giving to God's Work

Have your spouse read this information and then talk about how to set up a mutually acceptable plan on how you can give more regularly or more generously to the Lord's work.

If You Are Married and Your Spouse Is Not a Christian

1. See if your spouse would be willing to read this material, or

2. Identify any money you know you do have freedom with (read Luke 8:3) and set aside the first portion of this money to give to the Lord's work, or

3. Suggest to your spouse that you try this faith experiment for three months. Begin to give some money and then look back each Sunday to see if any special financial things begin to happen.

Giving off the Net or the Gross?

Pray and ask God which you should do. If he prompts you in your heart to give off the gross, go ahead and do this and trust him with the results. If giving 10 percent or more is a new experience for you, begin with giving off the net amount for a few months and see what happens. If after a few months you experience his creative care in your life, begin giving 10 percent or more off your gross.

If You Are a Parent

Help your children organize a place where they can set aside "God's portion" of any money they receive (i.e., allowances, work projects, gifts of money, etc.). Have them give their own church and ministry offerings from this money they set aside.

Here's a Faith-Building Exercise to Try

Read three Scripture passages on giving (see the following list for help). Then make it a priority to give the percentage of your income you believe to be God's will to the Lord's work each time you get paid or when you put a deposit in your checkbook. After ninety days, evaluate how God has worked in your life.

I wish you God's very best on this important journey in your spiritual life. May you be a believer who has been converted spiritually in your head, heart, and pocketbook!

For Further Study

Abraham gives 10 percent (Gen. 14:19–20)

Jacob's decision to give 10 percent to God (Gen. 28:20–22)

Moses and the people's gifts to build the tabernacle
  (Exod. 35:4–29)

Tithe of everything is the Lord's (Lev. 27:30)

Tithes support ministers of God (Num. 18:21)

Tithes, special gifts, freewill offerings (Deut. 12:5–7)

Set aside a tenth to learn to revere God (Deut. 14:22–29)

Hezekiah's generosity and giving instructions (2 Chron. 31:2–12)

Nehemiah's giving instructions (Neh. 10:35–37)

Holding back tithes and offerings is stealing from God
  (Mal. 3:7–12)

Jesus' affirmation of tithing (Matt. 23:23; Luke 11:42)

Elijah and the starving widow (1 Kings 17:8–16)

God gives people the ability to produce wealth (Deut. 8:18)

Honor the Lord with your wealth and firstfruits (Prov. 3:9–10)

Moses restrains people from bringing offerings (Exod. 36:3–6)

Malachi's rebuke for bringing bad offerings (Mal. 1:6–14)

Haggai's giving challenge (Hag. 1:4–11)

David's generous gift and giving challenge (1 Chron. 29:2–9)

Everything we have and give comes from God
  (1 Chron. 29:11–17)

Give and God will see that others give to you (Luke 6:38)

Rich generosity in the midst of extreme poverty (2 Cor. 8:2–21)

God loves a cheerful giver (2 Cor. 9:5–15)

Generosity is the pathway for more (Prov. 11:24–25)

A generous person will be blessed (Prov. 22:9)

Give and have enough; withhold and be cursed (Prov. 28:27)

Don't worry, but seek first the kingdom of God (Matt. 6:25–34)

Rich people giving and the widow's mite (Mark 12:41–44)

Give in proportion to the blessings the Lord has given you
  (Deut. 16:10, 16–17)

On the first day of each week, give according to God's blessing
  (1 Cor. 16:2)

Cautions about the materialism and the love of money
  (1 Tim. 6:6–11, 17–19)

No needy persons; sale of land and houses (Acts 4:34–37)

Share with God's people who are in need (Rom. 12:13)

Do you see brothers in need—help them (1 John 3:17)

A rich man turns away from Jesus (Luke 18:22–25)

Support financially those who teach you the Word of God
  (Gal. 6:6)

Helping the least of the brethren is helping Jesus
  (Matt. 25:35–40)

It is more blessed to give than to receive (Acts 20:35)

Other Resources

Check at your local Christian bookstore for the helpful resources listed below. We have included the direct contact information in the event that these materials are not available locally.

The Crown Ministries twelve-week financial Bible study that is available in English and Spanish across the country is a great tool to help you more fully understand God's blueprint for your financial future.

Crown Ministries Twelve-Week Financial Bible Studies and Video Series. 407-331-6000. www.crown.org

Books, videos, cassettes, materials, and study guides by Larry Burkett of Christian Financial Concepts. 1-800-722-1976. www.cfcministry.org

Books, resources, and video series by Ron Blue. 1-404-705-7000. www.rbc.com

"The Word for the Wealthy" by Brian Kluth. Personal or small group Bible study highlighting six hundred Scripture verses summarized into forty biblical principles about God's wisdom and warnings concerning wealth and generosity. 1-888-443-7407. www.kluth.org

Kingdom Seekers website (www.kluth.org) by Brian Kluth. Helpful resources and hotlinks on generosity and financial matters for individuals, churches, and ministries.

BRIAN KLUTH is a leading spokesperson, nationally and internationally, on issues of biblical generosity. He has ministered across America and on five continents. His written materials have been distributed to Christians in more than one hundred countries. His website, www.kluth.org, offers additional resources and insights into biblical financial and generosity matters. He is also the senior pastor at the First Evangelical Free Church of Colorado Springs, Colorado.

Servanthood

how can my life make a difference?

By Henry T. Blackaby

*T*o know God's will and to experience him working in and through our lives to carry out his will is the desire of every Christian's heart! This desire to know God's will is present in each of us because when God saves us he works in us to cause us to want to do his will and to enable us to do his will (Phil. 2:13). Therefore, even in wanting to do his will, we are responding to his activity of love in our lives.

Knowing and Experiencing the Will of God

From Genesis to Revelation we can see that God always takes the initiative to come to his people. Without him, we would all go our own way (Rom. 3:10–12) and lack understanding! God therefore takes the initiative and comes to us. God's desire is to reveal himself and his activities or purposes.

When we speak of doing God's will, we mean we know what he is doing or about to do and how he would accomplish his will through us. When we know what he is about to do where we are, we will then know how we must adjust our lives so he can accomplish his will through us. This was true of many Bible characters: Noah (Gen. 6:9–13), Abram (Gen. 12:1–4), and Moses (Exod. 3:7–10). With all those God used in the Old Testament, the pattern was the same. (1) he came to them; (2) he revealed his planned activity; (3) they believed him and adjusted their lives to him; (4) they obeyed him; and (5) they experienced God doing his will through them. This was also true of the disciples (Mark 1:16–18; John 15:16), Paul (Acts 26:13–19), and all those he used in the New Testament. It is just as true today in each of our lives!

Since Jesus is our pattern, it is instructive to remember that even he did not take his own initiative, but responded to the Father's activity. The Father loved the Son and showed him all he was doing (John 5:17, 20) so Jesus could know the Father's will and experience the Father accomplishing his will through him (John 14:9–11). He saw where the Father was working and joined him.

Every time God revealed his purposes and plans (his will) to persons, that revelation was at the same time his invitation to adjust their life to him. They learned what they were to do. Such an invitation brought about a major adjustment of their lives with God.

Look again at the lives of Noah, Abraham, Moses, the prophets, the disciples, and others in the Bible. None of these could remain where they were and go with God at the same time. Their lives could never again be "business as usual"! To know what God was going to do and to be a part of his activity always meant adjustment and change. Adjustment, however, made them available to God with a readiness for God to do his work, and accomplish his purposes through them.

Following the "adjustment to God," obedience to what God said next was crucial. To obey led to experiencing God at work through them, accomplishing his will just as he was revealed to them. It is in the doing of his revealed will that we know (experience) him and his will unfolding through us (Matt. 7:21–29; John 7:17; 8:29–32). This activity of God that follows our obedience brings clear affirmation in our lives that we are doing his will.

Thus, living as a Christian is living in relationship with a person—hearing him, obeying him, and following him. To know God's will, it is important to know when he is speaking. If we do not know when God is speaking to us, we are in trouble at the heart of the Christian life.

The will of God is God coming to us in his Word, in prayer, in circumstances, and in his church, revealing what he is doing and purposing, so we can adjust our lives to him, so he can do his will through us. When we obey him, we experience him working in us, around us, and through us.[1]

Being God's Servant

To be involved in God's work, you must be a servant. Many Scripture passages describe Jesus as God's servant. He came as a servant to accomplish God's will in the redemption of humanity. Paul described Jesus' servant attitude and commended it to us in this way: "Let this mind be in you which was also in Christ Jesus, who, being in the form of God, did not consider it robbery to be equal with God, but made Himself of no reputation, taking the form of a bondservant, and coming in the likeness of men. And being found in appearance as a man, He humbled Himself and became obedient to the point of death, even the death of the cross" (Phil. 2:5–8 NKJV).

We are to develop the servant attitude of Christ, which calls for humility and obedience. In his instructions to his disciples about servanthood, Jesus (the Son of Man) described his own role of service: "And whoever desires to be first among you, let him be your slave— just as the Son of Man did not come to be served, but to serve, and to give His life a ransom for many" (Matt. 20:27–28 NKJV).

Jesus also told us about our relationship to him, "As the Father has sent Me, I also send you" (John 20:21 NKJV). When you respond to God's call to salvation, you join him in his mission of world redemption. The call to salvation is a call to be on mission with him. In this new relationship, you move into a servant role with God as your Lord and Master.

Some would define a servant like this: "A servant is one who finds out what his master wants him to do, and then he does it." The human concept of a servant is that a servant goes to the master and says, "Master, what do you want me to do?" The master tells him, and the servant goes off by himself and does it. That is not the biblical concept of a servant of God. Being a servant of God is different from being a servant of a human master. A servant of a human master works for his master. God, however, works through his servants.

My understanding of a servant of God is more like the potter and the clay. God described his relationship to Israel: "The word which came to Jeremiah from the LORD, saying, 'Arise and go down to the potter's house, and there I will cause you to hear My words.' Then I went down to the potter's house, and there he was, making something at the wheel. And the vessel that he made of clay was marred in the hand of the potter; so he made it again into another vessel, as it seemed good to the potter to make. Then the word of the LORD came to me, saying: 'O house of Israel, can I not do with you as this potter?' says the LORD. 'Look, as the clay is in the potter's hand, so are you in My hand, O house of Israel!'" (Jer. 18:1–6 NKJV).

To be useful, the clay has to be moldable; once made into a vessel, it has to remain in the hand of the potter to be used. Clay that is not moldable is not useful. The clay has to be responsive to the potter so the potter can make any vessel of his choosing. Then the clay vessel has to remain in the potter's hand. When the potter has finished making the vessel of his choosing, that vessel has no ability to do anything whatsoever. It now has to remain in the potter's hand. Suppose the potter molds the clay into a cup. The cup has to remain in the potter's hands so the potter can use that cup in any way he chooses.

Human Servant and Divine Master

That is very different from the way a servant works for a human master. When you come to God as his servant, he first wants you to allow him to mold and shape you into the instrument of his choosing. Then he can take your life and put it where he wills and work through it to accomplish his purposes. Just as a cup cannot do anything on its own, you do not have any ability to do the command of the Lord except to be where he wants you to be. As you obey, he does his work through you.

A servant of God's has to do two things: (1) be moldable and (2) remain available for the Master's (Potter's) use. Then the Master can use that instrument as he chooses. The servant can do nothing of kingdom value by himself or herself. As Jesus said, "The Son can do nothing of Himself" (John 5:19 NKJV), and "Without Me you can do nothing" (John 15:5 NKJV). With God working through his servant, that servant can do anything God can do. Wow! Unlimited potential! Servanthood does require obedience. A servant of God must do what he is instructed, and he must remember who is accomplishing the work—God is.

If you have been working from a human approach to servanthood, this concept should change your approach to serving God. You do not get orders, then go out and carry them out on your own. You relate to God, respond to him, and adjust your life so he can do what he wants through you.

Expo 86

For six years I worked with the Southern Baptist churches in Vancouver, British Columbia. When the World's Fair (Expo 86) was coming to Vancouver, our association of churches was convinced that God wanted us to try to reach the twenty-two million people who would attend the fair. But we only had about two thousand members in our association's churches. How could two thousand people make an impact on such a mass of tourists from all over the world?

Two years before the fair, we sought the Lord's directions and began to set those plans in motion. The total income for our whole association was $9,000. The following year our income was about $16,000. The year of the World's Fair we set a budget for $202,000.

We had commitments that would probably provide 35 percent of that budget. Sixty-five percent of that budget was dependent on prayer and God's provision.

Can you operate a budget on prayer? Yes. But when you do that, you are attempting something only God can do. What do most of us do? We set the practical budget, which is the total of what we can do. Then we set a hope or faith budget. The budget we really trust and use, however, is the one we can reach by ourselves. We often don't trust God to do anything.

As an association of churches, we decided that God had definitely led us to the work that would cost $202,000. That became our operating budget. All of our people began praying for God to provide and do everything we believed he had led us to do during the World's Fair. At the end of the year, I asked our treasurer how much money we had received. From Canada, the United States, and other parts of the world, we had received $264,000.

People from all over came to assist us. During the course of the fair, we saw almost twenty thousand people come to know and trust Jesus Christ as Savior and Lord. You cannot explain that except in terms of God's intervention. Only God could have done that. God did it with a people who had determined to be servants who were moldable and remained available for the Master's use.

Elijah Was a Servant

Elijah was one of the great Old Testament prophets of Israel and a servant of God (1 Kings 17:1). Under the leadership of King Ahab and his wife, Jezebel, the people of Israel were being led away to serve Baal, a Canaanite fertility god. In 1 Kings 18:16–39, Elijah challenged the prophets of Baal to a public test to prove once and for all whose God was the true God. Elijah took a big risk in being a servant of God. He was outnumbered 850 to 1.

Elijah proposed that the prophets of Baal prepare a sacrifice and ask their god to send fire to consume it. He would do the same and appeal to the God of Israel for fire. Baal—who was no god—did not answer his prophets' pleas. Elijah repaired the altar of the Lord and prepared his sacrifice. God did answer by fire, consuming the sacrifice (and even the stone altar) as Elijah had proposed. If God had not displayed his own work by coming in fire, Elijah would have utterly failed. That would probably have cost him his life.

Throughout this process, Elijah had to stay with God and do everything God commanded him to do. In his prayer, Elijah said, "Let it be known . . . that I am Your servant, and that I have done all these things at Your word" (1 Kings 18:36 NKJV). Elijah was acting in obedience to God's command and not based on his own initiative. He went where God told him when God told him and did what God told him. Then God accomplished his own purposes through Elijah. Elijah attributed the work to God when he said, "You have turned their hearts back to You again" (1 Kings 18:37 NKJV). Elijah wanted the people to identify the Lord as the true God. That is exactly how the people responded!

Did Elijah or God bring down the fire from heaven? God did. What was Elijah doing? Being obedient. Elijah had no ability to do what God was about to do. When God, however, did something only he could do, all the people knew that he was the true God. God did this mighty work, but he acted through his obedient servant Elijah.

Ordinary People

When you begin to think about working with God on his mission to redeem a lost world, you may ask, "What can one ordinary person do?"

Peter and John Were Ordinary Men

Peter and John were two of the first disciples selected by Jesus. After Jesus' resurrection, God healed a crippled beggar through Peter. Peter and John were called before the Sanhedrin to give an account of their actions. Filled with the Holy Spirit, Peter spoke boldly to the religious leaders. Notice the response of the leaders: "Now when they saw the boldness of Peter and John, and perceived that they were uneducated and untrained men, they marveled. And they realized that they had been with Jesus" (Acts 4:13 NKJV).

All of the persons whom you see in the Scriptures were ordinary people. Their relationship with God and the activity of God made them extraordinary. Did you notice this statement—the leaders recognized that Peter and John "had been with Jesus"? Anyone who will take the time to enter into an intimate relationship with God can see God do extraordinary things through his or her life.

D. L. Moody Was an Ordinary Shoe Salesman

Dwight L. Moody was a poorly educated, unordained shoe salesman who felt the call of God to preach the gospel. Early one morning he and some friends gathered in a hayfield for a season of prayer, confession, and consecration. In that prayer meeting Henry Varley said, "The world has yet to see what God can do with and for and through and in a man who is fully and wholly consecrated to Him."

Moody was deeply moved by those words. Later, he listened to the great preacher Charles H. Spurgeon. Moody's biographer described how he responded:

"The world had yet to see! With and for and through
and in! A man!" Varley meant any man! Varley didn't say he
had to be educated, or brilliant, or anything else! Just a
man! Well, by the Holy Spirit in him, he'd [Moody] be one
of those men. And then suddenly, in that high gallery, he
saw something he'd never realized before—it was not Mr.
Spurgeon, after all, who was doing that work: it was God.
And if God could use Mr. Spurgeon, why should He not use
the rest of us, and why should we not all just lay ourselves
at the Master's feet, and say to Him, "Send me! Use me!"

Dwight L. Moody was an ordinary man who sought to be fully and wholly consecrated to Christ. Through this one ordinary life, God began to do the extraordinary. Moody became one of the greatest evangelists of modern times. During much of the nineteenth century he preached in revival services across Britain and America, where thousands and thousands came to Christ.

Could God work in extraordinary ways through your life to accomplish significant things for his Kingdom? You might say, "Well, I am not a D. L. Moody." You don't have to be a D. L. Moody. God doesn't want you to be a D. L. Moody. God wants you to be you and let him do through you whatever he chooses. When you believe that nothing significant can happen through you, you have said more about your belief in God than you have said about yourself. You have said that God is not capable of doing anything significant through you. The truth is, he is able to do anything he pleases with one ordinary person fully consecrated to him.

John the Baptist

Don't be surprised that God's standards of excellence are different from ours. How long was the public ministry of John the Baptist? Perhaps six months. What was Jesus' estimate of John's life? "For I say to you, among those born of women there is not a greater prophet than John" (Luke 7:28 NKJV). None greater! He had six months wholly yielded to God, and the Son of God put that stamp of approval on his life.

Don't measure your life by the world's standards. Don't do it. Many denominations are doing it. Many pastors and staff leaders are doing it. Many churches are doing it. Think about it. By the world's standards, a person or church may look pretty good, yet in God's sight be utterly detestable. Similarly, a person or church may be wholly yielded to him and very pleasing to him and in the world's eyes be insignificant. Could a pastor who faithfully serves where God put him in a small rural community be pleasing to the Lord? Sure, if that is where God put him. God will look for and reward faithfulness, whether the person has been given responsibility for little or much.

An ordinary person is who God most likes to use. Paul said God deliberately seeks out the weak things and the despised things because it is from them that he can receive the greatest glory (see 1 Cor. 1:26–31). Then everyone will know that only God could have done it. If you feel weak, limited, ordinary, you are the best material through which God can work!

The call to salvation is a call to be on mission with God as he reconciles a lost world to himself through Christ. This calling requires that you be a servant of God. Jesus gave you the best model of servanthood, which was both humble and obedient. As a servant, you must be moldable and remain available for the Master's use.

Even though you may consider yourself to be an ordinary person, God will prepare you; then he will do his work through you, revealing himself to a watching world.

Experiencing God Today

Do you want to be a servant of God? Do you want to see God accomplishing things through you that only God can do? Do you want to experience the rest and the success Jesus described in Matthew 11:28–30? If so, find out where the Master is—then that is where you need to be. Find out what the Master is doing—then that is what you need to be doing. Jesus said: "If anyone serves Me, let him follow Me; and where I am, there My servant will be also. If anyone serves Me, him My father will honor" (John 12:26 NKJV).[2]

HENRY T. BLACKABY has served as a music director, Christian education director, and senior pastor in churches in California and Canada; his first church assignment was in 1958. Following his local church ministry, Dr. Blackaby became a college president, a missionary, and an executive in the Southern Baptist Convention.

Dr. Blackaby formerly served on staff at the North American Mission Board in Alpharetta, Georgia, as special assistant to the president. Through the office of Revival and Spiritual Awakening of the Southern Baptist Convention, he provided leadership to thousands of pastors and laymen across North America. He also formerly served as special assistant to the presidents of the International Mission Board and LifeWay Christian Resources.

In the early 90s Henry Blackaby became one of North America's best-selling Christian authors, committing the rest of his life to helping people know and experience God.

The author of more than a dozen books, Dr. Blackaby is a graduate of the University of British Columbia, Vancouver, Canada. He has completed his Th.M. degree from Golden Gate Baptist Theological Seminary. He has also received three honorary doctorate degrees.

Henry Blackaby and his wife, Marilynn, have five married children and are expecting their twelfth and thirteenth grandchildren in November. He currently serves as the president of Henry Blackaby Ministries.

Caring

what does Christian love look like?

BY CAPTAIN JOHN CHEYDLEUR

I grew up as a normally selfish child and teenager in the comfortable but passive Christianity of the Episcopal Church. When I was seventeen, my parents began attending the Quaker (Friends) Church, where I was introduced to an activist youth group whose Christian focus was on projects designed to help other people.

At age nineteen, my parents' moral teachings and the influence of both of these churches came together when my life was abruptly changed by attending a Salvation Army Youth Council gathering in Atlantic City. There I made a conscious decision to accept Christ into the core of my life as my personal Savior.

I remember marching into the student dean's office at Swarthmore College and announcing to Dean Barr that I wanted to drop out of college and devote my life to caring for a lost and broken humanity through the Salvation Army!

Dean Barr was remarkably patient with my immature idealistic enthusiasm, as were the men and women leaders of the Salvation Army who would later become my mentors, disciplers, and friends.

The first crack in my newfound rush of enthusiasm to care for the whole world all at once came when I went home from college on a student break. I overheard my dad say to my mom, "I'll believe this new religious experience has substance when John starts to take out the trash for you without being asked."

Other similar revelations to me about my own selfishness, first with my parent's family and later in my young marriage to Judy, pointed me to the understanding that caring, like evangelism, must start in Judea, then extend to Samaria, before it can go to the ends of the earth. In practical terms, this means that caring must start at home and move outward from there to school, job, and local community before being applied to a wider environment.

When an inquirer challenged Jesus to pinpoint the greatest commandment, Jesus answered, "'Love the Lord your God with all your heart and with all your soul and with all your mind and with all your strength.' The second is this: 'Love your neighbor as yourself.' There is no commandment greater than these" (Mark 12:30–31).

The Lord commands us to love him supremely and then to love our neighbors as ourselves, but he does not ask us to love others in ways that violate our own personalities, or in ways that require abilities beyond our level of competence, education, or training.

As new Christians, each of us intuitively knows what our old self-centered lifestyle was like, but we do not immediately understand what our own individual new caring lifestyle would include.

In our search for this understanding, we often seek out potential role models. I remember helping a Salvation Army evangelist, Colonel Lyell Rader, when he stormed into the inner city area of north Philadelphia for a week of public evangelistic meetings for youth and adults.

His enthusiasm and deep caring for children and adults alike was so contagious that I was happy just to be around him—whether helping him push free tickets for a children's afternoon gospel movie through a school playground fence, or assisting him in setting up one of the scientific demonstrations that he used in his dramatic evening presentations.

On the last day of that exciting evangelistic week, as we were packing Colonel Rader's trunks before he left town, I blurted out, "When I grow up, I want to be just like you!"

"No you don't, son," the wise old evangelist replied, "you want to be just like you, because God designed you in a special way, and you need to be true to that design."

Over the years, I have discovered that the old Colonel was right. Whether I am caring for my family, my neighborhood, a stranger at an airport, or involved in a wider ministry focus, I have to care in a way that is true to my own spirit and design as God has created me.

The answer key for which we are all searching is contained in two words: "sustainable caring."

On-again, off-again caring is not the answer. Declaring our parents, spouses, or other difficult people off limits for our caring is not the answer.

I must care, and you must care, in ways that we can repeat and sustain. This is needed if we are to become consistent witnesses for Jesus and to serve as role models for our own family and others who seek to understand him by observing our imperfect lives.

Styles of Caring

There are (at least) seven different sustainable styles of caring that I have observed over the years. See if one of the following styles of caring describes you at your best moments. Then seek, in prayer, to have those moments of caring become increasingly frequent until you have developed a sustained pattern of Christian caring that is true to your own personality and godly design.

I have named each of these sustainable styles of caring after one of the spiritual gifts noted in Romans 12:6–8: Prophet, Teacher, Administrator, Giver, Doer, Exhorter, and a person who shows Mercy.

The Prophet Style of Caring

When a prophet personality is not founded on Jesus Christ, a person's extreme moral fervor may attach itself to non-Christian standards or causes, as Saul of Tarsus did when he persecuted Christians before his conversion to Christ and his born-again identity as the apostle Paul.

However, once he or she becomes focused on Jesus, a person with a prophet personality gains strength from learning true biblical standards and applying them to correct and uplift the people who are touched directly by this unique style of caring.

My wife Judy has a prophet personality. As such, she expresses her caring through advocacy on behalf of those who cannot protect themselves, such as senior citizens and small children. Once, when she saw a mother repeatedly slapping her six-year-old son in the supermarket, Judy intervened and told the woman to stop. When the woman complained that the abuse was a private matter between her and her son, Judy responded, "When you hit him in public, it becomes a public matter." The lady calmed down, and my wife was able to discuss child development with her and recommend some less harsh and more effective methods for appropriate discipline of her child.

Judy's sustainable style of caring is to be an advocate. Because it is God's plan and design for her life, it works well when she does it. Is this your style? Perhaps. Perhaps not. It is not my style. Read further, because God does have a sustainable style of caring that will work for you, one that you can maintain and in which you can grow and develop your Christian expression of caring to others.

The Teacher Style of Caring

Florence Townsend is an expert in day care, children's services, and family counseling. Her caring style is that of a teacher, which means that she is a very organized and detail-oriented person. Others can depend on her accuracy. I call this a "teacher" style of caring because she cares by providing information rather than by directing others through the use of power or position. Flo uses this information in a unique way: to help people apply it to their own growth in ministry.

Someone with a teacher personality who is not focused on Christ might be bothersome to others rather than dependable. If he or she is obsessive-compulsive about a myriad of small details, it doesn't really help anyone. For example, one lady in California became so obsessive about her house that she spent her whole life adding secret passages and stairs that go nowhere. The house is now a tourist museum, a quaint curiosity that helps no one.

In contrast, Major Townsend, whose whole focus is on Christ, has led a life of teaching and caring for needy children—organizing and supervising others to be child care providers, and now crafting meticulous standards to ensure the quality of care given to children in each of our hundreds of Salvation Army child-serving agencies and institutions. Her commitment to caring is shown in the careful details of every one of her projects.

The Administrator Style of Caring

Petra Decaille-Poleon has an administrator's style of caring, which means she is at her best when organizing the rest of us in the office around a common task or goal. Of course, she also takes responsibility for individual acts of caring for her husband, children, and parents, as well as organizing group projects at her church.

A man or woman with an administrator personality style who is not focused on Jesus Christ may invest great energy in projects that have no eternal significance, and may also be tempted to treat team members as "disposable equipment" rather than as the valuable God-designed individuals whom they are.

King Saul in the Old Testament may have had an administrator style of caring that allowed him to realize that David was the right person to fight Goliath. Later, however, he became jealous of David's popularity and tried to kill him. King Saul forgot that the prophet Samuel had anointed him to be king, not simply for his own pleasure or reputation, but to help the whole country. This would have included mentoring David and teaching him how to be a leader.

I have the same administrator style of caring as Mrs. Poleon. My daughter and two sons know that I am at my best as a caring administrator when we are stopping to help a stranded motorist together, working as a team on a new book, or undertaking a specific Salvation Army ministry project.

I express my caring by matching each person's abilities to the part of the project that will be most fulfilling to them or most valuable for their personal growth and development.

If you have an administrator style of caring, you will experience the paradox that you are most willing to care, to work hard, and to sacrifice yourself for someone else's benefit when you are in charge of the caring project.

The Giver Style of Caring

An immature "giver" personality who is not focused on Christ will often act as a "getter" more than a "giver." His or her focus on finance may be on obtaining wealth for its own sake rather than on developing financial resources as a steward for the betterment of others and the expansion of the kingdom of God on earth.

In the New Testament, Jesus tells the story of a rich man whose grain silo was filled with selfish gain when God told him this was his last night to live. What had his great ability to obtain and store up riches done for him, or anyone else, then?

In contrast to that story, Andrew Carnegie was an American immigrant who became a steel tycoon and made millions of dollars in his business life. He focused his later years in a giver style of caring by funding and founding a great network of hundreds of public libraries across the United States. His libraries have brought knowledge and inspiration to millions of people.

Ray Howell could have become a millionaire in private life with his outstanding financial and investment skills; instead, he used these skills to build a charitable empire of forty-one adult rehabilitation centers in the northeastern states. These centers care for almost seven thousand homeless and addicted men and women per year, at no charge to the residents, with a substantial annual operating budget funded entirely by collecting and selling old clothes and furniture.

The Doer Style of Caring

A doer personality expresses his or her caring through practical means more than through words or emotional demonstration. Doers are more likely to send a note, stir up some fudge, or carve a toy than they are to offer a hug to strangers or engage in emotional conversation.

An immature doer, or a doer without a spiritual focus on the value of his or her uniqueness in Jesus Christ, may actually be victimized by the excessive demands of others and may resent those who are not as practical or dependable as they try to be.

In the Bible, Mary's sister Martha came to Jesus to criticize Mary for sitting at Jesus' feet and listening to his teaching instead of helping Martha with the housework and meal preparation. Jesus responded that Mary had "chosen the better part" because Martha was focusing her attention on resenting Mary rather than on the joy of her own caring service to Jesus, even through her outward activities were virtuous and even praiseworthy.

Ruth Miller is a Salvation Army officer widow with a doer style of caring. Her late husband had an outgoing, engaging communication style, which made him very successful in ministry.

While her husband lived, Ruth supported him in many practical and dutiful ways, although she was almost victimized by losing her own identity in the shadow of his flamboyant adventures.

After her husband died, Ruth went into therapy to understand the value of her own unique identity in Jesus Christ. Later, she was assigned to the Salvation Army's Missing Persons Bureau in New York City, where she poured her love for Christ into reuniting family members who had lost contact with one another.

Today, Ruth has qualified to become a private detective in the state of New York. Her department uses custom-designed software to reunite hundreds of lonely family members through Ruth's practical ministry, tailored perfectly for her unique style of caring.

You may have a doer style of caring. If you do, and have recently accepted Christ as your personal Savior, you may find that you experience more change in your attitudes than in your behavior. You may already be doing many right and caring acts for others, although sometimes with a stubborn or resentful spirit.

People around you can tell if you have a doer personality style, expressing caring through practical means. Only you and God can know if your caring is growing more deep and real, and if you are experiencing fulfillment through what you do, since you may rarely express either love or frustration through superficial expressions.

The Exhorter Style of Caring

Even before finding God, individuals with exhorter personalities can be funny, charming, or motivational. However, they may use these skills to manipulate people for selfish gains, without regard for biblical ethics or the other person's welfare.

Jacob in the Old Testament was such a person. He sold his brother Esau a pot of soup in return for the family birthright, then later tricked his blind, aging father into giving him the blessing that really belonged to the oldest son.

However, those same people skills, flowing through a heart of love and compassion after a significant encounter with God, allowed Jacob to become Israel, the patriarch of the twelve tribes, and a loving father to both Joseph and Benjamin.

Once, during a time of great stress, I was helped by a legendary man with an exhorter style of caring, Andrew S. ("Andy") Miller.

I visited him in Chicago when I was in a time of vocational and spiritual crisis. When I arrived, Andy had only thirty minutes before he was scheduled to speak at a Rotary Club luncheon. He took me for a brisk walk around the block, listened to my concerns with care, and then, using a fire hydrant as an altar, we knelt and prayed until I could see a clear solution to my problems.

Andy's penchant for the dramatic has created many such wonderful memories for people like me who were loved in astonishing ways, the beneficiaries of his exhorter style of caring.

The Mercy Style of Caring

Immature persons with a mercy style of caring whose lives are not centered on Jesus Christ may tend to focus their sense of urgent emotional need on themselves, to the exclusion of consideration of anyone else's needs, hurts, hopes, or wants. When their lives are not focused on Christ, they may be subject to tremendous mood swings—sometimes from "super" to "awful" in as little as twenty minutes.

Often, their emotional vulnerability sets them up to become victims of emotional, sexual, or financial exploitation. The good news is that their emotional sensitivity, when surrendered to Christ, allows them to mature into wise and effective counselors for others as their lives are increasingly stabilized through devotion to Christ.

In the Old Testament, Naomi's daughter-in-law Ruth illustrates a mercy style of caring. She responded to Naomi with heartfelt loyalty after the death of both of their husbands. Later, Ruth's willingness to trust Boaz to treat her with respect the night she came to the threshing room to sleep at his feet displayed both love and courage, which resulted in her marriage to Boaz and in her becoming an ancestor of Jesus Christ.

Sylvia Rebeck has sustained a mercy style of caring for more than fourteen years of a very special ministry. In that time, she has led more than three thousand men and women prisoners to find Jesus Christ as their personal Lord and Savior.

Major Sylvia pours her heart and soul into her correspondence Bible lessons with these men and women behind bars. As she corrects their lessons, she also writes them personal notes and prays for many of them individually by name.

And what does this godly, mature "mercy person" do in her spare time? She leads an inner city Sunday school class and children's choir in East Orange, New Jersey, where she is as emotionally committed to each child as if they were members of her immediate family.

Developing a Sustainable Style of Caring

These seven people exemplify the seven most frequent styles of caring that I have encountered in more than thirty years of active counseling and Christian ministry.

Each one has learned the deeply important lessons of self-care and family-care, which are necessary for any style of caring to be sustainable for an extended period of ministry to others.

As you begin to transform the caring you have done in the past into a deeper, less selfish, and more sustainable concern for others because Jesus Christ is now your Lord and Savior, start with small expressions of caring. Begin with acts of kindness that are easy for you to do, that do not need to be sustained beyond your current ability or interest level.

As you continue to mature in Christ, read what the Scripture has to say about God's love for us and our love for others. In your sessions of prayer, allow yourself enough time to listen to the Holy Spirit speaking back to your own heart. In addition, consult with those leaders in your local church who have more experience in the Lord. Seek to discover, develop, and practice your own sustainable style of caring on a regular basis.

Sometimes when you care deeply, you will be hurt. Don't give up.

Sometimes you will feel you have not cared well enough. Don't give up.

Sometimes your motives will be misunderstood by those you seek to help. Don't give up.

Learn to express yourself in a caring style that you can sustain over time. God knows your heart. He knows your sincerity of purpose. He knows your desire to love others in Jesus' name. Your soul is an open book to God. He will guide you, step by step, in your new adventure of caring:

All the way
From earth to heaven,
He will guide you
With his eye.
—*Salvation Army Hymnbook*

CAPTAIN/DR. JOHN
CHEYDLEUR is the territorial
social services secretary for the
Salvation Army's 2014 Social
Service Programs in the Eastern
Territory, USA.

John is the author of four
books, including *Every Sober
Day Is a Miracle* and *Called to
Counsel.* He has written numerous magazine articles and
chapters for books, and produced a Christian mental
health TV series.

He has been married to his
wife, Judy, for thirty-six years.
They have three children and
five grandchildren. John and
Judy live in West Nyack, New
York.

One-Verse Evangelism®

is there a simple way to share my faith?

BY RANDY D. RAYSBROOK

*H*ere's an uncomplicated way to invite someone to experience God's love, using only one Bible verse.

We sat in the busy hamburger stand, explaining to Jeff how he could have a close, eternal relationship with God. Suddenly, tears welled up in his eyes. As he realized how he had been rejecting Christ's love, years of resistance cracked and dissolved. We offered to find a more private place where he could pray if he wanted to ask Christ to forgive him. "No, let's pray right here," he said. And so Jeff accepted Christ's love and decided to follow him that afternoon.

What was it that helped Jeff to understand Christ's love for him and his own need to accept that love? It was a simple illustration drawn on a piece of paper, clearly communicating how a person who has chosen to live a life apart from Christ can be forgiven and become a child of God.

On another occasion, I watched in dismay as a friend attempted to explain his faith to an unbeliever. As he jumped back and forth from the Old Testament to the New Testament, he used a multitude of verses but never explained clearly how to become a Christian.

Since then, I have decided that whatever I do in evangelism, I will never be fuzzy or unclear. I don't have the right to take a simple message and make it difficult. As a result, I've found a simple way to communicate the gospel using just one Bible verse and an easy-to-draw illustration.

Often, when a conversation turns to spiritual topics, I will ask the other person if he would like to understand the basic theme of the Bible. I tell him that if he is interested, I can draw him a picture that will explain all sixty-six books of the Bible in a practical way that he can easily understand. I assure him that it will take only ten to fifteen minutes.

People are usually curious and seldom resist this approach. Few have ever had someone explain the whole Bible to them, let alone in ten minutes. If the person agrees to listen, I proceed with the following illustration.

Wages

Open your Bible to Romans 6:23. While pointing to the verse, ask the person to read it aloud to you while you write it at the top of a piece of paper. (If you're at a restaurant, a paper napkin works well.)

Draw a box around the word WAGES, write the same word midway down the left side of the page, and draw a box around it there also.

I begin by saying, "How would you define the term *wages?*" (Wages are what we receive for what we have done.)

As I continue, I use this example: "How would you feel if your boss refused to pay you the wages that were due to you? Deep down, we all know that it is only right that a person gets

what he deserves. Similarly, we earn wages from God for how we have lived our lives."

Sin

Draw a box around SIN in the verse. Write SIN below WAGES on the left side of the paper, and draw a box around it.

"What do you think of when you hear the word *sin?*

"How good a life would a person have to live in order to get into heaven? Have you always lived a life like you just described? (This should help him to see that, even by his own definition, he falls short of living a good and perfect life.)

"Sin is more of an attitude than an action—it can be a hostile or apathetic response to God. In other words, we can either actively or passively keep God out of our lives. At any point in your life, has God seemed far away?"

When he answers yes, draw in the lines of the cliff on both sides. Explain that sin has separated everyone from God.

"Imagine that you have a friend, and you asked that friend to avoid doing something that hurts or offends you. But your friend goes ahead anyway, disregarding your request. Do you think that would create a distance in your relationship? Our sin, in the same way, creates a distance between us and God."

Death

Draw a box around the word DEATH, write the word on the illustration, and box it there.

"What thoughts come to mind when you think of death? Physical death means separation—when we die, our soul is separated from our body. Spiritual death is when a person chooses to reject God. That separation begins in this life and extends into eternity. The result is eternity in hell. Ultimately, the choice a person makes toward God in this life is one he must live with forever."

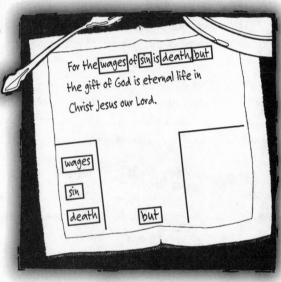

For the wages of sin is death, but the gift of God is eternal life in Christ Jesus our Lord.

wages
sin
death   but

But

Draw a box around BUT in the verse and write it in a box between the bases of the cliffs.

"This is the most important word in the verse because it indicates that there is hope for all of us. What we have talked about so far is bad news, but God has good news. What we're going to talk about now is a contrast to what we just discussed."

Gift

Draw a box around GIFT in the verse. On the right side of the cliff, write the word GIFT, boxing it there.

"What is the difference between a gift and wages?"

From now on, be sure to point back and forth to each side of the cliff to emphasize that the words contrast with each other.

"A gift is not earned by the person who receives it. Someone else pays for it. How do you feel toward someone who gives you an expensive gift?

"Some people try to earn God's favor by doing good deeds, living moral lives, or taking part in religious activities. But it is impossible to earn something that has already been bought.

"Say you wanted to buy a special gift for a close friend to show how much that person means to you. How would you feel if the friend refused to accept it without first paying you for it?"

Of God

Draw a box around OF GOD and write it on the right side of the cliff, across from SIN. Box it.

Point to SIN on the left side and then back to GOD on the right and explain that all of us have sinned, which means we have not lived life the way we were designed to. God is perfect, though, and never made any mistakes.

"God wants to give you a gift. I can't give it to you. A church can't give it to you. No one can give you this gift but God alone. Why does anyone want to give someone a precious gift?"

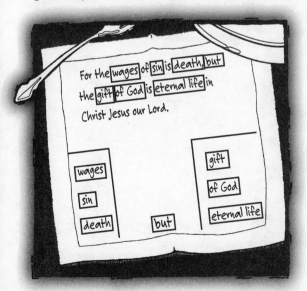

Eternal Life

Draw a box around ETER-NAL LIFE and write it on the right side of the cliff with a box around it.

"What do you think eternal life is?"

Point to DEATH on the left side and show that ETERNAL LIFE is the opposite.

"Eternal life means a relationship with God in harmony forever. Just as separation from God starts in this life and extends into eternity, eternal life starts now and goes on forever. No sin can end it."

Ask if he has any questions, or if there is any part that you have explained so far that he does not understand. Be sure that each point is clear before you proceed any further. If necessary, go back and explain each point that is not clear.

Christ Jesus

Draw a cross between the cliffs as a bridge. Box the words CHRIST JESUS in the verse. Write CHRIST JESUS (or JESUS CHRIST) inside the cross.

"Jesus alone is the means by which we can obtain the gift of eternal life. No one can offer a gift except the one who purchased it. He purchased it by paying for it with his life.

"Imagine that a police officer writes you a ticket for speeding and you go to court. The judge finds you guilty. But to your surprise, although you are guilty, the policeman pays your fine out of his own pocket. In the same way, Jesus paid the fine that you deserved: death. He experienced death so you would not have to."

Hold out a pen to the person and

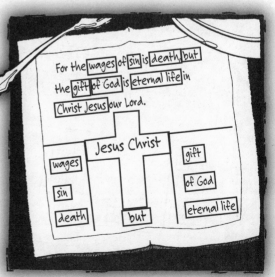

For the wages of sin is death, but the gift of God is eternal life in Christ Jesus our Lord.

Jesus Christ

wages
sin
death
but
gift
of God
eternal life

ask him to imagine that someone had bought it for him as a gift. As you hand it to him, ask him at what point the pen becomes his. (It's his when he accepts it.)

Trust

Write TRUST through the top of the cross.

"We have not lived life the way God would want us to. We deserve punishment for that, but if we trust—believe—that Jesus took our punishment for us, we are forgiven."

Draw a person on the left side of the bridge. Write GOD on the right side of the bridge.

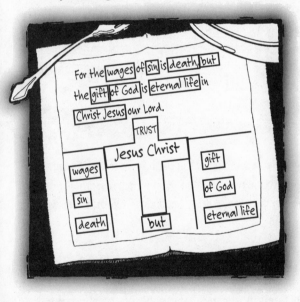

"As a person trusts God for forgiveness through Christ, he passes across the bridge. He begins a relationship with God and starts to experience a new and eternal life."

Draw an arrow from the man through TRUST to GOD.

"On the basis of what I have just explained, what must a person do to have a relationship with God and have eternal life?" (If he does not say "trust" or "believe" and understand what that means, go back and explain it until it is clear.)

"If you were to place yourself on the bridge, where would you be? Are you far off to the left—far away from God—or close to the bridge and eager to learn more about God?

"What must a person do to cross over the bridge to begin a relationship with God and have eternal life?

"Is there any reason why you would not trust God for forgiveness right now and begin to experience a close relationship with God and receive eternal life?"

If the person is ready to admit his need for forgiveness, help him to pray, but give him the freedom to use his own words. Remind him, though, that he is not forgiven because of how or what he prays, but instead because he trusts in Jesus.

To help your friend, you may want to say a simple prayer similar to the one you prayed when you accepted Christ. Ask him to repeat it after you, one phrase at a time.

Since "One-Verse Evangelism" was initially published our unevangelized audience has changed in major ways. People unexposed to a church rarely understand the concepts of sin, confession, forgiveness, or belief in Christ. People are increasingly skeptical of easy answers. And the gospel appears to many to be irrelevant.

In light of these shifts, it is even more important that any evangelistic tool we use remains personal and simple. Naturally, you will want to put the questions and explanations in this presentation into your own words.

Today, I would emphasize the importance of developing your own illustrations and metaphors when sharing. People respond to metaphors, and when you use your own stories, the presentation becomes a natural part of you.

These metaphors, or "word pictures," can be drawn from life experience, work, politics, economics, current events, and relationships. When developed by the person sharing his or her faith, they become personal and applicable.

Understanding our audience will increase our ability to communicate. Sometimes the most effective word pictures are those drawn from the personal world of the person we are telling about Christ.

Be sure to listen carefully as the person answers your questions. Try to understand where he stands in relation to the gospel and adjust your presentation to suit his personality and needs. As you explain, be alert to signs of confusion.

It might help if you practice One-Verse Evangelism with a Christian friend before you share it with an unbeliever. It is also a good idea to know at least one verse that backs up each step in the illustration in case the person needs further explanation.

Advantages to using the tool include:

- It is short. It can be used effectively when time is limited.
- It is expandable. Examples are optional, and you can make the presentation as long or as short as you wish, omitting the second example when applicable.
- It is easy for the listener to understand.
- It is easy to learn and use, since there is only one verse to memorize.
- There is no need to flip back and forth between the Old Testament and the New Testament, which can be confusing to the listener who is unfamiliar with the Bible.
- It gives you an opportunity to find out if the listener understands the gospel clearly by giving him or her two chances to tell you the steps necessary for salvation.

Most importantly, remember that the power to change lives is not in having an effective, smooth-flowing illustration. It is the Spirit of God who opens someone's heart to hear the message of salvation (see John 6:63–65).

But what a privilege we have in being able to colabor with God himself in reaching out to others. Let us sharpen our tools and be ready always to give a clear and simple presentation of the answer that every person needs.*

RANDY D. RAYSBROOK has been on staff with The Navigators since 1980. He is cofounder of Creation Resources, a national project of The Navigators that develops training and resources for Christian leaders and laypeople to improve their learning, teaching, and ministry innovation. With a master's degree in human communications and a Ph.D. in higher education, Randy teaches courses in communication, public speaking, and critical reasoning at several colleges and universities. Before joining The Navigators he worked as a police officer, lifeguard, ranch hand, model, and lumber mill worker. He has been married for twenty-five years and, with his wife Marilyn, has one daughter and four grandchildren. Randy and Marilyn live in Colorado Springs.

*Illustrations: Dale Johnson
"One-Verse Evangelism"® is distributed by Dawson Media, a ministry of The Navigators. For more information on this and other ministry tools, visit www.dawsonmedia.com.

Heaven

what will it be like?

By John Eldredge with Brent Curtis

*The door on which we have been knocking all our lives
will open at last. —C. S. Lewis*

My wife, Stasi, reads the end of novels first. Until recently, I (John) never understood why. "I want to know how the story ends, to see if it's worth reading," she explained. "A story is only as good as its ending. Even the best stories leave you empty if the last chapter is disappointing.

"But the opposite is also true," she added. "A really tragic story can be saved by a happy ending."

"But doesn't knowing the end take away the drama?" I asked.

"It only takes away the fear and frees you to enjoy the drama. Besides, some things are too important to be left to chance," she said, and turned back to her book.

A story is only as good as its ending. Without a happy ending that draws us on in eager anticipation, our journey becomes a nightmare of endless struggle. Is this all there is? Is this as good as it gets? On a recent flight I was chatting with one of the attendants about her spiritual beliefs. A follower of a New Age guru, she said with all earnestness, "I don't believe in heaven. I believe life is a never-end-ing cycle of birth and death." *What a horror*, I thought to myself. *This story had better have a happy ending.* Saint Paul felt the same. If this is as good as it gets, he said, you may as well stop at a bar on the way home and tie one on; go to Nordstrom's and max out all your credit cards; bake a cake and eat the whole thing. "Let us eat and drink, for tomorrow we die" (1 Cor. 15:32).

Our hearts cannot live without hope. Gabriel Marcel says that "hope is for the soul what breathing is for the living organism." In the trinity of Christian graces—faith, hope, and love—love may be the greatest, but hope plays the deciding role. The apostle Paul tells us that faith and love depend on hope, our anticipation of what lies ahead: "Faith and love . . . spring from the hope that is stored up for you in heaven" (Col. 1:5). Our courage for the journey so often fal-ters because we've lost our hope of heaven—the consummation of our love story. No wonder we live like Robinson Crusoe, trying to cobble together the best life we can from the wreckage of the world; we think we're stuck here forever. Of course, our less-wild lovers seem irresistible—we see them as our only shot at some relief. The reason most men, to quote Thoreau, "live lives of quiet desperation" is that they live without hope.

Several years ago I joined some friends for a weekend of fly-fishing on the Snake River in Jackson Hole, Wyoming. It was a last fling of fall, before the long winter set in with my heavy responsibilities at home, work, and in graduate school. I had looked forward to the adventure for months, but the weekend hadn't lived up to my expectations. The weather was lousy, the fishing dreadful. As the weekend drew to a close, I found myself tense and irritable, trying desperately to squeeze joy out of diminishing hopes. *This is it?* I thought to myself. *This is as good as it's going to be?* Standing together in the river Saturday evening, empty-handed, my friend announced almost as an afterthought that he had arranged a float down a wild section of the river with a famous guide for our last day together. The weather was predicted to be clear, and the fishing was practically guaranteed to be fabulous.

In a moment, everything changed. The evening light took on a rich, golden quality; the fall colors became vivid; I noticed the musical rushing of the waters for the first time, and my fishing buddies suddenly seemed to me a truly decent bunch of guys. The pressure I had placed on the vacation was lifted as my heart recovered hope. I was released by the promise of better things to come.

The story may seem silly (particularly for those who do not fly-fish), but it reveals one of the most important truths of the human heart: If for all practical purposes we believe that this life is our best shot at happiness, if this is as good as it gets, we will live as desperate, demanding, and eventually despairing men and women. We will place on this world a burden it was never intended to bear. We will try to find a way to sneak back into the Garden, and when that fails, as it always does, our heart fails as well. If truth be told, most of us live as though this life *is* our only hope, and then we feel guilty for wanting to do exactly what Paul said he would do if that were true.

In his wonderful book *The Eclipse of Heaven*, A. J. Conyers put it quite simply: "We live in a world no longer under heaven." All the crises of the human soul flow from there. All our addictions and depressions, the rage that simmers just beneath the surface of our Christian façade, and the deadness that characterizes so much of our lives has a common root: We think this is as good as it gets. Take away the hope of arrival and our journey becomes the Battan death march. The best human life is unspeakably sad. Even if we manage to escape some of the bigger tragedies (and few of us do), life rarely matches our expectations. When we do get a taste of what we really long for, it never lasts. Every vacation eventually comes to an end. Friends move away. Our careers don't quite pan out. Sadly, we feel guilty about our disappointment, as though we ought to be more grateful.

Of course we're disappointed—we're made for so much more. "He has also set eternity in the hearts" (Eccles. 3:11). Our longing for heaven whispers to us in our disappointments and screams through our agony. "If I find in myself desires which nothing in this world can satisfy," C. S. Lewis wrote, "the only logical explanation is that I was made for another world."

If faith and love hang on hope, if a life without hope is as Paul says "to be pitied" (1 Cor. 15:19), then shouldn't we devote ourselves to recovering a vision for the end of our story in as vivid colors as our imagination can conceive?

I knew a man who as a young boy hated the idea of heaven. He would puzzle and embarrass his Sunday school teachers by stating quite boldly, whenever the subject of heaven was brought up, that he didn't want to go there. Finally, one of them had the sense to ask him why. His answer? "I don't like peas." He had heard the familiar Christmas carol "Silent Night," with the lovely refrain "Sleep in heavenly peace," and thought it referred to the vegetable. Like any red-blooded boy, he figured there had to be better things to do.

Our images aren't much better. We speak so seldom of heaven, and when we do, the images are sickly: fat babies fluttering around with tiny wings, bored saints lazing on shapeless clouds, strumming harps, and wondering what's happening back on earth where the real action is.

The crisis of hope that afflicts the church today is a crisis of *imagination*. Catholic philosopher Peter Kreeft writes:

Medieval imagery (which is almost totally biblical imagery) of light, jewels, stars, candles, trumpets, and angels no longer fits our ranch-style, supermarket world. Pathetic modern substitutes of fluffy clouds, sexless cherubs, harps and metal halos (not halos of *light*) presided over by a stuffy divine Chairman of the Bored are a joke, not a glory. Even more modern, more up-to-date substitutes—Heaven as a comfortable feeling of peace and kindness, sweetness and light, and God as a vague grandfatherly benevolence, a senile philanthropist—are even more insipid. Our pictures of Heaven simply do not move us; they are not moving pictures. It is this aesthetic failure rather than intellectual or moral failures in our pictures of Heaven and of God that threatens faith most

potently today. Our pictures of Heaven are full, platitudinous
and syrupy; therefore, so is our faith, our hope, and our love
of Heaven . . . . It doesn't matter whether it's a dull lie or a
dull truth. Dullness, not doubt, is the strongest enemy of faith,
just as indifference, not hate, is the strongest enemy of love.[1]

If our pictures of heaven are to move us, they must be moving pictures. So go ahead—dream a little. Use your imagination. Picture the
best possible ending to your story you can. If that isn't heaven, something better is. When Paul says, "No eye has seen, no ear has heard,
no mind has conceived what God has prepared for those who love
him" (I Cor. 2:9), he simply means we cannot outdream God. What
is at the end of our personal journeys? Something beyond our
wildest imagination. But if we explore the secrets of our heart in the
light of the promises of Scripture, we can discover clues. There is in
the heart of every man, woman, and child an inconsolable longing
for intimacy, for beauty, and for adventure. What will heaven offer to
our heart of hearts?

Intimacy

Our longing for intimacy gives us the greatest scent of the joys
that lie ahead. Being left out is one of life's most painful experiences.
I remember the daily fourth-grade torture of waiting in line while the
captains chose their teams for the kickball games. As each captain
took turns choosing a player, descending from best to worst, our rank
in fourth-grade society was reinforced. Though others fared worse
than I—"Don't make us take Smitty, we had him last time"—I was
never the first to be chosen. No one ever said, "Wait—we get
Eldredge this time!" I didn't feel wanted; at best, I felt tolerated. And
then there was junior high cafeteria. After buying lunch, you carried
your tray out into the dining room, looking for a place to eat. There
was an unspoken hierarchy that determined where you could sit.
One day, I dared to test that caste system. With modest courage I
walked over to the table filled with the "cool" kids, but before I could

sit down, one of them sneered, "Not here, Eldredge, we're saving this for someone else."

These are some of the ways I learned the lesson that I was on the outside. Throughout our lives, each one of us lives with a constant nagging that we never quite fit in, we never truly belong. We've all had enough experiences to teach us that we will never be allowed into the "sacred circle," the place of intimacy. Even those who are chosen to be part of the "in" crowd are never chosen for who they truly are. So we hide parts of ourselves to try and fit in, or we kill our desire to be an insider rather than let our longing lead us toward the true intimacy for which we were designed.

On the other hand, there is the joy of having someone save a place for us. We walk into a crowded room at church or at a dinner party and someone across the way waves us over, pointing to a chair he's held on to especially for us. For a moment we feel a sense of relief, a taste of being on the inside. Now consider Jesus' words in John 14:2: "I am going . . . to prepare a place for you." Christ promises that he is saving a place in heaven especially for each of us. When we walk into the crowded excitement of the wedding feast of the Lamb, with the sound of a thousand conversations, laughter and music, the clinking of glasses, and one more time our heart leaps with the hope that we might be let into the sacred circle, we will not be disappointed. We'll be welcomed to the table by our Lover himself. No one will have to scramble to find another chair, to make room for us at the end of the table, or rustle up a place setting. There will be a seat with our name on it, held open at Jesus' command for us and no other.

Heaven is the beginning of an adventure in intimacy, "a world of love," as Jonathan Edwards wrote, "where God is the fountain." The Holy Spirit, through the human authors of Scripture, chose the imagery of a wedding feast for a reason. It's not just any kind of party; it is a wedding feast. What sets this special feast apart from all others is the unique intimacy of the wedding night. The Spirit uses the most secret and tender experience on earth—the union of husband and wife—to convey the depth of intimacy that we will partake with our Lord in heaven. He is the Bridegroom and the church is his bride. In the consummation of love, we shall know him and be known. There we shall receive our new name, known only to our Lover, which he shall give to us on a white stone (see Rev. 2:17).

George MacDonald, a theologian with a poet's heart, has explored the promises of heaven more richly than perhaps any other man. He explains what the stone implies:

> It is the man's own symbol—his soul's picture, in a word—the sign which belongs to him and to no one else. Who can give a man this, his own name? God alone. For no one but God sees what the man is . . . . It is only when the man has become his name that God gives him the stone with the name upon it, for then first can he understand what his name signifies . . . . Such a name cannot be given until the man *is* the name . . . that being whom He had in His thought when He began to make the child, and whom He kept in His thought through the long process of creation that went to realize the idea. To tell the name is to seal the success—to say "In thee also I am well pleased."[2]

The stone will free us to enjoy the riches of heaven, for in order to share in this heavenly intimacy, we must have the freedom of heart enjoyed by Adam and Eve before the Fall, who were naked and *felt no shame*. This is the freedom from sin, or as Kreeft has said, "from what makes us not ourselves. We will be free to be the true selves God designed us to be." Shame kills intimacy. The soul that still is in some way hiding cannot enjoy the fullness of knowing what characterizes the love between God and the saints in heaven. But then we shall be perfect; our loved ones will be perfect as well. All that has ever stood between us will be swept away, and our heart will be released to real loving. The intimacy that begins between God and his people will be enriched and echoed by our communion with each other. The deepest longing of our heart—our longing to be part of the sacred circle, to be inside—reveals to us the greatest of the treasures heaven has in store. For we were made in, and for, the most sacred circle of all. Lewis says, "The sense that in this universe we are treated as strangers, the longing to be acknowledged, to meet with some response, to bridge some chasm that yawns between us and reality, is part of our inconsolable secret. And surely, from this point of view, the promise of glory, in the sense described, becomes highly relevant to our deep desire. For glory meant good report with God, acceptance by God, response, acknowledgment, and welcome into the heart of things. The door on which we have been knocking all our lives will open at least."[3]

Beauty

"And they all lived happily ever after." Where? Doing what? As wonderful as it will be to have our longing for relationship filled to overflowing, it is not enough. Our heart has other longings that heaven draws forth. There is so much more to the human soul and so much more to the riches God has prepared for those who love him. In the same way that life sharpens our yearning to be welcomed into the sacred circle of intimacy, so it awakens another ache from deep within—our longing for beauty.

The Ritz Carlton Laguna Beach is one of the most luxurious hotels in southern California. Nestled on a bluff above its private cove with a white sandy beach, the hotel exudes romance. Its mediterranean architecture lifts the Ritz out of space and time, creating a fairy-tale ambiance. Arches and tile walkways lead to fountained courtyards and terraces with breathtaking views of the Pacific. The tropical climate nourishes a lush canopy of purple and red bougainvillea, whimsical flower gardens, rich green lawns, and swaying palms. Staying at the Ritz, one can almost forget, if for a moment, that the Fall ever happened. Stasi and I enjoyed a weekend of escape there thanks to a business conference I was asked to attend.

Late one evening I slipped away from the meeting to wander the grounds alone. I felt restless inside and thought a walk might be calming. Something drew me through the terraces toward the ocean. As I wandered over the beautifully manicured lawns, more luxuriant than any carpet, the sounds of music and laughter from parties inside mingled with the scent of the flower beds in the warm ocean breeze. My restlessness grew. Standing on the edge of the cliff with the crashing of the waves below and the shining of the stars above, I felt the restlessness swell into an ache. As Simone Weil said, there are only two things that pierce the human heart: beauty and affliction. I was run clean-through by the beauty of it all, overcome by an ache for a home I have never seen.

I have had this experience many times, whether walking along the Napali Coast in Hawaii, flying over the glaciers of Alaska, or noticing the simple rays of sunshine falling on the kitchen table. Yet it always takes me by surprise. We grow so used to living in a world soiled by the Fall that our soul's desire for beauty lies dormant deep within, waiting for something to awaken it. During a visit to Westminster Cathedral in England, a friend of mine got lost and by accident came into that glorious sanctuary by a rather commonplace side door. Stepping around the corner, he was totally unprepared for the majesty he suddenly found himself engulfed by: the sweeping architecture, the glory in stone and spire and glass. At that very moment a choir broke into song, their angelic harmonies filling the massive cathedral. "I don't know what happened," he later told me, "but I broke down and began to weep."

"Each and every instance of beauty," writes Mark Helprin, "is a promise and example, in miniature, of life that can end in balance, with symmetry, purpose and hope." We long for beauty and the promise that it speaks. Our revulsion to the ugly is the counterpart to our desire for beauty. I used to hate the part of my daily commute that took me through the worst sections of Washington, D.C.: abandoned buildings, burned-out cars, desolate neighborhoods. It was a symbol of the triumph of evil, chaos, and death. My heart grieved to see such devastation, and I breathed a sign of relief as I passed through the wreckage and drove into the farmlands of Maryland. But we must be careful here; as Lewis said, one of the mistakes we so often make when captured by an object of beauty, whether it's a place, a person, or a work of art, is to assume the longing in our heart is for the thing before us. The Ritz and Westminster and farm meadows—these are shadows of the realities to come. The beauty of the tabernacle carried by Israel through the desert was a type of the real item in heaven. So it goes with all things on earth: The beauty that so captures our heart and is so fleeting draws us toward the eternal reality.

We long for beauty, and when the biblical writers speak of heaven, they use the most beautiful imagery they can. You can almost hear the agony of the writer trying to get it right while knowing he falls far short of what he sees. In the Book of Revelation, Saint John uses the word *like* again and again. "And He who was sitting was like a jasper stone and a sardius in appearance; and there was a rainbow around the throne, like an emerald in appearance. . . . Before the throne there was . . . a sea of glass like crystal" (4:3, 6 NASB). The beauty cannot be captured, only alluded to by the most beautiful things on earth.

I believe the beauty of heaven is why the Bible says we shall be "feasted." It's not merely that there will be no suffering, though that will be tremendous joy in itself; to have every Arrow we've ever known pulled out and every wound dressed with the leaves from the tree of life (Rev. 22:2). But there is more. We will have glorified bodies with which to partake of all the beauty of heaven. As Edwards wrote, "Every faculty will be an inlet of delight." We will eat freely the fruit of the tree of life and drink deeply from the river of life that flows through the city. And the food will satisfy not just our body but our soul. As Lewis said, "We do not want merely to *see* beauty, though, God knows, even that is bounty enough. We want something else which can hardly be put into words—to be united with the beauty we see, to pass into it, to receive it into ourselves, to bathe in it, to become part of it."[4]

And so we shall.

Adventure

What will we do in heaven? The Sunday comics picture saints lying about on clouds, strumming harps. It hardly takes your breath away. The fact that most Christians have a gut sense that earth is more exciting than heaven points to the deceptive powers of the enemy and our own failure of imagination. What do we do with the idea of "eternal rest"? That sounds like the slogan of a middle-class cemetery. We know heaven begins with a party, but then what? A long nap after the feast? The typical evangelical response—"We will worship God"—doesn't help either. The answer is certainly biblical, and perhaps my reaction is merely a reflection on me, but it sounds so one-dimensional. Something in my heart says, *That's all? How many hymns and choruses can we sing?*

We will worship God in heaven, meaning all of life will finally be worship, not round after round of "Amazing Grace." The parable of the minas in Luke 19 and the talents in Matthew 25 foreshadow a day when we shall exercise our real place in God's economy, the role we have been preparing for on earth. He who has been faithful in the small things will be given even greater adventures in heaven. We long for adventure, to be caught up in something larger than ourselves, a drama of heroic proportions. This isn't just a need for continual excitement, it's part of our design. Few of us ever sense that our talents are being used to their fullest; our creative abilities are rarely given wings in this life. When Revelation 3 speaks of us being "pillars in the temple of our God," it doesn't mean architecture. Rather, Christ promises that we shall be actively fulfilling our total design in the adventures of the new Kingdom.

Act IV—heaven—is the continuation of the Story that was interrupted by the Fall. God made the earth and entrusted it to us, to bring order and increase beauty. We were to be his regents, reigning with his blessing and authority. That arrangement was corrupted by the Fall so that the earth no longer responds to our leadership as it once did. When Christ accomplished our redemption, he didn't do it to place us on the bench for eternity. He restored us to put us back in the game. He even subjected the earth to a time of futility until the day it will be "liberated from its bondage to decay and brought into the glorious freedom of the children of God" (Rom. 8:21). We will then coreign with Christ. "St. Peter for a few seconds walked on the water," Lewis reminds us, "and the day will come when there will be a re-made universe, infinitely obedient to the will of glorified and obedient men, when we can do all things, when we shall be those gods that we are described as being in Scripture."

Part of the adventure will be to explore the wonders of the new heaven and new earth, the most breathtaking of which will be God himself. We will have all eternity to explore the mysteries of God, and not just explore, but to celebrate and share with one another. Here is a remarkable thing to consider: Your soul has a unique shape that fits God. We are not all the same, but unique creations each of us. Therefore, as MacDonald says, "Every one of us is something that the other is not, and therefore knows something—it may be without knowing that he knows it—which no one else knows: and . . . . It is everyone's business, as one of the kingdom of light and inheritor in it all, to give his portion to the rest."[5]

This may be why the angels Isaiah sees flying around the throne room of God are crying "holy, holy, holy," not to God, but *to one another*" (6:3, italics mine). They are calling each other to see what they see of the majesty and beauty of God, so that their joy might be increased as they celebrate him together. Every experience of delight takes on a fuller dimension when we share it. This is why we so often feel in the midst of some wonderful moment, "How I wish my beloved were here."

The exploration of heaven shall also include our knowing of each other. How could it not? How can love be complete without the freedom to be naked and unashamed? More than unashamed, we shall be *celebrated*. It is one of the sorrows of our present life: the separation we feel even from those closest to us. Married people can be the loneliest on earth, not for some failure of the marriage, but because they have tasted the best there is of human relationships and know it is not all it was meant to be. In *A Tale of Two Cities*, Charles Dickens captures that sense of mystery each human soul is to another: "A wonderful fact to reflect upon, that every human creature is constituted to be that profound secret and mystery to every other. A solemn consideration, when I enter a great city by night, that every one of those darkly clustered houses encloses its own secret; that every room in every one of them encloses its own secret; that every beating heart in the hundreds of thousands of breasts there, is, in some of its imaginings, a secret to the heart nearest it!"

But in heaven that veil shall be removed as well, not to our shame and embarrassment, but to our utter delight. Remember, we will be perfect, meaning we will be the soul that God had in mind all along. And then, as MacDonald says, "We shall have the universe for our own, and be good merry children in the great house of our father. I think then we shall be able to pass into and through each other's very souls as we please, knowing each other's thought and being, along with our own, and so being *like* God. When we are all just as loving and unselfish as Jesus; when, like him, our one thought of delight is that God is, and is what he is; when the fact that a being is just another person from ourselves is enough to make that being precious."[6]

And there is, of course, the exploration of our own lives. We know a time will come for us to look back with our Lord over the story of our lives. Every hidden thing shall be made known, every word spoken in secret shall be uttered. My soul shrinks back; how will this not be an utter horror? The whole idea of judgment has been terribly twisted by our enemy. One evangelistic tract conveys the popular idea that at some point shortly upon our arrival in heaven the lights will dim and God will give the signal for the videotape of our entire life to be played before the watching universe: every shameful act, every wicked thought. How can this be so? If there is "*now* no condemnation for those who are in Christ Jesus" (Rom. 8:1, *italics mine*), how is it possible there will be shame later? God himself shall clothe us in white garments (Rev. 3:5). Will our Lover then strip his beloved so that the universe may gawk at her? Never.

However God may choose to evaluate our lives, whatever memory of our past we shall have in heaven, we know this: It will only contribute to our joy. We will read our story by the light of redemption and see how God has used both the good and the bad, the sorrow and the gladness for our welfare and his glory. With the assurance of total forgiveness we will be free to know ourselves fully, walking again through the seasons of life to linger over the cherished moments and stand in awe at God's grace for the moments we have tried so hard to forget. Our gratitude and awe will swell into worship of a Lover so strong and kind as to make us fully his own.

Arrival

Brent and I have tried to put words to many of the questions we believe every heart is asking. Well into the Christian journey, two new questions began to haunt us: Will I make it to the end? And, Will it be good when I get there?

Several years into our marriage, Stasi and I reached one of the lowest moments of our lives. Sitting over the breakfast table one morning, the subject of divorce was raised in a rather casual way, as if it were a question about the raspberry jam. We had drifted apart, I knew that, but until that moment I didn't realize just how far. Over the next few days I made an emergency plan. We would go to the mountains for a holiday in hopes of recovering some of the ground we had lost. We had honeymooned in Yosemite, and I thought that might be the place to look again for a lost romance.

We set out the day after Christmas on a warm and sunny morning. But as the hours wore on, a snowstorm was building in the mountains ahead. Evening fell and with it came the snow, softly at first, then heavier and harder. Our car began to slip and spin on the icy road. It was dark when we reached the entrance to the park. Up ahead, I could see the cars before us turning around and heading back down the mountain. *Oh Lord*, I prayed, *please—not now, not when so much is riding on this*. The ranger told us that the roads had become treacherous and a blizzard was raging higher in the mountains. Several cars had already slid off the highway. He recommended we turn back but left the choice to us.

"We're going on," I said. As the hours dragged on, the snow blanketed the road and dark woods all around. We were alone. *Will we make it?* I wondered to myself. *Can it possibly be good even if we do?* My knuckles were white from clutching the steering wheel. The tension in the car was thick, a palpable reminder of the reason we had come.

Just when I was about to abandon hope, twinkling lights appeared through the trees ahead. As we rounded the bend, the Wawona Hotel came into view—a gorgeous, white Victorian inn with garlands hanging from the balcony and a massive Christmas tree in the window. The snowfall eased, and the flakes were now falling softly, gently. We could see a fire roaring in the large stone fireplace, casting a romantic glow over the couples who lingered over dinner. Currier and Ives never printed a more beautiful scene. As I pulled our car into safety, a deer ambled from the woods and across the white meadow before us. The sense of arrival was almost too much to bear. We had made it! The beauty of it all seemed to speak the promise of a life restored. As we walked into our room, we discovered gifts some friends had sent ahead. That weekend we turned a corner in our marriage and began the healing we now enjoy.

For now, our life is a journey of high stakes and frequent danger. But we have turned the corner; the long years in exile are winding down, and we are approaching home. There is no longer any question as to whether we will make it and if it will be good when we get there. "I am going there to prepare a place for you," Jesus promised. "And if I go and prepare a place for you, I will come back and take you to be with me" (John 14:2–3).

One day soon we will round a bend in the road and our dreams will come true. We really will live happily ever after. The long years in exile will be swept away in the joyful tears of our arrival home. Every day when we rise, we can tell ourselves, *My journey today will bring me closer to home; it may be just around the bend.* All we long for we shall have; all we long to be, we will be. All that has hurt us so deeply—the dragons and nits, the Arrows and our false lovers, and Satan himself—they will all be swept away.

And then real life begins.

JOHN ELDREDGE is an author, counselor, and lecturer. For twelve years he was a writer and speaker for Focus on the Family, most recently serving on the faculty of the Focus on the Family Institute. Now John is director of Ransomed Heart Ministries, a teaching, counseling, and discipling fellowship devoted to helping people recover and live from their deep heart.

As an author John has had published *The Journey of Desire* and *Wild at Heart,* and he coauthored with Brent Curtis *The Sacred Romance,* which also has an accompanying workbook and journal. John lives in Colorado Springs with his wife, Stasi, and their three sons. He loves living in Colorado so he can pursue his other passions, including fly fishing, mountain climbing, and exploring the waters of the West in his canoe.

Afterword

While putting this book together I pictured real people, with serious questions and a pulsating desire to know some answers, sitting in a comfortable chair saying, "Oh I get it!" I hope that has been your experience.

The basics of the Christian life are found in this book. Allow me to summarize the entire book in 261 words.

By turning to Scripture, the inspired Word of God, you can soak in the delicacies of great doctrine. The Trinity, although difficult to comprehend, consistently appears in the ancient pages. God the Father, deeply in love with us, is almighty, and capable of ordering our lives for his glory. Jesus, his Son, by living, dying, sacrificing, and rising again, made it possible for us to say yes! to God. The Holy Spirit, living inside us, enables us to enjoy other Christians as we become part of the church universal, receive forgiveness for all our sins, anticipate our resurrection from the dead, and enjoy eternal life now!

Our lives, once we trust Christ, need to revolve around three big rocks: our passion, mission, and vision. Our passion is to make Jesus the first love of our lives; our mission is to make Jesus look great; and our vision is to make him well known. However, if we try really hard to live the Christian life, we will only frustrate ourselves; we must allow the indwelling Christ to live through us. If we do, we'll be able to discern his voice and obey, deal effectively with sin in our lives, view suffering as a tool in God's hand to remind us of the hellish existence we have escaped, and reflect God's glory in personal and corporate worship. As these "inner disciplines" deepen in our lives, we will find joy in prayer, giving, servanthood, compassionate acts, and sharing our faith. All this will prepare us for the glorious reunion, which awaits us in heaven.

Now, if I had allowed you to read this page before you started in this book, it wouldn't have made much sense! See how much you have learned! You have finished the book, but you are just starting a long race. Consider yourself "out of the starting blocks." Pace yourself, keep your eyes on the finish line, help your fellow runners, and share this book and the truth within with someone "a lap behind you." I can't wait to see you in heaven! Until then, SDG!

Glossary of Terms

The Old Testament was written in Hebrew; the New Testament was written in Greek; and many theological terms are in Latin.

Advent | Preparation to celebrate the birth of Christ with self-examination.

Agape | Selfless, unconditional love.

Agnostic | "We don't know. We're not sure if God exists." This thinking is counter to Christianity and to atheism.

Alleluia | Hebrew word for "praise the Lord."

Alpha and Omega | Greek—the first and last, the beginning and end. See Revelation 1:8, 21:6, 22:13.

Amen | Hebrew—it is reliable; it is true; yes, surely; I agree.

Anoint | With oil; set apart for divine service.

Apocalypse | Unveiling (Rev. 1:1). A book with colorful representation of the end times.

Apologetics | Defending the Christian faith in order to convince unbelievers.

Apostasy | Rebellion against God.

Armageddon | Revelation 16:16—the place of the final great battle.

Ascension | Christ was lifted up into heaven forty days after his resurrection.

Atonement | At-one-ment; reconciliation.

Blasphemy | To slander or insult or mock the power of God.

Body of Christ | Paul's term for the church. It is the body of Christ, not the body of Christians (Rom. 12:4–5; Eph. 1:22–23).

Born Again | The need to become a new person (see John 3).

Carnal   From the word meaning "flesh," worldly, materially minded.

Charismatic   From the word meaning "gift," having to do with the gifts of the Spirit. See Romans 12:6–8, 1 Corinthians 12:4–11, and Ephesians 4:11–16.

Cherubim   An angel; the most frequently named angel in Scripture.

Communion   The Lord's Supper (Matt. 26:26–30). Remember what Jesus did!

Conversion   To turn, to turn away from, to turn toward—to change (Matt. 18:3).

Covenant   A compact or agreement between two parties.

Creed   From the Latin *credo*, it means "I believe in," not "I believe that." It is a confession of faith.

Damnation   Condemned to a godless eternity.

Depravity   Total corruption is extended to all aspects of our nature.

Devotions   Spending personal time with God, also called "quiet time."

Disciple   A close personal pupil.

Doctrine   What the whole Bible has to say about a given subject.

Doxology   From the Greek *doxa*, meaning "opinion, glory," and the Greek *logia*, which means "an expression of praise to God."

Ecclesiastical   *Ecclesia*, Greek for "gathering" or "church." Ecclesiastical has to do with church.

Edify/
Edification   Romans 15:2; 1 Corinthians 14:3; 2 Corinthians 10:8, 13:10. It means to build up.

Election   God choosing us for salvation.

Epiphany   A disclosure—the first and second coming of Christ.

Epistle   Letter; many of the New Testament books.

Eschatology   The doctrine of the last things.

Evangelical   One who believes and proclaims the gospel.

Evangelism   Proclaiming the gospel.

Evangelistic   A person or event who shares the gospel.

Exegesis   The process of interpreting Scripture; to draw out.

Expository Preaching	Systematic preaching of the text.
Faith	Belief, trust (Heb. 11:1).
Fall	Adam and Eve's disobedience, leading humanity into depravity.
Fasting ·	Total or partial abstinence of food.
Fellowship	Participation, sharing, self-sacrifice, community.
Flesh	A figurative picture of the dynamic principle of sinfulness.
Fruit of the Spirit	The result of submission (Gal. 5).
Genealogy	A list of names of ancestors (Matt. 1; Luke 3).
Gifts of the Spirit	*Charisma*, a gift of grace (1 Pet. 4:10).
Gospel	*Evangeline*—good news.
Grace	Unmerited favor; God's riches at Christ's expense.
Great Commission	Command of Jesus to preach the good news to all people (Matt. 28:19–20).
Heir	Inheritance of the kingdom of God and the family of God (Rom. 8:17).
Heresy	A deliberate denial of revealed truth.
Holiness	Distinct, different, completely other.
Immanence	God's involvement in Creation. (Not imminence, which pertains to the fact that Christ could return at any time.)
Incarnate/ Incarnation	In the flesh; the eternal Son of God took on human form.
Inerrancy	Entirely true and never false, in all the original autographs.
Infallibility	The state of being incapable of error. The Catholic Church would say the pope and the church are infallible; the Protestant church would say only Scripture is.
Jehovah	Hebrew for *Lord*; see Yahweh.
Justification	Declared righteous before God.
Koinonia	Greek word for fellowship.
Laity	Historically those who are not ordained.
Mercy	Withholding that which one deserves.

Millennium	Latin for *a thousand years;* Revelation 20:1–10 reign of Christ.
Monotheism	The belief that there is only one God.
Omnipotent	All-powerful.
Omnipresence	Always present.
Omniscient	All-knowing.
Ordinance	Baptism/Lord's Supper were ordained or prescribed by Jesus.
Passover	The angel of death went over the door frames with the blood of the lamb (Exod. 12, 23:14–17). Jesus is the Passover lamb.
Propitiation	The turning away of wrath by an offering.
Reconcile	Estrangement overcoming disunity; unity is restored.
Redemption	The payment of a ransom.
Regeneration	Inner-recreating of a fallen person.
Repent	A contemplated change; turn about-face.
Righteousness	Straight, right, to do justice, to do the right thing.
Salvation	Rescue from the power and penalty of sin.
Sanctify/ Sanctification	To make holy.
Sola Fidei	By faith alone.
Sola Gratia	By grace alone.
Sola Scripture	By Scripture alone.
Soli Deo Gloria (SDG)	To God alone be the glory.
Sovereign	One who is king, in charge, and reigns supreme.
Testament	Latin word for the Hebrew word meaning "covenant"; two main divisions of Scripture.
Transcendence	Over and above all creation.
Trinity	One God in three persons: Father, Son, and Holy Spirit.
Witness	One who testifies to the truth with a testimony.
Worship	Worth-ship; honor rendered to God. A life of worship is a life of submission (Rom. 12:1–3).
Wrath	God's indignation toward sin.
Yahweh	The tetragrammaton—the four letters of the Hebrew Bible designating God's name YHWH. It means "I Am."

Notes

The Bible

1. W. C. G. Proctor, "Infallibility," in *Baker's Dictionary of Theology*, ed. Everett Harrison (Grand Rapids: Baker Book House, 1960), 284.

2. Carl F. H. Henry, "Inspiration," in *Baker's Dictionary of Theology*, ed. Everett Harrison (Grand Rapids: Baker Book House, 1960), 288.

3. Calvin Miller, *An Owners Manual for the Unfinished Soul* (Wheaton, Ill.: Harold Shaw Publishers, 1997), 41–44.

The Trinity

Taken from *Growing Deep in the Christian Life*, © 1986 and 1995 by CRS, Inc., used by permission of Zondervan Publishing House.

God the Son, Jesus Christ

1. Max Lucado, *God Came Near* (Sisters, Ore.: Multnomah Publishers, Inc., 1986).

2. Ibid.

3. Max Lucado, *The Final Week of Jesus* (Multnomah Publishers, Inc., 1994).

4. John R. W. Stott, *Basic Christianity* (Downers Grove, Ill.: InterVarsity, 1971), 50.

5. Max Lucado, *When Christ Comes* (Nashville, Tenn.: Word Publishing, 1999).

6. Max Lucado, *He Chose the Nails* (Word Publishing, 2000).

7. Max Lucado, *And the Angels Were Silent* (Multnomah Publishers, 1992).

Your Purpose

1. Several versions of this parable are on the Internet, including one from Stephen R. Covey, *First Things First* (Fireside Publishing, 1994), 88–89.

Sin

1. R. B. Girdlestone, *Synonyms of the Old Testament: Their Bearing on Christian Doctrine*, 1978 reprint of 2nd edition of 1897 (Grand Rapids: Eerdman's), 76.

2. W. Dyrness, *Themes of Old Testament Theology* (Downers Grove, Ill.: InterVarsity Press, 1979), 105–107.

Suffering

Taken from *When God Weeps* by Joni Eareckson Tada with Steven Estes (Grand Rapids: Zondervan Publishing House, 1997).

Prayer

1. Taken from *Lord, Teach Me to Pray* by Kay Arthur (Eugene, Ore.: Harvest House Publishers, 1982).

2. Taken from *His Imprint My Expression* by Kay Arthur (Harvest House Publishers, 1993).

Servanthood

1. *The Experiencing God Bible* (Nashville, Tenn.: Broadman & Holman Publishers, ©1994), 1,794–96).

2. *Experiencing God* trade edition (Nashville, Tenn.: Broadman & Holman Publishers, ©1994, 1998), 38–48.

One-Verse Evangelism

Taken from "One-Verse Evangelism,"® © 1996 Randy D. Raysbrook, used by permission of Dawson Media, a ministry of The Navigators, Colorado Springs, Colo.

Heaven

Taken from *The Sacred Romance,* © 1997 John Eldredge and Brent Curtis, reprinted by permission of Thomas Nelson Publishers.

1. Peter Kreeft, *Everything You Ever Wanted to Know about Heaven but Never Dreamed of Asking* (San Francisco: Ignatius, 1990).

2. George MacDonald, *Unspoken Sermons,* as quoted in *George MacDonald: 365 Readings,* C. S. Lewis, ed. (New York: Macmillan, 1947).

3. C. S. Lewis, *The Weight of Glory* (Grand Rapids: Eerdmans, 1949).

4. Ibid.

5. MacDonald, *Unspoken Sermons.*

6. *The Heart of George MacDonald,* Rolland Hein, ed. (Wheaton: Harold Shaw, 1994).